John Cooper

The science of spiritual life: or, The adaptation of Christianity to the nature and condition of man

Second Edition

John Cooper

The science of spiritual life: or, The adaptation of Christianity to the nature and condition of man
Second Edition

ISBN/EAN: 9783337261627

Printed in Europe, USA, Canada, Australia, Japan

Cover: Foto ©Lupo / pixelio.de

More available books at **www.hansebooks.com**

THE
SCIENCE OF SPIRITUAL LIFE.

PRINTED BY BALLANTYNE, HANSON AND CO.
EDINBURGH AND LONDON.

THE

SCIENCE OF SPIRITUAL LIFE;

OR,

THE ADAPTATION OF CHRISTIANITY TO THE NATURE AND CONDITION OF MAN.

BY THE

REV. JOHN COOPER.

SECOND EDITION.

LONDON:
SAMPSON LOW, MARSTON, SEARLE, & RIVINGTON,
CROWN BUILDINGS, 188 FLEET STREET.
1877.
[All rights reserved.]

PREFACE TO THE SECOND EDITION.

IT is now ten years since the First Edition of the "Science of Spiritual Life" was published. During these years many books on religious subjects have issued from the press, but though carefully watching, I have not yet seen any book which has attempted to deal with the wide and important subject to the elucidation of which this volume is devoted. A fertile region, therefore, I am sorry to say, is allowed in great measure to remain unproductive.

As indicated in the Preface to the First Edition, the book was written and put through the press under very disadvantageous circumstances, and in consequence blemishes were allowed to pass, which in other circumstances would not have found place. These blemishes have now in part been removed, yet this Second Edition is substantially the same as the First. The following are the main changes which have been made:—A new Introduction has been substituted. The substance of the Appendix has been inwrought into the chapter on the Power of Reconciliation, and the twenty-third chapter, entitled "Inspiration," has been recast, and now constitutes chapter third, and is entitled "The

Transmission and Reception of Truth." These are the principal changes which have been made in the book, at all events, the only changes which call for special notice.

I cannot allow this opportunity to pass without referring to the second chapter—a chapter over which it would seem many have been sorely exercised. This chapter I have still retained, for this reason, viz., the book is intended for those who are familiar with the style of thought which runs through that chapter, as well as for those to whom it is strange; the former may be able to appreciate it, the latter may pass on to the following chapters, and do little violence to the course of the argument.

A word to my reviewers. They may herein see how far their criticisms and suggestions have been approved of by me, and I would take this opportunity of thanking them for the courteous and, I may add, encouraging manner in which for the most part they have reviewed my labours.

The book, with all its imperfections, I now again send forth in the service of Him who accepts the feeblest efforts put forth for His glory, and for the good of man.

PREFACE TO THE FIRST EDITION.

THE principles evolved in this volume have received the attention of the writer for years. In venturing to give them to the world, he is not without the humble hope that they may (under the Divine blessing), be made instrumental in helping to establish the cause of truth, and to promote the glory of God. He regrets that the circumstances under which he has committed his ideas to writing, and thereafter passed them through the press, have not been of the most favourable character for the production of such a work. The statement of this fact will in some measure explain, while it does not excuse, and is not intended to justify, the imperfections of the book. A just and impartial criticism is not shunned, but will rather be welcomed. The work is put forth as a small contribution to the great cause of truth, and while, in the full consciousness of its imperfections, it is laid at the feet of the great Teacher of the race, it is at the same time offered for the perusal of thoughtful men.

CONTENTS.

CHAP.		PAGE
	INTRODUCTION	1
I.	MAN A RELIGIOUS BEING, IN AN IRRELIGIOUS EFFORT AND HELPLESS CONDITION	26
II.	TRUTH IN ITS HIGHER MANIFESTATIONS	40
III.	THE TRANSMISSION AND RECEPTION OF TRUTH	57
IV.	THE PRIMARY LAWS OF PERCEPTION, OR THE CONDITIONED OF HUMAN BELIEF	76
V.	THE PRINCIPLES OF THE DIVINE ADMINISTRATION	84
VI.	COMBINATION OR CAUSATION	94
VII.	THE POWER OF CHOICE	106
VIII.	TRIAL	121
IX.	RETRIBUTION	135
X.	INABILITY	151
XI.	RECONCILIATION	175
XII.	POWER OF RECONCILIATION	193
XIII.	MEDIUM OF RECONCILIATION	244
XIV.	CONDITION OF RECONCILIATION	259
XV.	AGENT OF RECONCILIATION	270
XVI.	CAPACITY OF THE HUMN FOR THE INDWELLING OF THE DIVINE	281
XVII.	RECEPTION OF CHRIST	291
XVIII.	THE INDWELLING OF THE DIVINE IN THE HUMAN	300

CHAP.		PAGE
XIX.	UNION OF THE HUMAN WITH THE DIVINE	309
XX.	UNION AND UNITY OF BELIEVERS WITH ONE ANOTHER IN THEIR UNION AND UNITY WITH CHRIST	316
XXI.	EXALTATION OF THE HUMAN IN THE SONSHIP OF BELIEVERS	326
XXII.	PERFECTION	338
XXIII.	DUTY AND RATIONALE OF PRAYER	346
XXIV.	CONCLUSION	369

Ἐγώ εἰμι τὸ φῶς τοῦ κόσμου·—JOHN viii. 12.

Ἐγὼ ἦλθον ἵνα ζωὴν ἔχωσιν καὶ περισσὸν ἔχωσιν.— JOHN x. 10.

Ἐγώ εἰμι ὁ ἄρτος τῆς ζωῆς·—JOHN vi. 35.

Ἀμὴν ἀμὴν λέγω ὑμῖν, ὁ πιστεύων εἰς ἐμὲ ἔχει ζωὴν αἰώνιον.—JOHN vi. 47.
The Master.

"Ὅτε δὲ εὐδόκησεν ὁ θεὸς" ὁ ἀφορίσας με ἐκ κοιλίας μητρός μου καὶ καλέσας διὰ τῆς χάριτος αὐτοῦ ἀποκαλύψαι τὸν υἱὸν αὐτοῦ ἐν ἐμοί, ἵνα εὐαγγελίζωμαι αὐτὸν ἐν τοῖς ἔθνεσιν·— GAL. i. 15, 16.

Ζῶ δὲ οὐκέτι ἐγὼ ζῇ δὲ ἐν ἐμοὶ Χριστός ὅ δὲ νῦν ζῶ ἐν σαρκὶ ἐν πίστει ζῶ τῇ τοῦ υἱοῦ τοῦ Θεοῦ τοῦ ἀγαπήσαντός με καὶ παραδόντος ἑαυτὸν ὑπὲρ ἐμοῦ.—GAL. ii. 20.

Ἐγὼ γὰρ ἤδη σπένδομαι καὶ ὁ καιρὸς τῆς ἐμῆς ἀναλύσεως ἐφέστηκε.   τὸν ἀγῶνα τὸν καλὸν ἠγώνισμαι, τὸν δρόμον τετέλεκα, τὴν πίστιν τετήρηκα· λοιπὸν, ἀπόκειταί μοι ὁ τῆς δικαιοσύνης στέφανος, ὃν ἀποδώσει μοι ὁ Κύριος ἐν ἐκείνῃ τῇ ἡμέρᾳ, ὁ δίκαιος κριτής· οὐ μόνον δὲ ἐμοί, ἀλλὰ καὶ πᾶσι" τοῖς ἠγαπηκόσι τὴν ἐπιφάνειαν αὐτοῦ.—2 TIM. iv. 6. 8.

Ὁ δέ· Οὐ μαίνομαι, φησί, κράτιστε Φῆστε, ἀλλ' ἀληθείας καὶ σωφροσύνης ῥήματα ἀποφθέγγομαι.—ACTS xxvi. 25.

The Slave who, in
the spirit of his bondage, realised the highest liberty.

THE SCIENCE OF SPIRITUAL LIFE.

INTRODUCTION.

JUDGING by the signs of the present day, it would appear that the time has now come when a scientific exhibition of the facts and principles of Christianity may be set forth with advantage; indeed, we may go further than this, and affirm that such a setting forth of the doctrines of Christianity has become an imperative necessity.

In many of the religious controversies which from time to time have agitated the minds of men, particular doctrines have been fully discussed, and the result has been in most cases a more exact estimate of their scientific value. This, however, is not exactly what is most required in the present day. The Christian apologist cannot afford always to be waging war on behalf of this, that, or the other doctrine of his religion; it is prudent and needful to bring together the whole of the ascertained facts and doctrines of his faith, and by making the best possible disposition of his forces, see what is the precise position which he occupies.

Scientific exhibition and development in all cases naturally follow an inductive period, a period which is longer or shorter according to circumstances. In the spiritual sphere few if any great outstanding facts remain to be gathered together, and the work of the scientist in this direction is to discover exactly in what direction these data point—what they enable him to affirm, and what to deny. He is not, of course, in doing so, to confine himself solely to the facts developed under Christianity; this no doubt is his main source, but he is at the same time to avail himself of all facts, from whatever source, that bear upon the task which he undertakes.

A clear conception of the religions of the world affords no small aid to him who would form a just estimate of the scientific value of Christian doctrine. Such a one will find that Christianity though new, yet in one sense is not new; he will find that in the religions of the world there are rays scattered and broken and unintelligible in themselves, which are gathered up into one grand luminous centre in Christianity. What in these religions is a dark enigma, is made plain in the light which Christianity has thrown upon spiritual being. In other words, Christianity brings to the spiritual in man what that spiritual had lost and was craving after, but in such a form as longing humanity could never have conceived of. The difference between the religions of earth and Christianity is this,—the religions of earth are the yearnings, the guessings, the gropings of the human after the Divine. Christianity is the Divine descending into, possessing, and moulding the human after Itself.

A strange use, or rather misuse, has been made of the forms in which the spiritual element in man has found vent before the coming of Christ. Judaism itself has not escaped the same kind of abuse at the hands even of some who profess great zeal for the religion of Jesus. Indeed, many seem to think it needful to show their zeal by dis-esteeming and practically cutting all connection between Christianity and the Jewish Cultus: we are, I trust, beginning to learn a more excellent way. The following extract glances at a profound truth: "What distinguishes man from all other creatures, and not only raises him above the animal world, but removes him altogether from the confines of a merely natural existence, is the feeling of Sonship inherent in and inseparable from human nature. That feeling may find expression in a thousand ways, but there breathes through all of them the unextinguishable conviction, 'it is He that made us and not we ourselves.' That feeling of Sonship may with some races manifest itself with fear and trembling, and it may drive whole generations into religious madness and devil-worship. In other countries it may tempt the creature into a fatal familiarity with the Creator, and end in an apotheosis of man or a headlong plunging of the human into the divine."*

Religious or spiritual life in its widest acceptation has taken many crude and even revolting and disgusting forms of expression; but the wise man will not be

* Chips from a German Workshop, i. 352.

scared away from his investigation on that account, any more than will a physiologist be driven away from his labours because they are at times the reverse of pleasant. It may indeed seem strange that the religious feelings of men should take such crude forms as we find prevailing in different ages, and yet, read in the light of the perplexity expressed on the subject of religion in our own day by not a few cultivated minds, there is nothing to be surprised at in all this. It requires no great stretch of imagination to picture to ourselves those who deny the Christian's God—men of the most advanced materialistic school, yet very angry at being charged with Atheism, inasmuch as they admit an unknown and unknowable something, which may, for all they know to the contrary, be God,—it is easy to fancy, we say, such men the grossest of all idolaters while as yet the taper of physical knowledge burned low. Extremes in such matters usually have a point of contact.

Be this, however, as it may, to us it appears that the crude and even revolting forms of which we speak are in part to be explained objectively and in part subjectively. It is all very well for such men as the late J. S. Mill (who was by far the ablest man of the school of thought to which he belonged) to say that the benefits of Christ's teaching, like that of other masters, whatever it amounts to, is now as a matter of fact our possession, and that such truths are strong enough of themselves to retain the belief of mankind after they have acquired them.* Ideas of this sort go far

* Essay on the Utility of Religion.

to lead men of certain tendencies in religion to deny that men ever possessed a clearer view than they now have of moral and religious truth. The affirmation of such men is that the course of man has ever been upward—he cannot sink and lose hold of truths once laid hold of. In opposition, however, to this, we hold by the superior wisdom and philosophy of one old writer when he says, "Because that, when they knew God, they glorified Him not as God, neither were thankful; but became vain in their imaginations, and their foolish heart was darkened. Professing themselves to be wise, they became fools, and changed the glory of the uncorruptible God into an image made like to corruptible man, and to birds, and four-footed beasts, and creeping things."

A downward course became a necessity, when men had separated themselves from very close fellowship with God. The difficulties which encompassed man on all sides at first, before he could have experience and make a history for himself, were necessarily very great, so great that nothing short of constant intercourse with God could have prevented him from falling into idolatry of the grossest kind. In the absence of knowledge and experience, even a pure heart could not have always proved a sufficient defence for man without close contact with his Creator. The very instrument of thought—viz., language—was itself misleading. How much our progenitors knew of the nature of God we are not

* Rom. i. 21-23.

in a position to say; but the highest view necessitated by the account of Creation given in Genesis does not carry us very far. And the fossils of language embedded in the Shemitic, Aryan, and Turanian strata, seem to indicate that the spiritual was better known and more clearly realised before these main stems put forth their many shoots than for long afterwards. Yet, as an instrument of spiritual thought, language was miserably imperfect. Let us listen to what an able linguist has to say on this point. After referring to primeval civilisation, Max Müller says: "And let us not turn away and say that this, after all, was but nature-worship and idolatry. No; it was not meant for that, though it may have been degraded into that in later times: *Dyaus* did not mean the blue sky, nor was it simply the blue sky personified; it was meant for something else. We have in the Veda the invocations *Dyaûs Pitar*, the Greek Ζεῦ Πατερ, the Latin *Jupiter*; and that means in all the three languages what it meant before these three languages were torn asunder—it means Heaven Father! These two words are not mere words, they are to my mind the oldest poem, the oldest prayer of mankind, or at least of that pure branch of it to which we belong; and I am as firmly convinced that this prayer was uttered, that this name was given to the Unknown God before Sanskrit was Sanskrit and Greek was Greek. As when I see the Lord's Prayer in the language of Polynesia and Milanesia, I feel certain that it was first uttered in the language of Jerusalem. ... Thousands of years have passed since the Aryan nations separated to travel to the North and the South, the West and the East. They have each formed their languages; they have each founded empires and philosophies; they have each built temples and razed them to the ground; they have all grown older, and it may be wiser and better; but when they search for a name for what is most exalted and most dear to every one of us, when they wish to express both awe and love, the infinite and the finite, they can but do what their old fathers did, when gazing up to the eternal sky and feeling the presence of a Being as far as far, and as near as near can be : they can but combine the self-same words and utter once more the primeval Aryan prayer, Heaven Father, in that form which will endure for ever, 'Our Father which art in heaven.'"*

In course of time, when men forgot God, when they not only wandered away from the cradle of humanity but from God Himself, language became from its poverty a snare to them, and gradually the words and names applied to God led to the pantheons of Greece and Rome, and the other degrading forms of worship with which we are acquainted.

What we are chiefly to bear in mind are the spiritual indications which lie embedded in all these varying forms, however wicked and absurd we may in many respects truly regard them. And it will be found that these indications outweigh a hundred-fold all the atheistic appearances which meet us in

* Science of Religion, p. 172.

history, and in part explain them; for to such an extent did the spiritual impulse within drive men at times, that many were led to ask if there could be any objective foundation for such fancies, and not being able to discover any, and identifying religion itself with these caricatures of it, they threw it aside altogether. They were atheists, therefore, not from rejecting the God of heaven whom they never knew, but because no god worthy of their worship was placed before them.

We have now to look at the position assumed by those who attempt to deal scientifically with the subject handled in this volume; and these resolve themselves, with all their minor differences, into two principal and opposing methods. A preliminary statement, however, may be necessary, and here the words of another are so applicable that no apology is needed for their insertion: "In these our days it is almost impossible to speak of religion without giving offence either on the right or on the left. With some, religion seems too sacred a subject for scientific treatment; with others, it stands on a level with alchemy and astrology, as a mere tissue of errors or hallucinations far beneath the notice of the man of science."* We have little in common with either party. We have no great idea of the intelligence of the man who cannot see that there are religious *facts*, as truly facts as anything which physical science in any of its departments has to lay before us. The superficial trifling which denies not only any given

* Science of Religion, p. 6.

explanation of these facts, but the facts themselves, can hardly be much longer tolerated; and in point of fact, this class of atheists is dying out, for the present at least. With such persons we can hold no intercourse, for in the present treatise there is no ground common to them and ourselves. We feel bound to take for granted from the first certain great spiritual facts, which to our mind are so established that they can easily bear all the weight of the superstructure which is herein raised upon them.

On the other hand, there are those who have a strange dislike to any and every attempt at dealing in a scientific manner with spiritual things, generally speaking. Such persons have no great sympathy with science in any way (they perceive not that the scientific handling of Christian principles is the only true safeguard from superstition on the one hand and rationalism on the other). Now, to quiet all needless apprehensions, we should say that truth does not fear a scientific exhibition, and has seldom suffered from such a thing. It may indeed happen that mistakes have been made, and a grain of truth may have led to the acceptance of a cartload of error; yet the mistake has inevitably been discovered sooner or later, and so shall it be in the present case. If the exhibition of truth herein contained is correct, then let us hope that truth shall be the gainer; but if not correct, then let there be a full discussion and ventilation of the subject. The formula ever on the lips of such persons is this—viz., preach the Word, as if, forsooth,

Christ cannot be preached in any way but that which approves itself to their minds. This is often mistaken for true Christian humility; but there is a humility which has the marks of a disdainful pride; and of all the offensive forms in which pride can appear, that is the worst which encases itself in a narrow dogmatism. Blinders may indeed keep unusual objects from scaring nervous persons, but they are not well adapted for strengthening the sight.

But the very thing so much depreciated by many, has helped to preserve intact the doctrines of Christ, and has cleared them time after time from the mists which threatened to settle down upon them. Who, for example, needs to be told that this has pre-eminently been the case with the doctrine of Christ's person, which for generations formed the subject of debate? The doctrine is now seen to rest on a sure foundation, and is more clearly apprehended than it otherwise could have been; and the same thing holds good in the case of other great doctrines that have been discussed.

Assaults, moreover, are made on the very foundations on which a scientific exhibition alone can rest, and as a matter of course the defence must in some measure be guided by the mode of attack. When a country is in danger of being invaded and overrun by the foe, men do not cry Peace, peace; they do not go on cultivating their fields and enriching the country; they, in preference, burn all before them, however pungent their pangs of regret. Now, so is it here; we must go out to meet the enemy: there is nothing gained by concealing the fact from ourselves that there is an enemy, but everything to be lost by so doing. Let us then take what vantage-ground we may, not indeed so much concerned about victory as about truth, yet, persuaded that ours is the cause of truth, let us do what we can to strengthen it. Moreover, it is well that men should know that Christianity is capable of being scientifically defended. There are many, not thoughtless persons, who strangely enough take their views of religion from others, and think that it cannot be defended in the manner indicated. We may be astonished why men should do so, but there are many things not readily accounted for; hence it is our duty to show such men, if possible, that they are in error, and in this way lead them to a healthful profession of faith, or leave them without excuse in holding by their second-hand and false views of Christianity.

Among those who in one way or another aim at presenting a scientific explanation or exhibition of spiritual life there are many differences—varieties, we would say, but bound together by some differentia which constitutes them species, separate and distinct. The first method we would refer to is that adopted by the entire school spoken of as evolutionists. At the head of this school, in England at least, stand Darwin, Huxley, Tyndall, Spencer, and a host of lesser stars—men who in some way happen to dominate the British Association and a portion of the London press. They constitute what Principal M'Cosh rather facetiously has designated a branch of that hackneyed club known all over the world as the Mutual Admiration Society, inasmuch as they are never weary in quoting each other as infallible authorities. These authorities may not all be satisfied at being regarded as advancing a scientific basis on which to exhibit spiritual life, but, with all the nescience of their theories anent spiritual things, this is precisely what they are doing.

It is not affirmed that these scientists present such a basis as a Christian can adopt; on the contrary, grant their assumptions, and the whole superstructure of Christianity falls to the ground. But for all that, these men, one and all, affirm the existence of religious feelings, though they are much exercised over their explanation. With one consent, however, they relegate them into the region of the dark unknown and unknowable. According to Tyndall, physical science cannot explain them, but yet physical science, as being the most enlightened guide, is entitled to the direction of these feelings. But as confessedly physical science does not lead up to God, then, unless our religious feelings do not lead to God, science must wrongly direct them. If these aspirations do lead upwards, common sense surely tells us that they should be under no such dominion as the Professor indicates. The truth is, religious feeling is a centre of force which Dr. Tyndall does not well know how to manage, and he does the best he can in setting a physical-science conscience over it. J. S. Mill in his essay on "The Utility of Religion" ascribes the great power which religious feeling seems to exert to the force of education, and his impression seems to have been at that time—though he appears to have changed his mind afterwards—that the world would have got on rather better without religion than with it. The feelings themselves, like everything else, he would resolve by his universal power—*inseparable association.*

In general the disciples of this school are more reticent, not indeed that they want the courage of their opinions, but they seldom come to speak directly on this point, though they clearly indicate the current of their thoughts. Huxley is cautious when in his review of Comptism he says—in reply to the question, "Does human nature possess any free, volitional, or truly anthropomorphic element, or is it only the cunningest of all nature's clocks?—Some, among whom I count myself, think that the battle will for ever remain a drawn one, and that for all practical purposes this result is as good as anthropomorphism winning the day." *

Mr. Spencer resolves, as is well known, all our necessary beliefs in a way which he and some others regard as more satisfactory than Mr. Mill's law of inseparable association, which, by the way, is no longer felt to be tenable. Mr. Spencer adds hereditary experience to the experience of the individual; in short, these necessary beliefs have been in process of formation since man was a monad. This author generously allocates the entire domain of the unknown and unknowable to the religious element in man; if it confines itself to this he will not meddle with it,

* Lay Sermons, &c., p. 164.

and in that region it may find something to feed upon. But, as M'Cosh pertinently asks, " why does he exclude a necessary belief in the existence of the unknown and unknowable, or absolute and unconditioned," from the sweep of the law aforesaid? may such a belief not be generated by the race ever coming to the knowledge of something hitherto unknown? Let us listen to a few sentences of this bleak and barren synthetic philosophy: " It must be remembered that while the connection between the phenomenal order and the ontological is for ever inscrutable, so is the connection between the conditioned form of being and the unconditioned form of being for ever inscrutable. The interpretation of all phenomena in terms of Matter, Motion, and Force is nothing more than the reduction of our complete symbols of thought to the simplest symbols; and when the equation has been brought down to its lowest terms, the symbols remain symbols still; hence the reasonings contained in the foregoing pages afford no support to either of the antagonistic hypotheses respecting the ultimate nature of things. Their implications are no more materialistic than they are spiritualistic. Any argument which is apparently furnished to either hypothesis is neutralised by as good an argument furnished to the other. . . . He" (the man who understands his book) " will see that though the relation of subject and object renders necessary to us these antithetical conceptions of spirit and matter, the one is no less than the other to be regarded as but a sign of the unknown reality which underlies both."* This is Mr. Spencer at best, but alas! he rides away from us on a nebulous cloud, know-nothingness, into a region whither we are unable to follow him, not being assured that it has any existence at all.

The method, then, adopted by this school may be called hypothetical, and it resolves itself into this— viz., within the domain of the knowable there is no evidence for the existence of a God—in point of fact, there is no God; but if beyond that sphere there is anything, which is unknown and unknowable, that may be God, and the religious element of our being, on the principle of sufficient reason, may be allowed to connect us in some mysterious way with this unconditioned unknowable Being. This is granted only because it is impossible meanwhile to find any other more tangible place for such feelings.

It may fairly be questioned how long this faint recognition of a Supreme Power will hold its own among an English-speaking population who may be led to entertain it. A basis of religious life such as this will not long be respected by a fearlessly logical mind, and the feelings themselves, along with their basis, must soon come to grief. A God unknown and unknowable, who neither hears nor heeds our cries, is for all practical purposes no God, and a later generation will soon find this out. There is small chance of the rising race of thinkers in this school respecting such a flimsy barrier raised between them and Atheism. They will rather imitate the more consis-

* Biology, i. 491, 492.

tent Germans, who even now look upon all such things as sheer sentiment and want of courage. May the God of heaven defend us from such a consummation!

Indeed, if Dr. Tyndall is to be regarded as the interpreter of his school, there is obviously a movement in the camp of the Materialists—they are finding their ground insecure and are abandoning their strongholds of a pure Materialism. In his preface to his last edition of his "Fragments of Science," he says that by matter he does not mean mere atoms and motion and force, but a certain something which can and does produce all the phenomena of the world—the basis of all phenomena or all potentiality—a formative force.

We may well ask of him, What is this certain something—this basis of phenomena—this formative force? and until he gives an intelligible definition, a definite idea of his meaning, we must hold him as falling back upon pantheism or advancing to spiritualism. This he makes the more apparent by his concession that he cannot conceive of how life can be developed from the lifeless, or how consciousness can be evolved out of physical organisation.

We have shown in chapter xiii. that matter cannot be the basis of all phenomena. In that chapter it will be seen that the recognised proportions of matter can by no effort of reason or flight of imagination be predicated of mind or spirit. The attributes of spirit are there shown to be the very reverse of the properties of matter. The Professor's notion of matter is too vague and general, as also his idea of it as a formative force, to be of any scientific value. Force is formative in its crystallising and vital power, but is it nothing more in its mental and spiritual operations?

Formative force in its crystallising operations is doubtless a developing or evolving power, but is it such *per se?* In its vitalising operations it is a selecting power; in its rational operations it is an outgoing power; and formative force in its spiritual operations is a combining, reflecting, self-approving, or self-condemning, an advising or dreading power.

What kind of consciousness may be in a plant we cannot imagine, but we know that consciousness in man is the most vivid reality of his existence. When we enter this region of human experience we cannot escape its clear and definite teaching; and thus we are not surprised that the Professor, leaving for a moment his material speculations, and entering into the realisations of his inner life, should come out with the declaration that in the phenomena of consciousness we find the rock on which materialism must inevitably split when it pretends to be a complete philosophy of the human mind.

No complete philosophy of human life can overlook the phenomena of consciousness, and no comprehensive science can refuse to investigate the character of such phenomena; and the scientific investigator of such will find no difficulty in perceiving that the phenomena of consciousness can never be unquestionably regarded as the phenomena of mere formative force. In volition, conscience, self-approbation, self-condemnation, adoration or dread, are the operations of mere formative force; a minute analysis of these, not to speak of others, will unmistakably show that there certainly are in man what can never be regarded as the phenomena of mere formative force.

It is time, however, to draw attention to the other method of dealing with this great subject. This which we may call the Christological method is spiritual in the highest degree; it enters into no complicated and dark reasoning anent the essential nature of substance, nor does it concern itself about metaphysical subtleties regarding the unknown and unknowable. Strangely enough, it is those who raise, and would perplex themselves and us with such questions, that accuse religionists of dealing in subtleties; but surely the religion of Jesus comes to us like springs in the desert after the sterility and death of cosmism as evolutionists call their system; but a cosmism in which the soul, weary with the burden of sin, and seeking rest, can see neither order nor beauty. This method postulates a personal God as one of its most fundamental ideas, indeed as *the* fundamental idea—a God who is not only distinct from nature but above nature—its Creator and Preserver. This method of which we approve repudiates alike pantheism, atheism, and all such bastard ideas as represent God as an unknown something, if we may even use the term something to what is indefinitely near to nothing. It further encourages us to look up and say, "Our Father who art in heaven." In this method a place is found for all bygone aspirations after God, and a good reason is assigned for them. These have all along been what we should have expected from those who have been made in the image of God, but have left their first estate, and no longer enjoy the good after which their spirits yearn.

In all ages and conditions of his being man has been striving after the realisation of the Divine impressed on him at first, and nothing short of a Godlike life can satisfy the craving which he feels. Explain it as we may, man is restless, ever striving after what is beyond, forgetting what is behind; in his best moods he is ever reaching forward to what lies before him, and every step gained is but the precursor to a further attempt. In this sense we recognise a glorious evolution, a development which is ever going forward, not from the pressure of environment but from the power that dwells within. Here there is no transmutation of species, but a perfecting of the species in a higher life, the spirit of God becoming the spirit of man's spirit.

Mere man-life is evidently imperfect,—the highest forms of it with which we are acquainted were anything but satisfied with themselves. Even our progenitors, when they had all that in their circumstances they could reasonably need, are represented as not satisfied with themselves or the position in which they were placed, and so in striving to rise above it, they fell far below even the possibilities of man-life. And thus has it happened in the case of all the efforts put forth by men for the furthering of their spiritual interests. The smoke of countless victims that ascended from ten thousand altars, the penances, the indefinite, perhaps indefinable, longings of heathenism all indicate disquietude and discontent with the life man was living, and his desire to escape at least into another state which they imagined to be better; but their attempts ever ended in miserable failure; they ofttimes made bad worse, and were never able to free those who made them from their entanglements.

When we examine these attempts in a sympathising spirit, realising that those who made them were men like ourselves, that they felt the sorrows of life as we do, and were walled in on either hand by the thick impenetrable darkness which hung around them, without a glimpse of the light and immortality which are our inheritance, we feel a sinking of heart; in their own way they were groping about for God, like as blind men grope for the wall, and yet they could not attain to Him, though He was not far from them. Our deepest interest is concentrated on these men; when we thus regard them they are brought near to our hearts; whereas, looked at as they too often are, they are separated from us by the entire diameter of feeling. When, however, we do them justice and bring them near to us, and as far as possible try to put ourselves in their position, we get a glimpse of where and how far they went astray.

Change, restless change, was the motto inscribed on

their inner life, hope in pursuit of some *mirage* alternating with despair when it was found that their hopes were not to be realised. In earlier stages monotheism was tried, but soon degenerated into polytheism, with occasional outbursts of atheism; but the result was ever the same—wild unrest and feverish anxiety for fresh change, that they might secure the good they did not feel, but which they rightly enough judged to exist; and in their strivings, strange to say, they lighted upon many deep spiritual truths. But why should we say that this is strange, when we reflect that their nature was spiritual, and ever striving after the realisation of these very truths? In confirmation of this, look, for example, at Buddhism, a system effete and materialistic to its very core. A competent authority says: "Buddhism has no God, it has not even the confused and vague notion of a universal spirit, in which the human soul, according to the orthodox doctrine of Brahmanism and the Sânklya philosophy, may be absorbed. . . . It confounds man with all that surrounds him, all the while preaching to him the laws of virtue. Buddhism, therefore, cannot unite the human soul, which it does not even mention, with a God whom it ignores, nor with Nature, which it does not know better."[*] This matter is painfully brought before us by Max Müller, when he somewhat mournfully and truly says: "In no religion are we so constantly reminded of our own as in Buddhism, and yet in no religion has man been drawn

[*] M. Barthelemy Saint-Helaire, quoted by Müller, vol. ccliv. chap. i.

away so far from the truth as in the religion of Buddha. Buddhism and Christianity are indeed the two opposite poles with regard to the most essential points of religion—Buddhism ignoring all feeling of dependence on a higher power, and, therefore, denying the very existence of a Supreme Deity; Christianity resting entirely on a belief in God as the Father, in the Son of man as the Son of God, and making us all children of God by faith in His Son. Yet between the language of Buddha and his disciples, and the language of Christ and His apostles, there are strange coincidences. Even some of the Buddhist legends and parables sound as if taken from the New Testament, though we know that many of them existed before the beginning of the Christian era." [*]

From all this we may learn how imperative even truth itself is, when not applied to the sinful heart by the agency which has been provided by God, to apply the benefits of Christ's redemption to the souls of believers.

We see here where these ignorers of God turned aside into a wrong path, for, first, as mighty waters let loose spread desolation far and wide over fertile fields, but gathered together into a fitting channel carry fertilising influences along with them, as they descend to furnish a way for trade and commerce, and the necessities of civilisation and advancement; so the religious element in man when ill directed is a source of woe, but confined to its proper bed is

[*] Science of Religion, pp. 242, 243.

the source of the greatest bliss that man can experience on the earth.

The Christian doctrine—a doctrine shadowed forth under the Mosaic dispensation—is this, viz., that man escapes from his felt imperfection by an exaltation of human nature, and that this exaltation is realised in union and communion with a nature higher than his own. In this exaltation human nature remains unmodified, it is still the same, just as gold is still gold after it has been subjected to a purifying process. It is well known how companionships affect men, raising or deteriorating them, and what happens thus daily before our eyes, takes place in a higher sphere when the companionship of God is realised in the soul. In this case, there is no more than in the former any confounding of the persons or lives. The soul does not become the dead conduit, but is the living, loving exponent of the Divine, and finds the virtue of its very constitution, its highest perfection, in union and communion with God.

In the foregoing we may find something which goes a little way, perhaps, to explain that monstrosity called pantheism. Pantheism, we opine, is little else than the shadow cast by the deep indefinable feeling, that man is only perfect in God. Men may begin by reasoning about the absolute and unconditioned, and land in pantheism; but it cannot be their reasonings about matters which, from their very nature, are confessedly unknown, that land them in such conclusions. There cannot be any real connection between premises and conclusions, and we are perforce driven to find the true explanation in something more tangible. Man cannot stand apart from God; the feebleness of his spirit shows itself in his very yearning after something on which he may rest and call God. Pantheism is a weak, mad plunge into this as soon as a man has found it; it is fundamentally a sickly cast of thought. True religion is more manly; it holds by individuality, not in opposition to the God which it finds, but because it feels that there can be no contradiction between its dependence on God and God's good pleasure, that it should always be distinct from Himself.

There is, perhaps, no religious error which has not some true point of departure; and because it is so, men are apt to become increasingly perplexed when, from any cause, they are unwilling to approach the subject of religion with a spirit of deep reverence. Self-satisfaction is a blinding power in any case, but most of all in religious search. The self-sufficient man need not begin the study of the religious problems of his life, his self-conceit is like a bandage of many folds bound over his eyes—he can only in such a case furnish another illustration of the fact, that not many wise men after the flesh are chosen as interpreters of God's ways; with men it is only the man who will do His will that can know of the doctrine whether it be of God.

In Christianity, the exaltation of which we have spoken as the door of escape from man's unrest, it is union and communion with God, through union and communion with one who is at once

God and man. The great object of the Gospel of Christ Jesus is to set forth such truths as shall throw light upon the condition of humanity. It homologates its aspirations, it explains the mysteries which ever haunt man's weary footsteps, and in the scheme of redemption it opens up a way of escape to the embrace of a loving Father, at whose right hand there are pleasures for evermore. And it leaves us standing, fondly, desiringly, looking into the vista of the future, in the full persuasion that by and by there shall arise out of the ashes of a purified world a lovelier paradise than that from which our progenitors were driven.

> "There happier bowers than Eden's bloom,
> Nor sin, nor sorrow know;
> Blest seats, through rude and stormy scenes,
> I onward press to you."

CHAPTER I.

MAN A RELIGIOUS BEING, IN AN IRRELIGIOUS EFFORT AND HAPLESS CONDITION.

It is now generally conceded that man is a religious being. The import of the religious element, the direction in which it points, and as a consequence, the nature of the obligation under which it lays us, are constantly giving rise to its discussion. But of the fact itself, that man is a religious being, no serious difficulty of opinion now exists among reflecting men.

Among devoutly religious men, the most profound and accurate thinkers believe, and have tried to establish the fact, that man is a religious being, because he is possessed of a God-conscious faculty, the direct function of which is to gaze upon God; and therefore they conclude that he is religious just as he is a social or a sentient being.

It is, however, no less clear that there is a conflict in human nature—a struggle between what are regarded as the higher and lower powers and capacities of man's being;—in other words, man possesses a religious nature which is involved in an irreligious strife; and this condition of things we believe goes far to explain many of the varied and perplexing phenomena of man's life.

Man everywhere, and in all ages, has had an impression of a Power above him, and of his standing to that Power in a relation of responsibility. This impression, it is true, in certain individuals may be so faint as hardly to be discernible to the individual himself, or to the student of man's nature, however keen his search, yet will it ever be found that time and the requisite circumstances are capable of unfolding it to the full consciousness of all concerned.

Man is not only aware of a sense of obligation to the Power above him, he is made to realise that this sense of obligation is the deepest and most enduring consciousness of his life. In the felt presence of this Power, he can be satisfied with himself only in as far as he is able to persuade himself that his deeds are in accordance with the will of that Power, and his life acceptable to it. Every man knows, that although the religious impressions and convictions of his mind are not at all times in the most effective condition, they are the most powerful and enduring of his nature; for should he in the moment of temptation disregard the authority of his conscience, and do what he feels he ought not to do, yet will conscience reassert her authority, dash the cup of pleasure from his lips, and make him feel humiliated in the consciousness of having done what he felt he ought not to have done. And although some men may become so brutalised as utterly to disregard conscience, they do not thereby extirpate it from their nature, they only add to its condemning power, when at length, like a subterranean fire, it upheaves the heavy load under which, intentionally or unintentionally, they have buried it.

This sense of obligation to the Divine is not only the deepest and most enduring consciousness of man's life; but, side by side with it, the yearning after God in the spirit of man is the first and most indestructible craving of his soul. The necessity for the indwelling of God in the spirit of man, is the most urgent and irrepressible requirement of his well-being. Man apart from God cannot but feel that he is unable to meet the underlying necessity of his nature; for should he, in the pursuit of his own ends, attain to all that his heart can desire of earth's possessions, still, if his religious cravings be not met, these cravings cause him to realise that he possesses not all that he needs. A religious nature can rest only in a religious life, and capacity for the indwelling of the Divine necessitates the presence of God in the soul in order to its permanent enjoyment. The void spirit of man can no more repose in the desertion of God, than can the feeling of thirst be satisfied without water; and as soon may the body burning with fever enjoy the harmony and comfort of health, as the spirit of man while animated by the diabolic enjoy repose.

And when once the idea of religion takes possession of the mind of a man, that man cannot let the subject of religion alone,—he must either place himself in opposition to all religion, or struggle to satisfy himself with some of the false forms of religion that exist, or he must find his satisfaction from repose in the true.

Man is thus a religious being, possessed of a religious nature, yearning after a higher condition of a religious life, and striving to attain to the end of his existence, in putting forth an effort to unite himself with the Infinite and Eternal. Man is capable of the indwelling of the Divine, he is gifted with powers susceptible of entering into fellowship with God, he is capable of religious impressions, he is the subject of religious aspirations and desires. He readily engages in religious efforts, and ever worships what he conceives to be the proper object of admiration. He has longings which can be met only in God. He realises the perfection of his life in a true likeness to God, and he can rest satisfied only when God dwells in his heart.

While this is true, as already indicated, man is at the same time a religious being in a fallen condition of life. The God-conscious faculty of his spirit is insensible, like the organ of breathing in the fœtus, it has no action until he is "born again." In his unregenerate state man has no immediate vision of God, no fellowship with his Father in heaven. He is averse to God, and strives to live without Him in the world.

Man's impression of the Power above him, and of his responsibility to that Power, does not draw him near in holy love and obedience to his Father, that he may receive the supplies of the Divine necessary to meet the wants of his nature, and to develop the constitution of his being. This impression of a Power above him rather leads man to endeavour, by means of sacrifice, penance, and supplication, to propitiate that Power. This impression exists in its truest condition while in its faintest form, for when it is unfolded in the human mind, irrespective of the light of revelation, it is developed in erroneous conceptions of the human, and in false and perplexing notions of the Divine. The experience of heathenism, the degenerating tendency of idolatry in man, the results of human speculation, the doctrines of the different schools of philosophy, and the tenets of the many sects in religion, exhibit the truth of this statement. In fact, wherever this impression has been unfolded in the human heart, apart from the influence of the Spirit of God, it has always developed itself in impious feelings towards God. The facts of heathen sacrifice, the endeavour of man in all ages to propitiate God, to alter His disposition, and change His purpose towards sinners, sufficiently establishes and illustrates the truth of this assertion.

The cherishing of such desire in the human heart shows that man has fallen from, and is striving to live beneath, the conditions of his own wellbeing. God, in His infinite wisdom and benevolence, could never have created man to desire that God would be, and do differently from what God Himself is and does. This would have been to have created man in a condition of conflict with the principles and obligations of his nature, the necessities of his spiritual life, and with the terms of his fellowship with and enjoyment of God. Man, by cherishing the desires of his natural heart, necessarily places himself in opposition to God, and removes himself from Him, acts in opposition to the deep necessities and immutable condition of his own wellbeing; and therefore he cannot be at peace with God, nor act in harmony with the requirements of his nature.

Human experience shows that man's sense of obligation is of no direct avail to him in his natural state for the discharge of his duty. It affords him no means of ascertaining what is right from what is wrong. On this all-important point, men from the beginning have differed. Man has no knowledge of right in the abstract, conscience can only approve when he acts in accordance with, and condemns when he wills in opposition to, his judgment. Hence one community and one age has approved what another has denied. Conscience, moreover, has not that supremacy in man's life to which it is entitled, it is a dethroned monarch; when passion rises conscience does not rule, but is suffered merely to warn or threaten. When assailed with temptation man does not immediately and unhesitatingly dismiss the tempter, but dallies with the temptation, and by so doing falls before its power. In his spiritual and rational nature, man acts more unworthily than does the brute creation. The inclinations of the inferior animals are in the direct line of the end of their existence, their instincts at once propel them to what is necessary to their wellbeing. Similarly the instincts of man's animal nature are true and urgent, but such is not the case with man's rational discernment and spiritual biases. In the spiritual of his being while in his natural state, man has no spontaneous risings of filial affection to his Father in heaven, no vivid discernment of the mind of God, no ardent and cherished desire to comply with the obligations of duty, no longing after any cherished delight in the consciousness of the Divine. And why are the biases of man's soul not Godward, unless it be that they are perverted?

Man has thus no true knowledge of the immutable principle of his wellbeing, viz., that the finite can never meet the necessities, fill the capacities, and energise the functions of his spirit—that nothing short of the indwelling of God can quicken and sustain him in his true life, that, secure what amount he may of the finite without the indwelling of God, he can only be the more restless and unhappy. In such circumstances, it is surely no great leap to conclude that knowledge of his wellbeing, if this is to be obtained, can only be reached by man through revelation. A holy being, without a direct perception of the end of his existence, and an intuitive knowledge of the Divine, is something like a contradiction. Surely the simplest and most satisfactory solution of the problem is, that man is not now what he once was.

And what is the history of man's religious endeavours, but the narrative of irreligious deeds? It is the history of a religious being struggling after the advantages of a religious life, while disinclined to comply with the only conditions of religious obligation and enjoyment. This is the true solution of the varied and conflicting phenomena of life. On the admission of man's fallen condition, the different and contradictory phases of human experience in man's present state can be adequately accounted for and satisfactorily explained. But on no other principle, so far known to us, can the restless and conflicting state of man on earth be cleared up.

Man, moreover, is not only a religious being in a fallen condition, he is in a helpless state, unable to rescue himself from the conflict of his own nature. In order to the restoration of a fallen religious being, there must be, as we shall afterwards see, a supernatural manifestation of the Divine. Apart from the peculiar grace of God, every manifestation of the Divine to the fallen must, from the nature of the case, be wrathful, and as such be provocative of opposition, and only drive the fallen farther and farther away from God. If man is to be drawn to God, the supernatural manifestation given to him must be of love, of merciful purpose, and of quickening grace, such as shall allure into the fellowship of the Divine. Such a manifestation of God as this, as a matter of course, must be given to man from without; for of himself he is utterly unable to ascend to such ideas of God, he can neither work out from his own inner self nor discover in creation a medium of delightful fellowship with his Father in heaven. Do what he will he cannot lay hold on such a manifestation of love and grace as is fitted to ravish his heart and bind him to the throne of the Eternal. Man cannot think of God as He is. To do so would be for the false and hating to produce the loving and true. Hence man cannot unveil to himself God in mercy, nor produce such a vision of the love of God as can bring him into fellowship with his Father in heaven, and promote the ends of his own existence.

Nor does this inability measure the helplessness of man. He is not only unable to produce the gracious of the Divine, he is averse to the holy and unwilling to attach himself to the heavenly. In virtually desiring, as man does, a change in the nature of God, he must falsely apprehend God; and in striving to elaborate an idea of God from materials supplied by his own faculties alone, he is necessarily creating an idol and forging for himself chains of darkness. The first duty of man in regard to spiritual things is not to search after truth, but to yield himself up to the guidance of the true. Rationalism is the most irrational attempt on the part of man; it is, in fact, the monstrous of human intellect.

Reason cannot approve of man's attempt to think God, much less can it justify him in his desire that God's nature were changed. Reason cannot allow that the wellbeing of man is compatible with false desire in his heart, or with erroneous conceptions in his mind regarding his relations with God.

How dark must be the mind that can entertain the idea of effecting a change in God! And does not the attempt on the part of man to propitiate God clearly prove the existence of such a conception and desire in man, and reveal the inner darkness of the human mind regarding man's relations with God? Nay, the very effort on the part of man to propitiate God discloses a deep consciousness in humanity of a difference between God and man. And what can this difference be but an opposition of entire life. The attempt to propitiate God also implies the existence of a vague notion in man that somehow he is able to rectify the disturbance between himself and God—that it lies with man to provide the medium of agreeable fellowship between himself and God—that the change necessary to agreeable fellowship is a change needed not in man but in God; and that man is more desirous than God for the re-establishment of agreeable fellowship between heaven and earth. Here is the acme of human self-righteousness, of the errors which underlie the religious efforts of man.

Moreover, the cherishing of such desire on the part of man shows that the direct manifestations of God in and to man are offensive; so much so, that instead of satisfying they disquiet his spirit. The cherishing of such desire surely shows that the manifestations of God to man, through the operations of nature in him, only intensify his consciousness of guilt, arouse the enmity of his rebellious spirit, and increase the conflict of his nature, and therefore are not and cannot be a blessing to him.

And reason must see that man in cherishing such a desire, and in endeavouring to propitiate God, can only render his condition worse; for such a desire and effort can only make him more unlike God and less sympathetic with Him, and in this way widen the gulf already existing between them.

Yet man struggles, and that persistently, to be religious after his own conception. He does not perceive that by such an effort he violates the first principles of the finite and religious—viz., that the finite must ever be dependent on the Infinite—in the measure of the nearness of his nature to God, and that the religious in man must feed itself only on the manifestations of the Divine. He perceives not that by his very effort to win the favour of God he denies the fact of his fall, and of his helpless condition before Him; for how can he meet the Divine approbation by desiring that God should be different from what He is, seeing that by so doing he creates to himself an idol, and sins against the living God?

The very effort of fallen man to commend himself to God by his own doings is inconsistent with the revelations of the fallen, and subversive of the fundamental principles of a gracious restoration. Grace requires of fallen man that he become acceptable to God not by doing but by believing. And herein we perceive the direct opposition between the religious attempts of men and the religion of God. The religious after man's conception does not perceive man's need of renewal through the quickening of the Divine. Instead of carefully examining the characteristics of his religion, to see if it be in entire conformity with the necessary conditions of grace to the fallen, he is rather disposed to take credit to himself for the excellence of that religion which has sprung up from within, and has proceeded from himself. He tests his religion not by the assimilation of his life to the Divine, and by the consciousness of the calm, deep, and ready power of principle which enables him to overcome temptation, raises him above fretfulness in reference to the seen and temporal, and preserves him in the realised sense of the Divine presence, not by this, but by the heat of his emotional fervour, the zeal of his prejudice, and the numerous deeds and burdensome character of his services.

And yet, after all, is there not a something underlying this desire in man that God's nature were other than it is, that deserves the most thoughtful study of man? Is there not a something here which foreshadows the bringing in of a better hope—a something which shuts man up to the dictates of a higher reason than his own, even to faith in a revelation from God? May there not be in this desire the first motion of a craving after that which is necessary to the restoration of spiritual life in man? Is there not in this desire a divine indication of the deep requirements of man's condition, an echo in the human soul of a higher voice than man's? Doubtless there is here the response of man's inner being to that voice which tells him that a change must be effected ere he can delight himself in God—a change in that very desire which he so ardently cherishes. And in order to the accomplishment of this change, there must needs be a change, not in the nature, but in the manifestations of God to the sinner.

And can this change needed by man be any other than a transition from the disturbed emotions innate in the fallen, to a tranquil and joyous repose of the soul in God, through means of a supernatural manifestation of the Divine? If the desire in man for a change in God proves that the manifestations of the Divine in man, or the revelation of God to man through the operations of nature in and around him, are so offensive that he cannot through means of them hold delightful fellowship with God, but must long for other manifestations, can these other manifestations be through nature? Must they not be such as, while acting upon man so as to harmonise the operations of nature in him, be supernatural in themselves?

If this desire in man does not furnish him with the evidence of a Divine voice speaking in him— if it does not warrant him to expect a supernatural manifestation of the Divine, it certainly should dispose him to listen with attention to the announcement of such a manifestation, and induce him to examine with care the credentials of that which claims to come to him as a revelation from God, which tells him that God has given to man a manifestation of Himself for the very purpose of effecting a change in him, and thus rescuing him from the conflict in which he groans and toils, but from which he labours in vain to escape. Should not this desire incline man to receive and readily obey this revelation, rather than to endeavour to reduce its doctrines to the level of his selfish dispositions and vain conceits?

What a spectacle in the universe of God is man! a being created with capacities boundless and enduring as the Eternal—endowed with a receptivity for the indwelling of God—possessed of a nature susceptible of rising to the loftiest condition of the finite, and a heart that ever yearns with an indestructible longing for the enjoyment of endless fellowship with the Infinite, and yet understanding not the deep cravings of his own immortal spirit, nor embracing the fair opportunities within his reach of knowing God and entering into rest. For what is the result of all his labours under the sun? They are only vanity and vexation of spirit even at best. Instead of finding God, excavating Him as it were from the womb of nature or the depths of his own consciousness, he only gives an ideal objective existence to his own inner disturbed state of thought and feeling—a phantom which, as he pursues it, leads him only farther and farther into ever-deepening gloom, and increases the unavailing conflict which already exists, and awakens more keenly within him the feeling of disquietude.

CHAPTER II.

TRUTH IN ITS HIGHER MANIFESTATIONS.

WHAT is truth? Truth is related to thought—its source and its expression. It is the harmony of thought with its object, and the agreement of thought with its expression—the agreement of the objective and subjective. When a witness is called to give his evidence on a matter in dispute, he is required solemnly to bind himself "to speak the truth, the whole truth, and nothing but the truth"—*i.e.*, to tell all that he knows of the case in hand, and to tell it exactly as he knows it. He is not to withhold anything, or to colour any of his statements. He is to embody his knowledge of the matter in such language as will convey to the mind of judge and jury an impression of the case the exact reflex of his own. And if in making his statement he is known intentionally to employ terms which cannot but mislead, or which in their nature are fitted to do so, he is held to be a false witness, or one who has not spoken the truth.

Moreover, the testimony of a witness, while faithful, may be inadequate to convey a correct conception of the matter under investigation. His observation may have been hurried, partial, or incomplete; and while he candidly declares all that he knows, his declaration may be found insufficient to represent the matter in all its exactitude and fulness. Such a witness has indeed spoken the truth; but truth in its widest sense implies not merely a faithful utterance, but likewise a correct and complete expression of the full acquaintance with the object or subject matter of knowledge. Man seeks in his knowledge to embrace all being in all its relations and conditions. Man has thoughts of himself and of other beings, and his knowledge of external existence is not merely historic, but scientific and vital —not simply an acquaintance with the facts, but a discernment of the laws and operations of being; and this knowledge is gained not merely by the perceptions of the mind, but also by the emotions of the heart and the realisations of the spirit. Man has a knowledge not only of physical nature, but of personality, of the principles and realisations of life. Thought is related to the outer of being and to the inner of soul, and truth is the harmony or correctness of this thought. To know truth in its entirety, we must not only acquaint ourselves with the whole of outer existence, but with the entire of inner being, and realise the relations of the inner to the outer, and of the outer to the inner of existence.

Truth is the medium of rational intercourse. Mind cannot hold intercourse with mind but through the medium of truth. If one mind in converse with another does not employ nor receive truth, then there is no communication between them. To the extent that error is involved in the converse of mind, to that extent the one mind is shut out from the other. If life does not act truthfully — *i.e.*, feed on its own proper aliment, and act in harmony with its constitution—it does not realise itself as it ought to do, nor through the consciousness of life in itself know what life is in another. If spirit does not meet spirit in truthful embrace, there can be no pure fellowship between spirits, no realised intercourse of soul. The knowledge of spiritual truth, then, is not mere intellectual perception of facts, laws, &c., of being, but the spiritual realisation of existence through the love of the Divine—conscious life in God. Truth has been defined "the reality of things;" it would be more correct to call it the reality of being. A knowledge of the objective, however correct and complete, cannot afford an adequate acquaintance with truth. To know truth we must know the subjective as well as the objective, and realise life in its relations to being.

We may set it down as an axiom, that if there be a personal God at all, He can bear testimony as well as man. The Infinite may express Himself as well as the finite. Man utters his thoughts in words, himself in life. If God utters his mind, we are to expect He will do so adequately and truthfully—in Word and Life. And for the adequate reception of such a revelation, there must be a pure reception of the Divine—a capacity for hearing the Word and a capability of receiving the Life.

Truth is essentially dualistic. Mind must have idea, and idea must have form. Thought is distinct from the thinking substance, and yet they are essentially connected. Thought can exist only in mind, and mind, which is essentially active, can act and realise itself only in thought. Mind must be conscious of thought, but that thought is not the mind itself. The subjective is necessary to the objective, and the objective to the subjective. Mind must express itself to itself, and mind can express itself to itself only by the subjective passing into the objective in consciousness. And the objective must be the express image of the subjective. The subjective of the Infinite Mind is the Divine consciousness of God's being, purpose, and enjoyment. The objective of the Infinite Mind is the Divine ideal, that of which God is conscious; and that of which God is conscious is in perfect agreement with and altogether worthy of the subjective Divine.

The ideal is the objective, the consciousness of the emotional and volitional is the subjective, of mind. The subjective may be in a harmonious or conflicting state towards the objective, as in the consciousness of guilt. In this state the affectional and volitional are not and cannot be in accord with the ideal or objective. If the subjective and objective are concordant, truth is in the mind to the extent of its consciousness. If they are in conflict, error is in the mind. If all minds had the same ideal, then would there be no difference in minds but that of individual personality. In the Infinite Mind, while as yet nothing was created, the objective proceeded from the subjective, and was derived from no foreign or external source. In the finite mind the objective is derived from the inner and outer — from intuition, observation, and experience.

Truth is subjective and objective, and objective and subjective. Mind is occupied with its ideal. The ideal is the objective, and the consciousness of the ideal is the subjective, of mind. The objective is the offspring of the subjective; the utterance of the objective is the embodiment in sound, form, or vitality of the subjective, and the perfect utterance is the true manifestation of the subjective in the objective. Truth is objective internal and external. While the ideal of mind exists only in the consciousness of mind, it is the internal objective of mind; but when it is expressed in its embodiment, it is the objective external; and when it is embraced by other minds in belief, it becomes the objective internal and subjective of such mind, and the consciousness of it brings the subjective of the mind embracing it into a oneness with the mind from which it originally proceeded. Truth subjective and internal objective in the Divine Mind is necessarily infinite; but can truth external objective to the Divine Mind be necessarily infinite, must it not be necessarily finite? The limitations of truth are in the forms and not in the essence of truth. If modern philosophic speculation would keep this fact in view, there would be less talk than there is of creation proving only the existence of an imperfect God.

Truth in God, or the objective internal and subjective of the Infinite Mind, is necessarily true—*i.e.*, the objective is the exact counterpart of the subjective, and the objective is the full measure or complete realisation of the infinitude of perfect being. But from this it does not follow that truth in the finite, while adequate to the exigencies of finite wellbeing, is necessarily infinite; and out of this then arises the possibility of a false objective and an erroneous subjective in the finite. It was therefore not without reason that some of the early fathers in the Church argued that there was necessarily the outgoing of the subjective into the objective Divine—the passing of the Infinite Mind into the consciousness of Itself in the generation of the Logos; and in this there was an entire satisfaction of the Infinite Heart with the Brightness of His own glory. God had a knowledge of His own Being, a consciousness of Himself, and this subjective Divine expressed Itself to Itself in the eternal generation of this Image of Itself. This objective of the subjective Divine could be expressed only in an eternal infinite Divine objective, an objective which was one with God. "In the beginning was the Logos, and the Logos was with God, and the Logos was God."

Truth is the external objective of the Infinite when it is the exact impress of the Divine ideal in the creation of the finite, the utterance of the Infinite concept in a sphere of being beyond the consciousness of God, the outgoing of the internal objective and subjective Infinite into the external objective and subjective finite. "And God said, Let us make man in our own image, after our likeness." "So God created man in His own image: in the image of God created He him; male and female created He them." "And God breathed into his nostrils the breath of life; and man became a living soul."

Truth in its totality is the infinite of the Divine, the concept of the Infinite Mind, the consciousness of that concept, the manifestation of that concept, the apprehension of that concept, the realisation of that concept, the fellowship of that concept. Truth is the infinite in the Infinite, the Infinite in the finite, the finite in the Infinite. Truth is the descent of the Infinite into the finite, and the ascent of the finite into a oneness with the Infinite—the fellowship of the Divine with the human, and of the human with the Divine and with the human. From the unbeginning ages of eternity there was in the Infinite Mind an ideal of the universe, a model concept of the contemplated workmanship of God. This model concept is the objective in the subjective, the ideal in the Infinite Mind. In this concept the objective and the subjective were one—the idea with the consciousness of it. There was a oneness or perfect agreement between them. There was no discord, opposition, or unlikeness between them. The concept was perfect and complete, all worthy of God. And when the Divine fiat in the act of creation gave substantive existence to the ideal objective of the Infinite Mind, the universe of material, intellectual, and spiritual being was the reflex of the Divine

objective, the written transcript of the Divine ideal.
In the act of creation, God, having as it were in
space the picture of His own ideal, gave beyond the
region of His own consciousness substantive existence
to His own objective concept, and displayed in the
mirror of the external the image of His own internal.
Divine wisdom, power, and goodness were adequate
to the production in external substantive existence of
the objective or ideal concept of the Infinite Mind.
Had it not been so, the Infinite must for ever have
continued within Himself all being—the objective in
the subjective, the finite in the Infinite; no objective
could have ever existed beyond the region of the
Divine consciousness; creation never could have
been, for God could never have given forth imperfection.
This of course does not mean metaphysical
imperfection. And Divine wisdom, power, and
goodness were not only adequate to the production
of a creation beyond the region of the Divine
consciousness, but were equal to the production of
this creation every way worthy of the exact counterpart
of the model concept of the Divine Mind. The
Almighty could have made it nothing else; for if
it was not the exact transcript of the Divine, then
did God not reproduce His own idea, but took the
model of His creation from some other than His own
ideal. If creation, as fresh from the Almighty hand,
had not been the exact transcript of the model concept
of the Divine Mind, then there must have been
imperfection in the workmanship of God. Creation
could never have met the intention of the Almighty,

God never could have surveyed His entire creation with satisfaction and pronounced it very good. But creation did reflect the model concept of the Divine Mind. God did survey it with His entire satisfaction and pronounced it very good. It was all that He desired it to be. It had a being as well as a beginning in perfect accordance with His design. There it hung in the presence-chamber of Jehovah the unique sketch of the Divine Artist, the perfect embodiment of the Divine purpose; there it lay traced on the parchment of space, in its substance and realisation the exact impress of the Divine intention, the perfect copy of the model concept of the Infinite and Eternal Mind—the fit transcript of the objective, the suitable outbreathing of the subjective, Divine. As the impression thrown from the stereotype plate answers to the page printed from the original fount, so did creation correspond with the ideal of God. The culmination or high perfection of this creation was immortal mind—spirit in the image of God—beings essentially active, capable of regulating their actions, of understanding their relations, and conscious of the high conditions of their wellbeing. The last stroke of creative skill and benignity was the gathering up into one bright image of God the scattered rays of His glory sparkling in the prior outgoings of the Divine, and breathing out from Himself into this finishing stroke the vital spark of infinite life. This immortal offspring of God not only imaged His own likeness in the constitution of their being, but in the conceptions of their minds and realisation of their spirits. They not only possessed in the substance and mechanism of their existence a counterpart of the objective Divine, but realised in their consciousness the reflex of the subjective God. Their whole nature moved in perfect sympathy with the Divine. The fellowship between the finite and the Infinite was perfect in kind, though not complete in degree; the spirit exulting in the fulness of its joy, the mind clear in its discernment of the light of the true, the soul joyous in the purity of its affections and satisfied with the bliss of the Divine. Man delighted in his being, and rejoiced in the presence of his God; and God, beholding in the objective and subjective of man the lovely reflex of His own being and life, rested with the entire satisfaction of His Infinite complacency in His first-born offspring. There was an interchange of affection, of thought, of confidence, of delight. Man received from God the fulness of his joy, the energy of his life, and returned the gratitude of his soul. God imparting to man the outgoing of His fulness, beheld in the human the exemplar of His design, the embodiment of His ideal, the perfection of His work, and received from man the full confidence of his love. Man had only, in the study of creation and in the fellowship of the Divine, to develop the capacities of his being, acquaint himself with the principles of his constitution, the end of his life, and to exercise the powers of his existence in communion with his Father, to advance to higher perfection, and ascend, in the endless progress of the reception of the Divine, to nearer and nearer resemblance to God and deeper consciousness of His life.

As man gazed on his own being, the nearest approach of the finite to the Infinite, he would perceive the objective Divine reflected in the objective human; as he realised life, he would become conscious of the subjective Divine being mirrored in the subjective human; and as he developed the powers and capacities of his life, he would ascend to a fuller fellowship, a higher enjoyment of being in himself, through means of his life in God and a more complete knowledge of the true. If creation reflected the objective Infinite and was summed up in man, then the human mind would receive, in its contemplation of the outer and realisation of the inner, an advancing impress of the objective Divine. As the body of the infant in the progress of growth approaches the maturity of manhood, so would the objective human rise in nearer measure to the objective Divine. If the inner of man imaged the inner of God, then as man read in his own being and life, and realised more of existence in his fuller consciousness, the subjective of man would pass into a nearer oneness with the subjective of God, as the consciousness of infancy in the development of life passes into a fuller knowledge of humanity. And thus the fellowship of man with God would grow in measure as he advanced into the deeper and fuller realisation of his own being and life, the subjective finite would pass into a closer oneness with the subjective Divine, the inner life of man into a nearer realisation to the life of God.

Man, the child of God, the heir of the Infinite and Eternal, the student of the Divine, would come to know the truth, to bask in its radiance, to realise its bliss, and to reflect its glory. Truth to be fully known requires not merely a completed objective, but a perfect subjective. If the subjective should be diseased—*i.e.*, morally disordered, conscious of guilt— the objective would be appalling to the subjective, and struggled against by the subjective. The subjective could not rest satisfied with this objective, however faithful an exemplar of itself, but would strive to bring it into such a condition as would satisfy it. And thus error and discordance would necessarily be generated in the mind. The mind could not be in a condition of truthfulness.

As long as fellowship was enjoyed with God, truth was known by man. Life was realised by him in the development of the human, through the indwelling operations of the Divine. Man was a possessor of truth, a student of truth, a witness for the truth. It is only in the fellowship of the Divine, and in the consciousness of the life of God in the soul, that truth can be known; not in the mere scientific study of nature, nor in the speculations of the human mind, but in the realisation of spiritual vitality. In spiritual life, the subjective human is one with the subjective Divine, the objective perceived with the objective real. Truth cannot be known in the consciousness of a discordant condition of existence, however clear the individual's perception may be of the relations and laws of being. If, then, in the mysteries of being, there were to arise in the deep recesses of the soul an aversion of heart from God, then truth would cease to be known, if the slightest misgiving were to enter into the consciousness. If a sense of guilt were to be realised, there then would be no longer a oneness of the subjective human with the subjective Divine, of the objective human with the objective real. There would be in the subjective of such consciousness a fall, a falsehood, a contradiction; and if from this cause there should arise on any account a necessity of a curse or blight, even for a time, spreading itself over creation, then the universe would no longer be the exemplar or faithful transcript of the model concept of the Infinite Mind, the true offspring of God. If, then, there be in the nature of free agency the possibility of a creature violating the obligations of his wellbeing, and if this possibility should become a reality, then that creature would be no longer what God had made him; his subjective and objective would be no longer one with the subjective and objective Divine, and the beauty of creation, as influenced by his standing in it, would be marred and its perfection destroyed. The world would be no longer the mirror in which was reflected the objective Divine, the human consciousness would no longer be the counterpart of the subjective of God. The human personality would be no longer one in conscious enjoyment with the Divine personality, the individual will would be no longer in harmony with the end, the principles and obligations of life. The concord, vigour, and bliss of human existence would be gone, and man at most would only remain a splendid ruin.

Into this most dire of all possibilities we may plunge, and grope amid innumerable suppositions, and stumble upon endless guesses, from which we can discover no outlet. Through this labyrinth we can trace no path; analogy itself is inadequate. The fall of man, the extinction of the Divine life in the soul, is the anomaly of man's existence; hence the absurdity of attempting any explanation of it, in accordance with the rules of logic. The only distant approach of analogy which, in the wildest suppositions of imagination, can be conceived of as bearing in the least upon this dark enigma, is the monstrous formations of the womb, the *lusus naturæ* which occasionally meet the eye. Admitting the fact of a disruption in the world—a fact which no philosophy can disprove, and a fact which no scepticism can disannul—it must be clear that the subjective human is no longer one with the subjective Divine, the objective human with the objective real. Just as the corrupt or mutilated text of a printed book is no longer one with the pure and correct manuscript of the written work, so the diseased frame of man, the rebellious spirit, the fallen world, is no longer one with the new-born creation which God pronounced to be very good. And should this disturbed order of being be read as the pure text of revelation, with the view of ascertaining from it the mind of God—if this fallen condition of humanity should be studied with the view of becoming acquainted with the real workmanship of God or the true nature of man, a grave error is committed, and a false impression of the will and design of God is received. If the guilty conscience and the rebellious spirit of man be read in the light of consciousness, in order to learn the true character of the soul, the real nature of spiritual life, and the original manifestation of the Divine in the human, the result must be error and confusion.

And this is the very error into which rationalists and many scientific men are continually falling. They study the existing order of things, the present state of the world, with the view of coming to a correct conception of the work of God, the original manifestation of the Divine to man, and expect by so doing to arrive at a knowledge of truth, of being, of God. But they perceive not that the sympathies, sentiments, desires, and consciousness of man are not what they originally were; that the development of the nature, the unfolding of the principles, the invigoration of the powers, the exercise of the functions, and the realisation of the life of man are not what they were when fresh from the hand of God. It is thus impossible for them in such a study to arrive at a knowledge of truth. Those who would thus study do not see that their perceptions must necessarily be obscure, perplexing, and contradictory. Hence the error and conflict of the contending schools of philosophy and sects in religion. The world may be in substance what it originally was, but is no longer what it was in its relations, operations, and realisations.

In the study of humanity, as made known to us in the life of man, we may arrive at a knowledge of the elements, faculties, existing relations, and actual experience and known consciousness of man; but such a knowledge cannot afford a clear insight into the original condition of man, much less can it supply a right conception of the purpose of God in creating man. As soon may we from the study of a dead body obtain a correct idea of life, as from the present condition of man acquire a correct conception of the life of God in the soul. Discordant humanity can afford no clear revelation from God; it can supply no medium of communion with God; it can furnish no power of enjoying God. God is not in the heart and life of man, and therefore cannot be discovered in the nature of man. From the parchment of humanity the original revelation of God has been obliterated, and the legendary tales of the fathers written in its stead.

Fallen man is not the manifestation of the Divine, the record of the True. He cannot be the manifestation of the Divine, for his subjective is no longer the counterpart of the subjective of God, and thus he realises not as God realises. He sees not in the light of the true, for his objective is no longer one with the objective real. He realises not the power of the truth, nor can he possibly realise the power and the enjoyment of the truth, for his efforts to realise the power and enjoyment of the truth are not in accordance with the truth. What condescension, then, is in God to reveal Himself to man, to quicken him with the

Divine life, and enable him to enjoy the fellowship of the inner circle of the Sonship! The sculptor who chisels the marble into the noblest form of material beauty, the painter who traces on the canvas the divine countenance of man in all but the glow of life, do illustrious deeds, and win for themselves merited fame. If they could confer life and animate their work with the thrill of soul, how much higher, more illustrious, and noble would their work be! Could the highest genius on earth confer on his favourite animal his own ideal, emotional, vital—his own genius in the highest form in which it could be transferred—and enter into the nearest, most endearing intercourse of life with the subject of his own vitality, he could not confer a higher gift on that creature. What, then, is the condescension of God in creating man with a capacity for his own ideal, emotional, vital—quickening him with His own life, and training him in the reception and interchange of the Divine subjective. Yet fallen man, in his speculative efforts and carnal endeavours, is ever labouring to frustrate this high and most God-like design of the Eternal Father, by attempting to bring down the lofty conception of the Infinite Mind, the divine workmanship of the great God of heaven and earth, within the narrow limits of his own fallen ideal and carnal desires.

CHAPTER III.

THE TRANSMISSION AND RECEPTION OF TRUTH.

HAVING in the last chapter considered truth in itself, it may now be profitable to inquire into matters connected with its transmission and reception.

In order to the transmission of truth the subjective to which an objective is addressed must be able to receive it in the comprehension of it. If the subjective be in affinity with the objective presented, a very slight hint will lead to the perception of it; but if, on the other hand, the subjective be averse to truth, no manifestation will lead to the full comprehension and reception of it. The history of the inductive sciences afford brilliant illustrations of the former of these facts. The slow progress in study of those who set about it as an unpleasant task sufficiently establishes the latter. Spiritual truth follows in its transmission the laws which govern other truth. In the enlightening of man in the things of God there must be presented to him an objective suited to his condition, and at the same time there must be a quickening of his subjective into an affinity with the objective presented to him. Here indeed is the keystone of the arch. Man in his fallen condition is not able of himself to attain to a true knowledge of God; he has no affinity for such knowledge, and when spiritual truth is presented to him, he is repelled by his dislike from it, and the great work of God in man's recovery is the production within him of a receptivity for Himself.

If a creature has no capacity for the indwelling of God, in the manifestation of Himself God cannot reveal Himself to that creature; if the creature has no receptivity for the manifestation which God gives of Himself, this creature can have no acquaintance with God through means of such manifestation. In order to the intercourse of the creature with God there must be a manifestation and a suitable receptivity. Mediation is thus a necessity of communion between the Infinite and the finite. The inner or unknown of the Infinite must become the manifestation of the Divine and the knowable of the finite— *i.e.*, the subjective of the Infinite must become the objective in revelation, and the objective of revelation must become the subjective of the human; and the manifestation of the Divine must be conditioned to the circumstances of man, and the subjective of man must be made sympathetic with the revelation of the subjective of God. There must be a pure receptivity in the human ere there can be an incarnate life of the Infinite in man; in other words, a communion of the finite with the Infinite through the indwelling of the Son of God. Were a manifestation of the Divine or a revelation of the subjective of God given to man which was not cognisable to the spiritual perception of man, God would not through means of it be known to man; and if man had no organ of God-consciousness, or inner eye of discernment, he could receive no immediate manifestation of God. On the other hand, if the organ of God-consciousness is dormant, and the heart preoccupied with a spirit of antagonism to the Divine, man cannot close in with the manifestation of God or enter into delightful fellowship with Him. Were a human being born into the world destitute of the bodily senses, he could hold no intercourse with his fellow-men—he would be shut up within himself and isolated from all around him; but if one after another of the senses were imparted to him, then as each was bestowed he would be elevated in the scale of existence, and enabled to enter into correspondingly enlarged intercourse with his fellow-men. Again, if his senses were in such a diseased and perverted state that their exercise could only afford to him pain, and if the objects coming into contact with his senses could only intensify that pain, then would he turn away from such objects and shut up himself within himself, and seek to occupy himself with anything that might relieve him of his pain. On the other hand, if a being were created with a hundred senses, and placed in the centre of blank space with no object near him on which he could exercise his senses, then, however acute or perfect those senses might be, he could not exercise them.

But take now the case of an individual who possesses all his senses in a high state of cultivation, and who is surrounded with all that is necessary to their proper exercise, such a one would as a matter of course possess the means of high enjoyment and agreeable intercourse. And thus it is with the mind and the spirit of man; for if an individual is born into the world and continues all his time in it in a state of insanity, he is excluded from the higher regions of intellectual life, and from the exercise and enjoyment of rational fellowship. Or were he endowed with the highest genius, but destitute of an adequate manifestation of the Divine—in other words, left entirely to himself in this matter—then would he have no suitable employment for his lofty powers in things pertaining more nearly to God; he could have no fellowship with the Father of spirits through means of the interchange of thought and affection. But further, supposing that innumerable manifestations of the Divine were displayed around him, and endless gifts of eternal love bestowed upon him, yet were the God-conscious organ of his spirit blind, he could have no fellowship with God. The God-conscious faculty can never of itself attain to the needful manifestation of the Divine, it cannot penetrate the inner recesses and discover the secrets of Godhead. The intuitional consciousness can read only what is in man, the intellect can only contemplate the facts and operation of nature, and reason can legitimately infer only rational results; faith, however, beholds the manifestations of the Divine, and fellowship enlarges with experience. If, then, there be no distinction between nature and God—in other words, if there be no personal God, there can of course be no communication between God and man; but, on the contrary, if nature be the creature of God, and man the offspring of the Father of spirits, then as the human father can communicate his will to his son, so may God reveal Himself to man; or as a medical practitioner may act on the brain of the insane so as to draw out his thoughts into lucid order, so may God act on the heart of the sinner to turn him to Himself.

The subject-matter of a revelation to fallen man must be supernatural, a communication from God to man of that which is out of and beyond man's power of discovery. God can hardly be supposed to communicate by supernatural means to man anything within the reach of his natural powers. Man with pen and ink can trace his thoughts on paper, he can combine the mechanical powers so as within certain limits to accomplish his will, he can reproduce his image and train his offspring in his own life. Now, if man can do so much, why should we limit God? He can thunder in the heavens, and may He not whisper in the ear? He can paint with the frost on the polished glass, and may He not depict on the mind of the seer? He can regenerate the soul, and may He not suggest to the spirit? He created the intuitional consciousness of man, and may He not elevate it to read inner visions afforded to the spirit? He produced the God-conscious faculty in the human soul, and may He not quicken it with His spirit? He incarnated His Son, and may He not reveal Himself to man? Man through means of his senses receives impressions from material things, by means of his mind he receives eternal, immutable, and indestructible ideas, and may he not through the elevation of his intuitional consciousness perceive the objective and subjective Divine, and by the quickening of his God-conscious faculty see God? External things with external evidence come to him through his senses, mathematical ideas with demonstration come to him through his intellect, and moral truth with conviction comes to him through his conscience, and may not revelation from God come to him through his realisation of the Divine? In sleep one part of man's nature is dormant while another is active, and while man is asleep the action of thought in him is occupied with delusions. In the realities of being there is nothing corresponding with the ideal of the sleeper. In Scripture sleep is an emblem of the natural or unregenerate state. In the natural state man only dreams of the Divine, his ideal of the Divine has nothing corresponding to it in the realities of God. Waiving the question as to whether an unfallen creature, irrespective of Divine communication, can sound the deeper depths of Deity, must it not be evident that with his God-conscious faculty dormant, his subjective averse to the holy, man will be separate from God and perceive the Divine only in dreamland? If his intuitional consciousness discern only the fanciful, his ideal of the Divine cannot correspond with the realities of God. And does not human experience prove that such is the case? Man, irrespective of the light of revelation, has not arrived at correct conceptions of God; and even with the aid of revelation, men, speculating instead of believing, reach not conceptions which satisfy the intellect and the heart-knowledge in which all agree. And why not? Because of the aversion of the subjective of man to its own disturbance and to the objective of God. Man has clear conceptions of abstract truth, but not of God and Divine things. If, then, we hold to the doctrine that all truth comes from God, and that all truth is in God, how can we account for the fact that man possesses clear conceptions of abstract truth, but has no correct idea of God and Divine things? Does God reveal Himself in abstractions to the spirit of man and not in divine quickenings? Man's spiritual is disordered, and as the lunatic refuses to acknowledge his lunacy and the prejudiced his prejudice, so does man refuse to acknowledge his "carnal."

Man of himself has no discernment of God or agreeable intercourse with Him, yet man is conscious of a spiritual in his life—*i.e.*, he is conscious of a supernatural force within which acts on his physical so as to impel or restrain its operations. The distinction between the subjective and the objective of the spiritual and physical is involved in the very nature of things, and made much more apparent by sin. If man possesses not only an intuitional consciousness but also a God-conscious faculty, he must possess a capacity for immediate communion with God; and were he to be for ever deprived of the enjoyment of fellowship with his Father in heaven, he could not be a son nor realise the filial life.

If, then, God is to reveal Himself to man, how is

He to do so? Is He to force on the averse subjective that which it dislikes? Such cannot be the case, it is much more likely that God shall reveal Himself in a manner suited to the condition of man's subjective, and also do so with a view to quicken that subjective into harmony with the manifestation given. As the educator must present instruction to the child level to his capacity, and the physician administer medicine suited to the condition of his patient, so must God reveal Himself in a manner level to the capacity and suited to the circumstances of the sinner. And as truth contains in itself what is level to the capacity of the child and what is beyond the comprehension of an archangel, so must that revelation which discloses the deep things of God to man be both level to the capacity of man and be beyond the present apprehension of finite intelligence. And as the child would be esteemed very silly and precocious who might refuse to submit to the teaching of a parent because he could not in his first lesson comprehend all that was meant, in like manner should be esteemed the man who, because he cannot in his first glance of revelation comprehend the deepest depths of the Divine, should reject that revelation. And as the child would be sure only to err who would only receive such instruction as was pleasant and agreeable to him, so must it be with the man who, instead of yielding up implicitly his heart and mind to the truth of revelation, endeavours to bring the doctrine of God into conformity with his tastes and previously-conceived notions. And how presumptuous is it in man, who cannot comprehend his own being in the movements of his own life, to refuse to listen to the voice of revelation because it informs him of things which is beyond the sphere of his comprehension! God may employ humanity to emit certain sounds, use man as a dreamer to dream particular dreams, as a seer to see and describe heavenly visions, as a herald to convey His message, as a reasoner to reason out His suggestions, as a body for His Spirit to dwell in. Personality and its individualities enter into the very nature of man; and as the construction of a trumpet affects the sound that passes through it, the character of the dreamer the dream, the acuteness of the eye of the seer the vividness of the vision, the intellect of the reasoner the character of the reasoning, so does the personality of the inspired the phase of the inspiration that passes through him. This is manifest in all the aspects of revelation from Balaam to John.

The visual discernment of the seer did not surmount the objective manifestations and quickening operations of the Divine. The Spirit's communications were conditioned to the manifestation of the Son; for if the Son be the revelation of the Father, if He be the subjective and objective of the Infinite and Eternal, if "in Him dwells the fulness of the Godhead bodily," then he who sees the Son must see the Father; and if it be the province of the Spirit in His revelation of the Divine as He quickens the human to take the things which are Christ's and show them to the believer, if the function of the Spirit in inspiring the apostles was to bring to their recollections whatsoever Christ had spoken, then the Spirit's communications, in the inner revelations He affords to the disciple, must wholly harmonise with the manifestations of the fulness of the times. And thus the manifestations of the Son will be apprehended by man only as he is quickened in the organ of his God-consciousness by the Spirit; and as the final end of all revelation is to make "every knee to bow, and every tongue to confess that Jesus Christ is Lord, to the glory of God the Father"—*i.e.*, to display the Son as head over all—all Divine revelation must be prefigurative of and subservient to the manifestations of the Son. And thus there can be no inner visions from God to man, or internal revelations of the Divine to the believer that in any way differ from the outer revelations of the Son to the world. The province of the Spirit is not merely to reveal Christ, but, in order to His reception in the inner life, to produce a receptive subjective in man; and this work of the Spirit is not completed all at once, as is apparent in the experience of Peter, who, after he had announced the reception of the Gentiles into the Church, required the vision of the sheet let down by the four corners to prepare him for preaching to Cornelius.

Man's tendency to the formal and corrupt, and his aversion to the spiritual and divine, have been manifest in all ages. In man's fallen condition sense has ever been struggling to absorb soul. Christ Himself found it a most difficult work to enlighten the minds even of His disciples. His complaint to them was,

"I have many things to say unto you, but you cannot bear them now." He had to wait for favourable moments in their states of receptivity to communicate to them His truth, and to adapt His statement of it to them as they were able to receive it. If, then, a revelation capable of lifting man out of his downward tendency was to be afforded him, it was necessary that this revelation should be communicated in such a manner as was most fitted to counteract the biases of his fallen nature. The "diversity of gifts," the "sundry times," the "divers manners" in which God spake to the prophets, the numerous forms, the many individuals He employed, were all necessary to the adequate conveyance of the truth to man, and all subservient to the Church's arriving at correct understanding of the revelation of God. Diversity in form and variety in letter affect not the unity of the Spirit nor the oneness of the truth. Sounds, signs, and words are necessary to the transmission of ideas: the formal, ritual, and ceremonial to the spiritual; the Jewish dispensation to the Christian Church; the body to the indwelling of the soul. The letter is not but for the idea, the manifestation is not but for the Spirit; and the manifestation is in accordance with its Spirit, the language in accordance with the idea, and the body is moulded by the soul which animates it.

While God is superior to the manifestations He gives of Himself, and is not necessitated to manifest Himself, yet if He does reveal Himself, then the revelation He gives must be conditioned by the mode

He adopts. As the flame is contained in and conditioned in its brightness by the atmosphere in which it burns, as the soul is contained in and conditioned in its operations of physical life by the faculties of the body, so in transmission the idea is contained in and also conditioned by the language in which it is expressed. The Logos or Son of God is contained in the Son of man, and conditioned in His manifestations of the Divine to the world by the sayings and doings of the Man Christ Jesus.

Thought or idea, in passing from the Infinite Mind to the finite mind, must be conditioned by the medium of conveyance. But if the Divine be communicated without a medium of transmission, if it be made known directly by God, is it conditioned in its transmission and qualified in its reception? Does God reveal Himself only or chiefly in thought? Does He not communicate Himself supremely in love? Is not the finite dependent on the Infinite for all, and especially for its most direct communings with God? Does not the spirit of man receive directly as well as indirectly from God; and is not the spirit of man capable of immediate contact with God, of direct reception and immediate indwelling of the Spirit of God? An incarnation of the Divine has taken place. All communication from God to man is subordinate to the indwelling of God in man. The spirit of man was created in the image of God; and if so, it must contain in it a capacity for the Divine and possibility of God's indwelling. And may not the spirit of man, through the quickening of its organ of God-consciousness, look directly on God; and may not God communicate to the quickened spirit without the intervention of a medium what the world cannot have revealed to it? And if so, must not such communication be more immediate than any transmission through language? What is life? has it a form? Is the filling of the believing spirit of man with "all the fulness of God" accomplished through means of forms? May not the Spirit of God flash upon the eye of the soul what cannot be uttered in form or expressed in language? Did not Paul in the third heavens come into contact with the unutterable?

Truth is one in God, but are the manifestations of truth in its outgoings from Him invariable, and is truth in its apprehensions by man uniform? Is the spirit of man in his fallen condition capable of apprehending the higher phases of truth? Was not a subjective quickening, even in the case of some of the prophets, necessary to their becoming the vehicles of the higher forms of Old Testament revelation, to their reception of the inbreathing of the Divine, to their beholding the visions of the Son of God? And was not a higher degree of subjective quickening necessary to the apostles for their more spiritual apprehensions of the higher visions of the risen One, that from their own realisations of the Divine they might communicate visions and revelations to the Church? And is not a regeneration or quickening with the Divine still necessary for the reception of spiritual truth? Is it not, and shall it not ever be, that just as we come into a oneness of Spirit, we shall come into a oneness of mind, a knowledge of the truth, a consciousness of the life of God?

The letter can neither express nor give full utterance to the Spirit, nor can the God-conscious faculty in man, while in its diseased state, see God. Some aspects of philosophic and scientific thought, by the manner in which they treat these lofty themes, would lead us into error. We cannot but regard all speculation respecting the undisclosed things of God as an attempt to spell from the alphabet of creation in the light of nature the name of God, and from the present condition of life in man to deduce the character and learn the mind of God. But no finite can fully express the Infinite, and no condition of the creature can adequately make known the Creator, much less can a disturbed creation and a fallen finite. Science and speculation must for ever fail in their attempts to extract from the *un* and *anti* Divine condition of humanity an adequate conception of the being, perfections, and character of God; but faith, beholding as with open face in a glass the glory of the Lord so as to be changed into the same image, can comprehend the love of God, and is able to grasp the manifestation of the Divine.

Faith is the yielding up the heart to God in the reception of the Divine, it is the recognition of God in that revelation which discloses His purpose and, makes Him known to man; and thus through faith's reception of the truth the spirit of man becomes conscious of the Divine life, the believer in Christ receives the Spirit, lives the life, possesses the mind of God, and will hereafter "know as he is known," "see face to face," and "be filled with all the fulness of God." But man on earth cannot see God, flesh and blood cannot inherit the kingdom, corruption cannot put on incorruption. Affinity of nature and identity of life are necessary to community of mind and intercourse of soul. A stone cannot realise a sensation, a brute cannot comprehend an argument, or an angel live a renewed life; and why? because they have no receptivity for these things. Revelation is the manifestation of the Son of God; but the Son of God is not fully disclosed in the written Word, nor was He fully seen, known, or comprehended by any of His disciples in the days of His flesh, nor has He since been seen alike by any two believers. The four Evangelists did not see Him alike, nor did they severally exhibit Him in the same *phase* of character.

Nor is this difference peculiar to man's contemplation of the Divine, it enters more or less into all human belief. No two individuals ever gazed upon any one object so as to receive the exact same impression from it, nor is the same realisation by two or more disciples necessary to faith in Christ and fellowship with Him. It may be desirable to have the same realisations, but this state has not yet been reached, nor will it probably be attained to on earth, nor is it necessary to saving acquaintance with Christ. Humanity is one and the same in all the different individuals of the race, but no two of the human family possess it identically alike; human life is essentially the same in all men, but no two men realise life alike or live the exact same life.

In adapting the revelation of Himself to the present condition of man, it was necessary for God to restrain as far as it was possible the corrupting tendencies of the human heart from perverting the spiritual to the purposes of the formal. And probably this is one of the ends contemplated in the numerous and peculiar modes employed by God in giving to man a revelation of Himself. Diversity in the statement of the same thing may lead different individuals to a like conception of it. Is not this actually realised by the spiritual in Christ of the different denominations? Are they not far more one at the throne of grace, in their realisations of spiritual life and in their apprehensions of Christ, than they are aware of or will acknowledge when engaged in their denominational strifes, or actuated by their sectarian feelings? This fact surely warrants us in coming to the conclusion that the different statements of the same truth, or varied modes of presenting the same thing, may lead different individuals to the same conception of it. Do not the four Gospels help us to a fuller, clearer, more correct and uniform view of the Son of God than any one of them could have done?

Certainly the same statement of any subject of discourse does not lead all that listen to it to the same conception of it. The speaker in a discourse is one, his discourse as uttered by him is the same to all his hearers; the ideas expressed, the words spoken, are the same to all the assembly, but the impression or conception of the discourse is not exactly the same in any two of his audience. Could he in uttering his discourse employ a variety of style and diversity of expression, he would lead the different individuals in the same assembly to a more uniform conception of the spirit of his discourse.

The end of revelation is the disclosure of the Divine to the human, and the instrument which God employs for the accomplishment of this end is the inspired presence exhibiting Christ to the eye of faith. Are the inspired writers, then, in the illustrations which they draw from nature, providence, and creation, bound to make use of such expressions as fit exactly in with the past, present, and future views of scientific and philosophic men? Surely not. They have one object in view, and whatever is best fitted to gain that end they will certainly employ. Style in inspired composition, or the suitableness of this word over that, is not thought of. In fervid thought or intense writing, the words arise in the mind as the spirit kindles and the heart glows, and the words which thus arise are the most suitable clothing for the ideas which spring up in the inspired mind. The glowing strains of poetry do not exhaust the sublime enthusiasm of the poet, and much less does the dull and unimpassioned mind of the mere prosaic reader, in perusing the eloquent effusions of the poet, realise the spiritual of his verse. Is there not in the lofty mind what language cannot express, and is there not in the sublime utterances of high themes what dull spirits cannot perceive? Doubtless, diversity of utterance does assist different minds in coming to like conception, and this fact throws light on the difference of style and diversity of mode employed by God in revealing His will to man. No two statements in Scripture of the same thing, nor any two references to the same event, discourse, or saying, nor any one quotation in the New Testament from the Old, are verbally alike. Now, are we to regard this fact in the composition of inspired Scripture as the result of carelessness or accident? Surely not; it is doubtless designed to teach us that it is the spirit and not the language of revelation that is the truth of God.

The controversies, then, about the modes and forms of revelation, the verbal or plenary nature of inspiration, or the scientific correctness of certain expressions in particular portions of the sacred volume, are after all but of secondary importance; without the quickening of the Spirit no form even of inspired truth will lead man to a spiritual knowledge of God, and in the quickening of the Spirit the form most suitable to the case in hand will be applied in order to bring men severally to conviction. There is, doubtless, in the numerous phases of the fallen heart, a need of the varied modes of revelation; and the employment of these varied forms of inspiration displays in richer manner the Divine condescension, and teaches men to look to the Spirit of God for aid in the study of Divine truth, and to come to the conviction that as the mind of the inspired penman yielded up to, and for the time being was lost to himself in, the spirit of inspiration, so the carnal life of the believer is destroyed in the measure of the indwelling of the Divine in his soul. The end of inspiration was to prepare for the coming of, and to express the sayings and doings of the Son of God; and as the end of revelation required that the mode adopted should most effectually exclude the influencing tendencies of the mediums through which it passed, so must the Divine life in the believer rise superior to all the retarding of "the carnal," and absorb the soul. Inspiration in its final is the inbreathing of the Divine into the human, the incarnation of the Son of God in the Son of man.

CHAPTER IV.

THE PRIMARY LAWS OF PERCEPTION, OR THE CONDITIONED OF HUMAN BELIEF.

FROM the very constitution of our minds we are forced to the conclusion that there is an eternal, indestructible distinction in the nature of things. We cannot rest satisfied in the notion that there is a sameness in all life and conduct. We cannot rest even in a state of doubt concerning the matter. Nothing short of absolute conviction can possibly satisfy us here. The law which conditions man's thinking shuts us up to this belief.

The human mind does, however, rest satisfied in the belief of an essential distinction in the nature of things. And man needs no argument to convince him that such and such a result takes place in accordance with the nature of things. The human mind does not fret at the conviction that it cannot push an inquiry beyond the perception that such a result happens in accordance with the immutable laws of all operation.

It is not in the power of sophistry to expel this conviction from the human mind, nor can man persuade himself that even Omnipotence can alter or destroy the necessary properties of being and annihilate the essential distinction of things. Man cannot by any process of sophistication persuade himself or convince others that being and not being are one and the same thing. Do what he will, man cannot believe any such thing; he cannot, for example, believe that a straight line is a curve, and that a circle is a square. Man cannot persuade himself that cause differs in nothing from effect. Do what he will, man cannot convince himself that wisdom is the same thing as folly, that love is the same thing as hatred, that right is identical with wrong, that virtue and vice are synonymous.

No; do what he will, man cannot persuade himself that there is not an indestructible distinction between these things. Neither can he convince himself that this distinction does not lie in the very nature of things. Man universally has an indestructible conviction that contrary qualities belong to contrary states of being. He is persuaded that the terms which are employed to point out these distinctions are terms which have always been employed to designate real qualities or essential distinctions in things, and that these qualities and distinctions have their foundations in the very essence of existence.

And just as man cannot believe that one and the same substance can be in two contrary states or conditions of being at one and the same time, so neither can he believe that a substance can pass from one state of existence into an opposite without losing the qualities of the former and acquiring those of the latter state. It is, in fact, the possessing the qualities of a state that determines a substance or individual to be in that state. And it is in the acquiring the qualities of one and in the losing the qualities of the other that a substance passes from the one state to another. It is only through our perception of a substance possessing the qualities of a state that we can rationally declare it to be in that state.

If we contemplate a straight line, and think of it as assuming the form of a curve, we cannot any longer think of it as a straight line; it no longer indicates the shortest distance between the points in which its ends may be laid. If we inscribe a circle within a square, and in thought try to make the periphery assume the form of a square, then to the extent to which we do so it is clear the circle loses its properties; all straight lines drawn from the centre to its periphery would no longer be equal to one another, and *vice versa* if we inscribe a square within a circle. Our apprehension of all such truths is conditioned by an absolute necessity or immutable law of thinking, a necessary principle or fixed condition in the nature of intellectual being. And this law of thinking is involved in the very nature of mind. And as there is no sufficient reason for believing that our intellectual being is other than a reflex of the Divine, this law of thinking, or condition of belief, must have its origin or seat in the immutable principle of the uncreated essence of the Infinite and Eternal Mind. And this law, which necessitates the method of our thinking, appertains not merely to the domain of matter or of mathematical forms, we are also convinced that it has a place in the sphere of morals, and that it as really belongs to the region of spirit as to the domain of intellect. On what ground, for example, can it be affirmed that spiritual life is less exact or immutable in its essential conditions than are mathematical properties or material forms? Is the being of God, the nature of Spirit, or the principles which determine that nature in its depositions, volitions, and consciousness, less exact and definite than the properties of the circle or of the square? We think not. The constitution of humanity is surely not less real and immutable in itself in all that appertains to it than the forms and principles of mathematical science. Existence, life, justice, harmony, beauty, and bliss are not less real, though men may differ about them, than the forms of the circle and the properties of the square. Men, for the most part, admit that there are necessary truths, eternal relations, and distinctions which nothing can destroy; but while many admit this in regard to mathematical and logical forms, they are not so clear about it in regard to other forms of truth. It is impossible, however, that we can rest here. The very perception of necessity in one department of truth naturally leads us to look for the like necessity in other departments.

There are in the regions of idealism constitutional forms and model conceptions separate and distinct from any one actual existence, and thus it is with humanity. We do not say that this ideal type or model concept of humanity exists in the human mind in as clear a form as does its conception of the arch or the square, but surely we may affirm that this concept of man existed in the Divine Mind as definitely as does exist the concept of any mathematical figure in the human mind. If so, then surely the concept was perfect, and man as he came forth from God's hand was in harmony with it. And man, in the measure in which he comes up to this model concept or recedes from it, must from the nature of the case be perfect or imperfect. And if man was created by God in complete accordance with this model concept, he must have sprung from the hand of his Creator perfect and entire. And every human being is perfect or imperfect, just in the measure in which he comes up to or recedes from this typal form of humanity in the conceptions of God.

And who will venture to say that it is impossible that the race of mankind can have passed from a condition of conformity into a state of discordance with this model type? Now, in the event of such a transition taking place, it is clear that man would no longer be what he was when he came forth from the hand of his Creator. And as we are unable to believe that the human body can pass from a state of perfect health into one of sickness and still retain the vigour, beauty, and buoyancy of health, and as we cannot conceive the possibility of the human mind passing from clear views of truth into perplexity of error and still retaining the satisfaction of lucid perceptions, so we cannot imagine that the human heart can pass from love of the Divine into aversion to the Godlike, and still enjoy the love of the Divine. In fine, we cannot realise the possibility of man passing from a conscious oneness of life with God into the realisation of the evils of a fallen state, and still retaining communion with God.

Moreover, just as we are unable to believe that the human body can be in a state of sickness without experiencing more or less of the prostration which disease invariably entails, as the human mind cannot be in a condition of ignorance and error without more or less partaking the perplexity that inevitably flows from ignorance and error—so we are unable to believe that the human spirit can be conscious of wickedness without realising more or less of the upbraidings of conscience. In other words, we are unable to believe that a human being can be in contrary states at one and the same moment—a human body at once in a state of sickness and of perfect health—a human mind at once in a condition of ignorance and of clear perception of law and duty—a human heart at once ardently loving and bitterly hating the same being, principles, and ends of life—in short, that a human soul can at one and the same time be spiritually dead and alive. And why is this? surely it is because the law of human thinking, the principles of the Divine administration, and the nature of things, compel us to it—we feel the impossibility of its being otherwise.

We know that man can pass from one condition to another—the body from a condition of health to a state of sickness, the mind from a condition of discernment to a state of prejudice, and the spirit from the consciousness of the rectitude of its doings to the conviction of the wrongfulness of its deeds, or the converse. But we cannot believe that a man can be in both these contrary states at one and the same time, or that he can be in either state without possessing the qualities of the state he is in, or that he can realise the conditions of any state without being in that state.

If, then, we find that humanity is destitute of the qualities of a pure and holy life, and that man desires and struggles after the benefits of a perfect condition while manifesting the properties of a fallen and sinful life, must we not in these circumstances come to the conclusion that he has passed from the one state to the other? And the question, What is man's natural or original state? is a momentous one. With a view to its solution we may point out the fact that his judgments are not as correct as his instincts, his dispositions and desires are not what his reason approves of; nor are his deeds worthy of his powers, means, and opportunities. His views of being, life, and destiny, are not clear and cloudless; nor are his supreme affections Godward. He does not rest in the love of God, nor is he supremely desirous of being conformed in life to the Father of his spirit. His conscience often condemns him. He has misgivings about the future, and dread of retribution. We may well ask, what are the ideas of God which idolatry in man has evolved, the ideas which infidelity, rationalism, and speculation, have sketched? Why are men ever striving to bring the teachings of revelation into conformity with their likings, instead of their conceptions into agreement with the teachings of a pure and holy faith? These facts, we think, indicate that man is in a fallen condition. How, or by what particular influence, instrument, or agency, a spirit passes from one state into its opposite, belongs to a region of inquiry which is little known to us, and in its higher domain is far out of sight. In the belief of the possibility of such a transition, there is involved no absurdity or contradiction. The acquaintance with, or realisation of, the results of such a transition is near to us, at our very door—it lies in our deepest consciousness.

There is, then, in man a necessary law of belief, a conditioned form of thinking. He must, when the matter is brought under his notice, believe in an immutable and eternal distinction of things. He is shut up to such a belief by the constitution of his mind; and do what he will, he cannot escape from this law of thinking. He must believe that the state and the qualities of the state are inseparable, and that, if a man passes from one state to another, he must lose the qualities of the one and acquire those of the other.

CHAPTER V.

PRINCIPLES OF THE DIVINE ADMINISTRATION.

GOD reigns over a threefold kingdom by a duality of law. His Sceptre is twofold in its sway. His reign is perfect and universal. The principle of duality pervades the entire administration of the Most High. By a twofold force God governs His universe. By force, negative and positive, attractive and repulsive, centripetal and centrifugal, God governs the material universe. By truth and error, by knowledge and ignorance, by conviction and doubt, God rules over the universe of mind. By love and hatred, by desire and aversion, by consciousness of right and conviction of wrong, God reigns over the universe of spirit.

No existence can escape the control of God. No heavenly body, however erratic, can wander beyond the limits of space, or escape from the influence of the law of attraction or repulsion; fly where it may, it must always move in space, and under the influence of its primary laws. And as the planet is ensphered in space, so is the finite embosomed in the Infinite.

The harmonious operation of this twofold law

preserves the beauty, order, and progress of the material universe. The increment of one power over another causes disturbance and ofttimes dissolution of the several parts, but not the annihilation of any one of the elemental powers. The storm may rage, the elements may battle, mountain chains may be dislocated or upheaved, individuals may die and families perish, yet in earth's greatest natural strife, and in times of most sweeping devastations, not one atom of matter perishes, nor alters in the least in its essential nature. Mind, however capricious, cannot surmount the sphere of intellect and escape the region of thought. It cannot divest itself of the influence of truth and error, of knowledge and ignorance. It must move in light or in darkness. If mind moves or thinks at all, it can only do so under the influence of the true or the false. The movements of mind under the influence of truth are harmonious and satisfying, its movements under the influence of error are disuniting and distressing; and its movements under the contending influence of truth and error are conflictive in the direction and degree of the prevailing power of the movement.

In the struggles of mind with truth and error, in the descent of mind under the bondage of falsehood, there is no distinction of its intellectual constitution nor annihilation of its individuality. Mind, even in its degraded condition, still remains the sphere of thought, the only difference being, that it has become the arena of struggle and conflict, the subject of contending ideas.

Spirit, again, however rebellious, cannot escape the domain of consciousness; it cannot divest itself of the influence of love and hate, of the consciousness of the rightfulness or the wrongfulness of its deeds, of satisfaction or dissatisfaction with its condition of existence. The movements of Spirit under the power of the love of the Divine are elevating and joyous, its movements under the hatred of the true are degrading and tormenting. The consciousness of the rectitude of our doings is the realisation of strength and delight to the Spirit. The consciousness of the wrongfulness of our deeds is the realisation of weakness and woe to the Spirit. Do what it may, Spirit must exist in a state of love or hate, or under their contending influence. Exert itself as it may, it cannot escape the conditions and obligations of its endless existence.

Every atom, then, that moves must move under the law of attraction or repulsion. Every mind that thinks must think under the sway of truth or error. Every spirit that acts must act under the influence of love or hatred, must realise the consciousness of the rightfulness of its doings, or the wrongfulness of its deeds, or be tossed between their contending sway. These we hold to be the eternal laws of finite existence. In one or other of these states, the spirit of man must ever exist, and by no possibility can it escape this necessity of its being. In the harmonious operations of their principles, peace continues, vigour rules, and bliss is realised. In the opposition or contention of these principles conflict prevails, weakness arises, suffering is felt, and degradation is secured.

We sometimes speak of states of indifference, and matter, mind, and spirit, may for the moment be so poised as to appear to be under the control of neither of their opposing influences, but for the time being they are equally under the sway of both. The equilibrium, however, can only be of brief duration. The one or the other must ultimately triumph. As a matter of course, we do not here speak of states, the normal condition of which is that of equilibrium.

The principles by which God governs His loyal subjects, the manifestations by which He dwells in and holds fellowship with His obedient children, are love, truth, and the consciousness of the rectitude of being and life. The powers by which He reigns over His rebellious subjects and governs His disobedient offspring are enmity, error, and the consciousness of the wrongfulness of their being and doing; He thus dwells in the consciousness, and rules over the life of His faithful children, while He dwells outside of the consciousness and rules over the life of His rebellious offspring.

Man must exist and realise within the sphere of truth or error, love or hatred, consciousness of the rightfulness of His doings or the wrongfulness of His deeds. He may abandon the light of the true, and fall from the love of the Divine; he may deprive himself of the consciousness of the rectitude of his doings and betake himself to a life of ungodliness, but escape from any pair of these correlated conditions at one and the same time he cannot. He must, if he exist at all, exist either in the consciousness of the one or the other, or partly in the one and partly in the other. In the one condition his heavenly Father smiles upon him and blesses him, and imparts to him a sense of His favour and presence. In the other God frowns upon the sinner, and inflicts the penalty of His law upon the transgressor, removing him to a distance from Himself.

Love is an attracting principle of life; it unites the soul in which it reigns to whatever is beautiful, or is conceived to be beautiful, in being and blissful in life. Love of truth draws us truthward, and leads us to the investigation of the true. Love of what is purely imaginary, delusive, and false, leads to a belief in what is fictitious, and produces a strong tendency towards it. In like manner love of the Divine draws us Godward and assimilates us to the Holy, and love of the false and evil draws us towards the evil one, and ends in the degradation of ruin and life and being.

Enmity is a repelling principle. We are averse to what we dislike. Dislike of the true and aversion to the Holy removes to a distance from the elevating influence of the Divine. So also the dislike of the illusive, a hatred of the false, keeps us at a distance from the imaginary, false, and misleading. Enmity is a tormenting power. In the presence of what we hate we are disturbed and pained in the degree of the intensity of our hatred.

We do not love the evil and the false because they are evil and false, *i.e.*, under the belief that they are evil and false. Neither do we hate the true and shun the good because they are true and good, *i.e.*, under the belief that they are true and good, but because at the moment we are under the impression that the true is not true, and the good is not good, and that the evil and false are not evil and false. Man seeks not evil for its own sake. The avaricious and selfish seek benefit, distinction, &c., for their own sake; and these things are good in themselves. It is not the exercise of power in the pursuit of these, but the wrong use or perversion of power in the obtaining of such, that is evil. It is when the motives, principles, and ends, are not what they ought to be, that wrong is done in the pursuit of these things. When the motive is not obedience to the will of God but preference of personal will, when the end is not general good but self-gratification, evil and not good is the result.

But gratification, benefit, &c., are not in themselves evil, but good. Again, the true and good are not disliked for their own sakes, but because the true often pains us by revealing to us what we dislike, and the good by requiring of us at times an amount of self-denial we are disinclined to, are imagined to be evil. Thus light and medicine are not disliked in themselves, but because of the pain which they at times subject us to. Light is not looked upon as evil in itself, but is felt to be so, and shunned by the diseased eye. Medicine is not thought to be an evil in itself, but because of its bitterness it is disliked by the sick.

In affording us the love of the godlike, God comes into us and dwells in us in the measure in which we cherish this love; and we, in cherishing this love, rise into the fellowship of the Divine, and draw near to God in the vision of His glory. "He that dwelleth in love dwelleth in God, and God in him." In giving us up to the dislike of the true, God abandons us to the power of evil; and we, in cherishing dislike to the godlike, descend into the conflict of darkness and woe. "We have loved strangers, and after them will we go." "The way of the transgressor is hard."

Truth is that which reveals God, and manifests the Divine. It is that in which the Divine comes down to the human, and in which the Infinite reveals Himself to the finite. Truth is that by which the finite ascends into the presence of the Infinite, and holds fellowship with the Divine. The Infinite, by means of truth, condescends to the finite, and, through the apprehension of truth, the finite ascends to the Infinite. In the revelation of the true, the Infinite comes within the apprehension of the finite. In the belief of the true, the finite rises to the embrace of the Infinite, to the delight and enjoyment of the Divine. They who live in the love and belief of the true, dwell in the light of God's countenance.

Error is that which presents the false to the mind in the semblance of the true, the form in the place of the substance, the shadow instead of the reality of being. Error is that which the fancy and imagination, instead of the senses and perception, present to the mind. In the belief of error, the subjective of the individual believing separates itself from and becomes unlike to the objective real. The subjective perception of the believer in error is of the objective imaginary, and not of the objective real. In the belief of the false the objective unreal becomes to the believer in the false the subjective real. In the belief of the false the mind of the believer enters into union with, and becomes moulded by, the false. And thus, while an idol is nothing in the realities of being, it is a terrible reality in the imagination of the idolater. The consciousness of the rectitude of our doing is a strengthening realisation in the soul. In bestowing this consciousness upon us, God manifests to us His admiration of our obedience, comes into us with the reward of His presence, and gives us to realise a pure and elevating joy. The consciousness of the wrongfulness of our deeds is a weakening power in the soul. In the consciousness of the wrongfulness of our deeds we are restless and helpless; we struggle in vain to escape from the consciousness in which God gives us a sense of His displeasure with our life, while He inflicts upon us the reward of our transgression, and causes us to realise the penalty of His law.

These are eternal principles by which God reigns in and rules over the life and being of man; principles which He never has and never will in the least alter or annul; and every attempt to alter them, or to efface the consciousness of them from the life while necessarily living under their power, is the highest of all absurdity.

In creating man a rational being, God has made him capable of union and communion with Himself, through the medium of love, truth, and the consciousness of the rectitude of his being. And in the manifestation of Himself in the revelation of the true, God comes to man and invites him to enter into fellowship with Himself. And, in the faith of the true, He has ordained that we shall realise this fellowship.

These considerations throw light on the present condition of man. They show the folly of his endeavour to satisfy himself with the seen and temporal, show the necessity of a revelation from God and of man's giving implicit attention to whatever God reveals to him, if he is to attain to wellbeing. It is clear to every observant eye that man is neither in a condition of hopeless despair, nor of perfect bliss. While selfish and opposed to God as the creature, he is generous and self-denying as the parent, child, and relative; while frequently perplexed and utterly unable to rescue himself from evil, he is capable of comprehending much of his real condition, and anxious to escape from it. And all this is accounted for, on the principle that he is the subject of right and wrong motives, principles, and ends of action—of love and enmity, of truth and error, and that God is dealing with him so as to let him know something of the bitterness of evil, and to lead him through the love of the Divine, the knowledge of the true, and the consciousness of the rectitude of his being, into the pure bliss of fellowship with Himself.

The sum, then, of what we have said on the principles of the Divine government may be thus briefly expressed. God gives bliss to the heart of man through means of love, and He gives this bliss in accordance with the nature of the object, and in the measure of the intensity of the love.

God gives pain to the heart of man through means of the emotions of hatred; and He does so in accordance with the nature of the object of the enmity, and in the measure of the intensity of the hatred.

God gives power, vigour, enjoyment to the mind of man in and through means of the belief of the true; and He does so in accordance with the nature of the truth, and the strength of the faith of him believing it.

God gives perplexity and distraction of mind to man in and through ignorance of truth and belief in error; and He does so, in accordance with the nature of the truth of which man is ignorant, and the character of the erroneous belief which he entertains. He gives light and energy in the measure of our knowledge, and in accordance with the nature of its objects.

God gives joy and energy to the spirit of man, in and through means of the consciousness of the rectitude of his life; and He gives, and ever will give, anguish and dread and weakness to the soul of man, in the consciousness of the wrongfulness of his deeds.

And, finally, these facts of human experience throw light on the present condition of man. They prove that man is neither in a condition of perdition nor of bliss, but in what may be regarded as an intermediate state of probation.

CHAPTER VI.

COMBINATION OR CAUSATION.

CAUSATION, as distinguished from creation, denotes combination and change. Creation proper, is the bringing into being what previously had no existence. Causation, is the bringing already existing substances into new combinations, and thus leading to new results. Creation belongs to, and is only in the power of, the Infinite. Causation belongs to, and is in the power of, the finite as well as of the Infinite. No limit can be set to Creation but the will of the Creator. No limit can be set to combination but the ingenuity, skill, power, and intention of the combiner. Qualities are susceptible of being brought into endless varieties of relations of harmony and discord. In the combinations of harmony there is scope for the display of power, wisdom, and goodness. In the combinations of discord there is scope for the manifestations of mistaken conception, of evil disposition, and malignant design.

Atoms, lines, colours, sounds, and substances, are capable of being brought into endless combinations of form and relation in the mechanical operations of nature and art. Words in the power of genius are susceptible of indefinite combination in language;

and dispositions, ideas, intellects, and spirits, may be combined into numerous relations in the activities and conscious realisations of life. In combination there may be the apparent, but not the real, distinction of power. A power may be suspended or held in abeyance, while the substance in which the power resides is placed in an altered relation, but the substance has only to be restored to its former condition in order to show that the power is there just as before. This fact has been demonstrated, and is expressed in the general formula, "the conservation of force."

Atoms, minds, and spirits, are necessarily created with primary properties, and the susceptibility of combination enters into the very nature of these properties. In bringing about a new result, there is nothing more than the forming of new combinations. Thus, a new machine is invented, and what is there in this invention but the perception, on the part of the inventor, of how certain results may be produced by a new combination of powers. A law of nature is discovered, and what is there in this discovery but the perception by the discoverer of how certain powers of nature may be brought to act in a given combination with a determinate result. It is by means of combination that the different properties and susceptibilities of being, in the course of their development, become known to finite mind. The higher laws of being hold the inferior in check, and direct their action. As a well-known illustration of this, we may point to the fact that the presence of life, or the restraint of its power on the action of the chemical laws of matter in the body, prevents the decomposition of the human frame.

The laws of nature are nothing else than the invariable operation of qualities in any given combination. Thus when certain chemical powers are brought into a particular combination, they act or operate in a particular manner, and produce a particular result, and however often the very same powers are brought into the exact same combination, they operate in the exact same manner, and produce the exact same results. And so of mechanical and vital powers. The invariable laws of nature are nothing else than the invariable requirement or obligation of the properties of being in invariable combination. General laws are the requirement of properties in general combination, and particular laws are the requirement of properties in particular combination. Alter the combination however little, and to that extent you alter the requirement, and consequently the operation of the properties in combination, and thus bring about a different result by making a difference in the combination. And the reason why one machine acts so differently from another, is simply due to the fact that the combination of forces which constitutes the one is different from that which constitutes the other. And this principle applies to all combination of forces, whether chemical, mechanical, or vital.

If, then, but one atom had been created, and if it had possessed but one property, it must have remained for ever in the same condition. But as numerous atoms have been created with the power of influencing and being influenced, these atoms, as a matter of course, will act on one another in accordance with the manner in which they are combined; and their operations in the different combinations into which they are brought will lead to the development of their powers, susceptibilities, and possibilities: and this holds good of the whole realm of nature. The letters of the alphabet are capable of being formed in all but endless combination, but they cannot of themselves go into combination. They can only be placed in combination by an agency external to themselves. One letter taken from, or added to, a syllable, remains the same, but the syllable is altered. One syllable taken from, or added to, a word, remains the same, but the word is altered. One word taken from, or added to, a paragraph, remains the same, but the paragraph is altered. One chapter taken from, or added to, a volume, remains the same, but the volume is altered. And so of all combination of any sort whatsoever. And things added to, or taken from, a combination, will affect the character and result of that combination, while, in themselves, the constituent elements remain the same. This is strikingly seen in the case of numerals or figures. If one or two figures be added to, or taken from, a line of figures, it greatly increases or diminishes the amount indicated. It is thus that by changing the number and relation of elements, properties, and powers in combination, we bring about widely different results.

The combination of one property with another may

aid, restrain, or neutralise the operation of another property, or bring into being a new property altogether; but the combination cannot destroy or annihilate the original property, or act upon it contrary to its susceptibility of being acted upon. The aid, restraint, or neutralisation takes place not through means of violence done to the powers or susceptibilities of the bodies combined, but in perfect accordance with their nature or capacity for being so influenced. And as in the combination of matter, so in the combination of mind and spirit in individual and social life. Individuals, with equals, or with those of a higher order of life, may be so combined together as by their co-operation to secure a given result; but in this combination they influence one another in such a manner, that their free agency is not interfered with or in any way injured, but preserved intact. Particular results are secured through means of the presence or absence of particular agencies. Matter may be brought into combination, and thus made to operate; but not spirit in its normal condition; it may be led into combination, but cannot in the combination be compelled to act, or to act in any one particular way. It is essentially free and endowed with power over its own action. It can enter into combination with higher, equal, or inferior powers, and by its presence affect the result; but in its influencing the operation of the combined forces by its aid or hindrance, it acts in the unfettered freedom of its nature.

Matter is capable of indefinite combination in

chemical, mechanical, or vital relations; it develops its powers and capabilities, but into all its combinations it must be brought—it cannot of itself form any new combination; whereas spirit can and often does so. Matter may be combined so as to form a globe or a planetary system with its appropriate mechanism. Atoms may be combined with vitality so as to produce a vegetable kingdom, or they may be so combined with vitality as to produce an animal kingdom; and matter, mind, and spirit may be so combined as to produce a world; but in all this there is nothing more than combination, a display of skill in combining the primary properties of created substances, a weaving of the higher threads of spirit and mind into the woof of matter. The whole of the rich variety which we see in creation is simply due to the skill shown in combining the different elementary substances of being. One creature differs from another in a difference of constitution, and, consequently, of life; and this difference of constitution and life is merely a difference of combination in its formation and life.

The simpler forms of vitality, as in vegetable and in animal existence, possess the power of construction or of non-discretionary combination. Their germs appropriate the nourishment on which they feed, and, by so doing, construct a vegetable or an animal, as they develop the mechanism or constitution of the seed or embryo in which they inhere. But a higher power of combination belongs to rational or spiritual agency; personality is endowed with the power of discretionary combination. An individual can select the elements he combines with the perception of their suitability or unsuitability for this or that combination. One individual combines certain sounds or notes in music, and is the author of an air, or tune; another individual combines colours in a particular manner, and becomes an artist, the author of a celebrated painting or admired design; another combines straight lines and curves, and sketches the plan of an edifice, and is thus an architect; another combines certain ideas, and becomes the author of a book in literature, science, or philosophy. These individuals claim to be the authors of their several productions, and are fully entitled to the merit of the claim; and so an individual, in the development of his personality, combines particular motives and volitions with certain ideas and dispositions, and thus he becomes the author of his actions, the framer of his character.

Agents act in the order of co-ordination and of subordination as soldiers in an army, and in this manner order is preserved in the movements of the army and in the achievements of war. There is a subordination of ranks as well as a co-ordination of agents. And, ascending from the lowest to the highest agent through the different orders of subordination, we at length arrive at a Supreme Agent who acts of Himself, and over whom there can be no superior. This Supreme Agent being over all, can form any combination of agents, powers, substances, He pleases, and thus secure any result He chooses; He can be under no law but His own will as moved by His own nature. If His power and resources are infinite, He can create and combine, re-create and re-combine as He pleases. And in this He can advance from the simplest to the most intricate and complex of combinations, and thus produce the simplest or most complicate results, none possessed of right or daring to say, What dost Thou.

What, then, is the bearing of these facts on the doctrine of general and immutable law? To answer this question we must inquire, What is general and immutable law? And for the answer we must again inquire, What is law? Law, as we have already defined it, is requirement or obligation. And this obligation arises out of the nature of the subject of law. Thus an atom of matter possesses the power of acting, and the susceptibility of being acted on by another particle. If the atoms remain alone, these properties remain latent, but if they be brought near to one another, then the one atom will attract or repel the other; and will do so in accordance with their inherent power and susceptibility. When the loadstone is remote from the steel its powers are latent, but whenever it is brought into contiguity with steel, then arises a requirement or obligation of its powers to attract the steel, and this requirement or obligation arises out of the nature and relation of the loadstone to the steel. And so of more complex nature and relations.

We speak of chemical, mechanical, vital, intellectual, and spiritual law, also of human and divine law, and in every case law denotes requirement or obligation, arising out of the nature, the constitution, and the relation of the subject or subjects of the particular law. We cannot conceive of an absolute simplicity of substance, *i.e.*, in the actual existence of substance or essence without any quality. Do what we may, we cannot believe in matter without form, or in the existence of spirit without activity. We cannot conceive of the existence of one particle of matter devoid of both substance and force. If matter had no power of attraction and repulsion, its particles would not unite with nor act on one another, but would remain without motion or adhesion as they were brought together. But if matter be possessed of these properties, not to speak of others, if it be essential to matter even in its simplest condition that its particles attract and repel each other, then when they are brought together they must act on one another, and they must do so in accordance with the relations under which they meet. And thus it will be seen that the law of action arises out of the nature of the combination, and the relation of the subject of law. By combination of particles, of properties, of natures, we bring law in its simple or complex forms into operation. Thus, when we combine colour of one shade, the particles will unite and produce a more consistent body of colour, or an intenser hue; and if we combine particles of different shades of colour, they will unite and produce a shade of colour exactly in accordance with their proportion, *i.e.*, in accordance with their nature and relation to one another. If substances of a cohesive nature be brought together, they will unite, and the result of their union will be in accordance with their nature and relation in combination. And if substances of repulsive properties be brought together, the result of the combination will be different, but at the same time in accordance with the nature and relation of the properties and substances in combination.

If a seed still vital be placed in nutritious soil, and moistened by the dew or rain of heaven, and warmed with the heat of the sun, in other words, if its vitality be combined with other productive powers, it will grow and produce a plant in accordance with its kind. If a seed of another species or genus of plants be placed in like circumstances, it will grow into a plant of a different kind; and if the same description of seed be placed in different descriptions of soils, in different climates, while producing the same kind of plants they will do so in different forms of vigour and size. And why? simply because of different temperatures of climate, and different descriptions of soil, in other words, a different combination of circumstances. If eggs of various species be placed under proper heat, they will be hatched each after its own kind. If animals of the same species be brought together to produce, they will bring forth after their own kind; if a male and a female of different species propagate, they will bring forth an offspring different from either species to which they belong. And it will be seen in all this that the result is after the nature of the combination. In like manner if a life be lived, whether that life be animal merely, or rational and spiritual, it must in all cases be manifested according to its nature and circumstances.

The finite cannot produce or create substance, or impart to substance primary qualities or original powers; but finite agency can combine chemical, mechanical, and vital substances, and thus bring forth certain results; and who can set limits to the skill or originality of man in forming combinations. Now, if this be so, who will, *a fortiori*, presume to assign limits to the Creator's skill and power to create and combine, to form and produce, or who will show that God (not to speak of creating) cannot, in combining, so contrive as to produce any result He chooses, and produce that result in entire accordance with the nature, constitution, and relations of the substances He brings into combination. Does He not ever act in accordance with the being or law of operation, either particular or general, of the substances, or agents He employs? God surely is not fettered in His doings by any operation of law. Is it not more philosophic to regard Him as guiding law, and through means of law itself working out His own gracious ends, than to look upon Him as fettered in His doings by any law of nature?

There can be no other notion of general, immutable law than the idea that the same agencies, in the same combination, will ever produce the same results; and if brought into other combinations, will produce other results. This is the true conception of invariable law; and in passing we may say, that it can in no way militate against the true doctrine of miracles; for a miracle is nothing but a new combination of existing elements, or the creation of a new element, and causing it to enter in and operate along with already existing elements in a new combination. And God can at any time do this as the Supreme Agent. He can at any moment form any combination of existing elements, create a new element, and combine it with already existing elements, or reveal Himself in a new form of manifestation to whomsoever He will. No theist can refuse to acknowledge the power of God in any of these forms; and, as it appears to us, no correct apprehension of the doctrine of theism can stand in the way of the belief in miracles.

CHAPTER VII.

THE POWER OF CHOICE.

GOD has placed man amid endless motives to action, and has given to him the power of choice in reference to objects of affection, of thought, of manner, and of life, and holds him responsible for the choice he makes in reference to these. God has given to man the option of whether he will live in the love of the Divine, or in the love of the selfish; whether he will think in the light of the true, or in the obscurity of the false; whether he will act in the consciousness of the rectitude of his doings, or in the conviction of the wrongfulness of his deeds. That man possesses the power of choice in regard to the manner of his life, *i.e.*, in reference to his dispositions and motives, an appeal to the consciousness of mankind is at any moment sufficient to prove.

Let us therefore inquire what consciousness has to say in regard to the matter. When, for example, we ask an individual to make a choice in reference to any matter, we do so in the full conviction that he has the power to make that choice, and that he is not attracted to the object we present, nor repelled from it, as is the north pole of one magnet attracted to the south pole of another magnet, and repelled from the similar pole. On the contrary, we ask him to make the choice in the conviction that, back and behind all the elements which operate on the man in influencing him to the choice of the particular object, the power of finally determining lies with himself. Consciousness ever persistently declares that choice is a personal act, and this view of the case is that by which all mankind regulates the affairs of daily life.

On the other hand, what is the consciousness of the chooser in making the choice? Not, surely, that he is blindly hurried into the choice, but that he can choose at once, or delay with a view to the consideration of the choice. He can deliberate on the consequences of choosing this or that object, or of not choosing at all, and then choose or not choose. He is conscious of a power by which he can place different objects before his mind, examine them minutely, weigh their different qualities, and weigh what will be the result of choosing or not choosing, or of preferring one object to another. He is at times conscious of a sense of duty drawing him one way, and a desire of gratification inclining him in another; he is also conscious that sometimes he chooses on the side of conviction of duty, and that at other times he chooses on the side of gratification, and in the face of the doubt of its being right; in fact, in spite of a strong feeling that it is wrong for him to choose as he does. He is conscious in all the choices he makes, that, back and behind all the influences acting on him, he is possessed of a self-determining power of will, and that the determination or choice in the matter is really his own.

And what is a man's reflection on the choice he has made? If he made the choice in the conviction that it was right in him to make it, and if the result of the choice proves advantageous, he realises a pure satisfaction in the consciousness that he made that choice and not another; he feels that the satisfaction of having made the choice is really and truly his own, that he is fully entitled to entertain the satisfaction that he would not only do himself an injustice, but would act inconsistent with the principles of eternal right were he to discard the satisfaction. If, however, he is conscious of having made the choice from selfish motives, from a desire for gratification in opposition to his conviction of duty, then, however advantageous its results may be, his satisfaction in the enjoyment of these results is neither pure nor unalloyed; a disquietude interrupts the satisfaction, and poisons the pleasure with which they are enjoyed. If, on the other hand, the results of the choice should prove disadvantageous, still, if the chooser is conscious that when he made the choice he acted from a sense of duty, then will that conviction sustain him under the pressure of its disadvantageous results. He will feel strong in the conviction that when he made the choice he acted from a sense that it was right and proper in him to do so. But if he is conscious of having made the choice from wrong motives, and the results of the choice prove baneful, then will he not only realise these results to be bitter in themselves, but the bitterness will be greatly intensified by the consciousness that when he made the choice, he knew that it was wrong in him to make it. And this feeling of self-condemnation in the consciousness of having made the choice from wrong motives will repel every attempt to persuade him that the choice was not really his, that he could not help making the choice, that behind his own will there was an influence which necessitated the choice, and that while he was under that influence he could not help making it. He will not allow himself to take shelter under such a notion; conscience in such an hour will scorn such subterfuge, and repel with indignation every such attempt to silence her accusing voice. The man smarting under her lash knows full well that the choice, in the strict and proper sense, is his choice. Memory may for a time allow the consciousness of the motive which led to the choice to fall into oblivion, but the moment the consciousness of the motive becomes vivid, the personal consciousness will brook no denial of the choice being really and truly the choice of the individual himself.

And what is the judgment of mankind in regard to the personality of choice? In awarding praise to an individual who, in pursuit of an illustrious career, has performed noble deeds, do men admire and laud the circumstances into which he has fallen, or the man's display of skill and perseverance in these circumstances? Do they look upon him as the mere fortunate instrument of propitious influences, or do they feel persuaded that he is not only an actor in, but the author of his own successful career, that behind all the propitious circumstances and influences, aiding and abetting in the choice, he is the chooser of the end, the selector of the means, and the active agent in guiding these to their appropriate results. What they admire is the man himself in his deeds, and what they feel is that he is entitled to the praise they award to him. Again, in blaming an individual for his wrong-doing, men do not feel persuaded that after all he could not help doing what they blame him for doing, they do not believe that he was only the passive instrument of influences he could neither avoid nor control, nor do they in blaming such an one experience any misgiving about his deserving their blame.

And let an individual, while censuring others, read carefully his own inner conceptions and feelings, and he will soon perceive, whether he can, at the bar of his conscience, vindicate his own wrong-doing on the plea that he could not help himself, but had to yield to the influences which were pressing on him at the moment; he will at once perceive that such an attempt is a delusion which will not bear the light of his own judgment. He will perceive that the judgment that he passes upon others is the judgment he must pass upon himself, for, when he reflects carefully on what passes within himself, he will perceive that the judgment which he passes on the conduct of others is the dictate of his unbiassed reason—a dictate which he must apply to his own case.

And what is the judgment of God as recorded in

human experience regarding man's power of choice? Do we not see that God has attached a sense of joy in the human heart to the consciousness of doing what is felt to be right, and a feeling of pain to the consciousness of doing what is felt to be wrong? Now, why is this, unless it be that man has a personal power in the matter of choice? It is a reward bestowed upon the right choice, and a punishment directed against the wrong choice. If individuals are the mere passive instruments of influences over which they have no control, why has God placed in them that fearful and indestructible voice of self-condemnation? Or why has He made them the subjects of those repeated and unavailing efforts of self-vindication in the heart of the transgressor? The voice of self-condemnation is not the voice of warning, neither is it the voice of timorous restraint, but the voice which speaks to man *after* his deed of transgression is done, is the most dreadful of all voices in man. Its pangs are the most prolonged and lacerating of which man is the subject, and they are indestructible by mere human effort. To us it seems incredible that self-condemnation, remorse, and despair can fall to the lot of man, were it not that he is a free agent. If man has not the power of choice in reference to objects, his constitution is a lie. Divine government is a fiction. Divine goodness a groundless fancy, and the moral nature of man a contradiction and absurdity.

Let us now proceed to inquire as to whether or not

a man has the power of choice in regard to ideas, opinions, and beliefs. When an individual endeavours to alter the ideas, opinions, and beliefs of another, what is the state of mind with which he makes the attempt? As is well known, he does not approach the person on whom he would operate, as the compositor sets about the correction of a proof-sheet, with the feeling that the man is a mere passive instrument or organ of the truth he brings to bear upon his mind; he does not address him with the conviction in his own mind that the man must conform to the truth which is set before him, and that he must do so in the measure in which he lets the light of it fall upon his understanding. On the contrary, he addresses him with the conviction in his own mind that, back of the evidence he brings to bear upon him, his auditor possesses a power in himself through means of which he deals with the truth and the evidence placed before him. Every orator addressing an assembly does so with the feeling that his hearers can give or withhold their attention from what is addressed to them; that they can give their attention divided or undivided, longer or shorter, and that they can weigh the evidence advanced partially or impartially, distractedly or calmly, and that they can yield themselves up to or resist the risings of conviction. It is well known that an individual can institute an inquiry into a subject when urged upon him by another, or when suggested by his own reflection, and that he can prosecute this inquiry or desist from, as his likings or dislikings urge or restrain him. Now, why this fact of human experience, if a man has not a power over his beliefs? And because it is so, the public instructor not only endeavours to enlighten the minds of his hearers, but also to persuade their hearts. When we would alter the opinions of others, we seek not merely to arrest their attention and to enlighten their understandings, but we also do what we can to move their wills; and the very effort we make to do so clearly shows that there is an inherent conviction in man—that men possess a personal power over their ideas, opinions, and beliefs, and that they stand to these in a very different relation from that in which they stand to the colour of their skin and the height of their stature.

Human consciousness, the judgment of mankind, and God, in all that we know of Him, hold man responsible for his belief. Every man has within him an indestructible conviction of possessing a power over his opinions, and a sense of responsibility in reference to his beliefs. All men avow a readiness to change their opinions whenever they are furnished with a sufficient reason for so doing, and this avowal clearly implies the conviction on their part of a power in them to do so. As a matter of fact, all men are very sensitive about the light in which their opinions are regarded by others. They are ever ready to show dissatisfaction when charged with holding unworthy and erroneous opinions, and are prone to resent all such charges. And why this displeasure and resentment if men are not conscious of possessing a power over their beliefs? An individual may wish to possess a different size of body or colour of skin, but he is not conscious of possessing a power over them as he knows he possesses over his opinions and beliefs. If an individual's colour or size subjects him to disadvantage, he feels the defect; but instead of expecting blame on account of the defect, he is rather an object of sympathy. But man does take shame to himself when charged with unworthy beliefs.

How, then, are we to account for man's belief in the possession of a power to alter his opinions when he sees fit, or for his sense of shame when conscious of clinging to unworthy sentiments. That such are facts of human experience is beyond dispute, and they can be accounted for only on the principle that man is conscious of possessing a power over his beliefs. If man be unable to alter his opinion when the erroneous character of such is laid before him, then there is no accounting for the consciousness in him that he is able to do so. On this supposition man's consciousness deceives him; and if consciousness deceives man, he is the dupe of lies, and can have no means of arriving at a knowledge of truth. The universal sentiment of mankind holds man responsible for his ideas, opinions, and beliefs. Men do not only distinguish between opinions—disapproving of some and approving of others—and blame individuals for adhering to one class, and praise them for holding by another; but they especially blame men for clinging to opinions in the face of evidence sufficient to convince them of the erroneous character of the opinions they cling to. We all know what prejudice is, but prejudice is only possible on the ground that men are possessed of a power over their opinions. If a man has no power over his opinions he cannot prejudice a case or hold to a sentiment in the face of its refutation. The fact that men do blame one another for prejudice and clinging to refuted errors, is an irrefragable proof of the fact that man is believed to possess a power over his opinions.

This disapproval of individuals for clinging to erroneous conceptions is grounded in the universal consciousness of mankind. When individuals are charged by others with entertaining false or unworthy opinions, they do not lament that they are altogether unable to alter them; on the contrary, they endeavour to show that their opinions are true and honourable, and that it is because they are such that they abide by them. If men are not possessed of a consciousness of power to alter their opinions, when supplied with sufficient evidence of their falsehood, they would not adopt this mode of defence. If they were not possessed of power to yield to evidence, mankind would blame the insufficiency of the evidence, instead of blaming the man for his unworthiness. This would be the rational course to pursue, but men do not blame the evidence for not convincing, they blame the individual for not being convinced.

God holds men responsible for their ideas, opinions, and beliefs. He treats with man through the medium of, and in accordance with, his opinions, ideas, and beliefs. He conditions discernment, energy, and enjoyment, also obscurity, vacillation, and suffering, on a man's ideas, opinions, and beliefs. Through the medium of individual belief God frowns or smiles on man, confers His favours or withholds His gifts; this mode of dealing with men on the part of God is an established fact in the experience of human life, and it is a law written in every man's constitution. To certain ideas, opinions, and beliefs, God attaches light, energy, success, satisfaction, and enjoyment; to their opposite He has joined darkness, weakness, failure, dissatisfaction, and pain. If man possesses no power of choice in the matter of his ideas, opinions, beliefs, is it conceivable that God would inseparably connect benefit with the one, and harm with the other class? Neither is it conceivable that God would attach a sense of shame and unworthiness to the one, and satisfaction and joy to the other; or that He would refuse to man deliverance from the shame, or deny him satisfaction, save by means of a change in his ideas, opinions, beliefs. Refuse therefore to concede to man the power of choice, and all God's dealings with him become an inexplicable enigma. Neither God nor man can be understood. On the opposite view all is consistent and clear. The very sense of shame we realise in holding to certain opinions, and the very satisfaction we feel in clinging to others, is a proof in man that God holds him responsible for his belief.

Let us now inquire if man has the power of choice in regard to dispositions, motives, and principles of action. Every man is conscious of cherishing certain dispositions, of preferring certain motives, and of acting on certain principles; he is likewise conscious of a satisfaction in cherishing what he knows to be right dispositions in preferring what he knows to be right motives, and in acting on what he believes to be right principles; he is also conscious of a sense of degradation, in cherishing what he knows to be wrong dispositions, in preferring what he knows to be wrong motives, and in acting on what he believes to be wrong principles. These facts of man's daily life are attested by universal experience, and are secured in their operations by the established law of his constitution. And man is peculiarly jealous of the light in which his fellow-men view his dispositions, motives, and principles, and he is ever ready to vindicate these. Now, on what ground can a man feel so satisfied with himself in cherishing one set of dispositions, in preferring one kind of motives, and in acting on one class of principles, but on the ground of his conscious possession of a personal power over them? And why should he be so peculiarly jealous of the light in which his dispositions, motives, and principles are viewed by others, if not on the ground of the abiding connection, that he is held responsible for them both in the sight of God and man?

This judgment of the individual consciousness of mankind is indorsed and manifested in the readiness with which men blame individuals for cherishing wrong dispositions, preferring wrong motives, and acting on wrong principles; and also in the readiness with which men praise others for cherishing right dispositions, preferring right motives, and acting on right principles. Thus men in praising or blaming others recognise a distinction between what is right and beneficial, and what is wrong and baneful; and also between what is right and difficult, and what is wrong and easy; and the praise which they award to an individual for doing what is right in the face of formidable difficulties is not only regarded as the highest, but is always rendered with promptitude and cordiality; while the condemnation pronounced against individuals who before the slightest temptations give way to base dispositions, mean motives, and selfish principles, is equally prompt and hearty, but at the same time with opposite feelings. Again, men are ever ready to avow what they believe to be good dispositions, worthy motives, and beneficial actions; while they are eagerly anxious to conceal what they conceive to be base dispositions, wrong motives, and selfish principles. This readiness to avow the one class, and to cherish delight in the consciousness of meriting the praise which is rendered to the man possessing that class; and the eagerness to conceal the other class, and shrink from the consequences which its possession entails, can only be fully accounted for on the supposition that man is conscious of a power over his dispositions, motives, and principles of action. If man possesses no power over these, this experience and practice is an anomaly—a contradiction in man, and an unaccountable providence of God.

And God holds man responsible for the dispositions

he cherishes, the motives he prefers, the principles on which he acts. God comes into the heart of man or withdraws from it in virtue of the dispositions he cherishes, and God bestows joy or grief, a sense of dignity or a feeling of degradation, through means of the dispositions, motives, and principles, which have their seat in the heart. This is an immutable law of God's fellowship with man—He bestows satisfaction or dissatisfaction, praise or blame; He favours or frowns on this principle of intercourse—He ever has done so, and He ever will do so. No man may look for agreeable and delightful fellowship with God while cherishing ungodly dispositions, motives, or principles; and let no individual dread the displeasure or abandonment of God, while cherishing those of which He approves. And why does God deal thus with man? Surely on the ground that He holds man responsible for these things. And why does He hold man responsible for these, unless on the ground that He has given to him the power of choice in regard to them?

Man's power over his dispositions would seem to be more immediate and direct than over his opinions and principles. In his choice of objects, man is influenced by his ideas, and in his choice of ideas he is influenced by his dispositions, and in his dispositions he displays his inner self; hence the keen sensitiveness, the special jealousy, with which he regards the light in which his dispositions are viewed by others, and the care which he takes to make his conduct, especially, in so far as it is influenced by his dispositions, appear to be correct in the view of his fellows.

Man, then, as read in the light of his own consciousness, evinces the fact that he is possessed of the power of choice in reference to objects, opinions, motives, and dispositions—that he is a free agent, and responsible both to God and man.

CHAPTER VIII.

TRIAL.

THE gift of the power of choice, as a matter of course, involves the possibility of its abuse, the responsibility of its use, and light for its guidance. The power of choice without the implied possibility of its abuse would be a contradiction. If the one scale of the balance be able to go up, the other must be able to go down.

Irresponsible power can be the trust only of absolute perfection, not of fallible being. The possession of the power of choice, necessarily involves the possibility of a right or a wrong exercise of it. If the power of choice could be exercised without the possibility of choosing wrong, then would there be no real, but merely a formal choice. If the result of any and every choice were the same, there could be no scope for the exercise of moral choice; and to regulate the exercise of the power of choice, a principle of nature and a rule of life are necessary. This principle of nature is the love of wellbeing and welldoing. The love of wellbeing and of welldoing is the deepest, most enduring, and indestructible principle of all moral existence. If the love of wellbeing and welldoing be not the deepest and most indestructible principle of all moral nature and life, then there must be another; and thus the moral creature would not be constituted in the most favourable manner for virtue and holiness. And to enable man to act in accordance with this principle of moral nature, he must be furnished with a rule of action, and this rule of action must be the expression of God's will, for no being but God can be the absolute judge of right and wrong; for none but the Omniscient can trace the consequences of any action down the stream of time, and over the broad ocean of eternity, and perceive all the possible, as well as all the actual results that flow from it; and without being able to do this, no being can be the infallible judge of the right and wrong of action. That man is incapable of being the infallible judge of his own actions is clear from the fact that what appears to him at one time to be trivial, often turns out in its consequences to be the most important event of his life, whereas many of the results of individual action, which are looked forward to with deepest anxiety, turn out in their consequences to be insignificant and worthless.

The highest reason of action in the creature is the will of the Creator. This will is not only supreme in authority, but absolutely right in itself, and ever productive of the harmony of all nature and life. In acting, then, in accordance with the will of God, the creature preserves his subjective in oneness with the subjective of God. The principle of implicit obedience is the bond of union between man and God.

The authority or expressed will of God is that in which God comes down to man, and the recognition of this authority, or implicit obedience to the will of God, is that in which man assimilates to God. The will of God is expressed in the constitution of the universe, it is uttered in the conscience of man, and is re-echoed in the pages of revelation; and a holy creature will ever be ready to do the will of God, that he may realise his supreme delight in conforming himself in heart and life to God.

In a state of holiness, or perfect condition of life, the innocent child of the Father of spirits dwells in the bright visions of the Infinite, in the clear light of the true, in the ready perception of the suitableness of God's authority. In this state there is no jarring emotion to disturb the security of his peace, no shade of obscurity to darken his visions of the Divine, no apprehensions of fear to awaken disquietude within. With holy harmony reigning within, and perfect order without, obedience is as easy as the inhaling of pure air by the healthy organ of breathing, as delightful as the outgoing of love. Temptation can only be realised when there is a power adequate to obscure the vision of God in the heart of the subject of temptation, and impair the sense of obligation to the Divine. This power may consist in the ability to present the objects of sense so as to captivate the imagination and inflame the desire, and thus withdraw the attention from what is going on in the subjective, and by this means magnify the objective so as to falsify its relations to the subjective, and thus allure the will.

And in a state of trial, and condition of moral probation, there must be in the subject of temptation, whether in an unfallen or fallen sphere of life, a possibility of realising an obscuration of the vision of God; and such a possibility might be realised through means of giving an undue attention to the outer; yielding to the fascination of the external, and allowing it to allure the attention from the watchfulness due to what is taking place in the internal.

In dallying with temptation there is a yielding to the power of the tempter, a realisation of the increasing influence of the outer over the inner, of desire over the perception of right, duty, interest; and this will ever increase in its influence in the tempter if he does not at once dismiss the tempter by instantly turning to God. In yielding to temptation, the objective is allowed to obscure the subjective, and the desire to obtain the imagined good prevails over the fear of doing what is doubtful or injurious. And in resolving to secure the *imagined* good, there is a departure from God, and a violation of the necessary conditions of wellbeing. There is the closing in with the suggestions of the tempter, instead of indorsing the promptings of the Spirit of God, and co-operating with Him in working out what He works in man to will and to do. And thus departure from the law of rectitude may take place at once, or, after a prolonged struggle, it may be brought about heedlessly, rashly, or deliberately; but in all cases there is more or less anxiety and inner conflict. Bias may blunt the perception, desire may obscure the judgment, and passion may carry the will, but there is always the consciousness of a personal act, preferring self to God, and this consciousness is a witness that the volition is not adopted for the glory of God in the maintenance of the order established by Him.

In yielding to temptation—in resolving independently of, and in opposition to, the will of God—there is the formation of a new combination, the introduction of an element of conflict, the termination of the harmonious order of the Divine, the commencement of an endless strife in the human. In willing without God, and, of course, in opposition to Him, there is the introduction into the consciousness of an element which disturbs the inner life and sets the internal powers into conflict, and an abiding conviction of sin and guilt is the result; and escape from this conviction is impossible to man, for he can neither deny his sin, nor change its character, nor alter its results. In resolving to act as he has done, the sinner has deranged the harmony of nature, and frustrated the benevolent design of God; he has violated the inner requirements of his own wellbeing, and acted in opposition to the first principles of the constituted order of the universe; he has shut himself up in the consciousness of having done what he should not have done, and this conviction cannot but be the tormenting demon of his recollection.

By the preference man has given to temptation he has banished God from the inner of his soul; and by so doing he has lost the direct vision of the Holy One, the consciousness of innocence, the agreement of will and desire with the will and law of God. The harmony of God's work within, and His administration over the sinner, is no longer realised in a consciousness of perfection of being and life. The enjoyment of a blissful fellowship with the Father of spirits in the consciousness of a oneness of subjective and objective with the objective and subjective Divine is no longer possessed. The approach of God, in the more immediate manifestations of Himself, is no longer delighted in as the drawings near of an approving Father, but dreaded as the descent of an avenging Judge. There is likewise an acquisition as well as a deprivation, viz., the acquisition of the feeling of separation from and unlikeness to God, and of conflict with Him; also a realisation of inner strife and woe. In this experience then is the realisation of a void, an inner derangement, a dread, a conflict, and a bondage to self.

Through transgression the sinner disturbs and deranges God's order of combination, and forms a new and different one of his own. But in this new combination in the consciousness of the transgressor, there is no creation of original substance or faculty; there is, however, the creation of a new power, the conviction of having resolved falsely is a new element in the inner existence of man, and a tremendous power for evil. In the formation of this combination, there is the commencement of new operations, and the inner of the disturber of order becomes the scene of disorder, conflict, and woe. The affections of the transgressor are no longer in sympathy with the

Divine, his thoughts are no longer in harmony with the true, nor his will any longer in union with the right, he is alienated from the Divine and enslaved to the false, he is in conflict with God and with his own conscience. "The way of the transgressor is hard," and he is utterly helpless in his efforts to escape from this struggle. "There is no peace for the wicked." "Dead in trespasses and sin," unable to appropriate the immediate manifestations of the Divine so as to nourish his soul on the "Bread" of life, he is sold to self.

Transgression cannot but deprive the transgressor of the loveliness of innocence and the image of God. No creature can act in opposition to the end of his existence and remain in the image of God. Transgression must deprive the transgressor of the consciousness of the rectitude of his doing. No individual can do what he doubts to be right, or fears to be wrong, and still retain the consciousness of the rectitude of his doings. Transgression must awaken in the sinner a sense of the unworthiness of his doing and being, it must arouse within him the operation of the reactionary principles of his life, and the condemnation of his conscience. Every moral creature possesses a sense of right, an inward satisfaction in doing what is right, and an inner dissatisfaction in doing what he knows to be wrong, and the consciousness of doing what he knows to be wrong must arouse this feeling of dissatisfaction, and produce in him the loss of harmony with the Divine. The evil doing of the transgressor must disturb the relations of his being, and deprive him of the consciousness of innocence and delightful fellowship with God, it must awaken the feeling of unworthiness and the effort to escape from his inner condemnation and distress, it must quicken consciousness so as to make him feel the disturbance he has produced. The evil doing of the transgressor must separate him from his Father, and bring him under His displeasure, and create a hungering in the deeper instincts of his spirit. If God be not a mere abstraction, if there be in Him a recognition of the obedience and disobedience of His creatures, and an approval of the right, and a disapproval of the wrong, then the transgression of His law must awaken in Him displeasure towards the transgressor, and He cannot fail to manifest His displeasure by the withdrawal of all sense of His approbation from the violator of His law, and to awaken within him the consciousness of wrath, and thus a separation must take place between the transgressor and God. The transgressor cannot delight in a frowning God, and God cannot regard with complacency the breaker of His law.

Has man, then, transgressed the law of his life, or has he made the right use of the power of choice? Has he kept himself in the love of God, endorsed and carried out the Divine rule of combination set before him in the established order of the universe? Has he preserved, in a holy life, his harmony of being, his rectitude of will, his fellowship of spirit with his Father? Is the subjective and objective of the human one with the subjective and objective Divine. Does man in his inner being move divineward, and only divineward—cherish right, and only right dispositions—entertain correct, and only correct ideas—act on just, and only just principles? Does he undeviatingly pursue the one end of his existence in the exercise of the power of choice, look only to God for direction, and seek to live in the consciousness that he can be blessed, and glorious only, as his subjective is one with the subjective of God.

Let universal consciousness, the prevailing sense of mankind, the incessant efforts of man answer the question. These cannot say that the feelings of humanity move in harmony with the will of God. Man's consciousness does not testify that his most fervent affections, his most eager aspirations, are ever Godward, that his conceptions of being and observations of life are at all times correct; that his motives, principles, and actions, are what they should always be what he himself conceives they ought to be. No, the accusations and struggles of his conscience, the immoralities, crimes, and experience of his life, clearly establish the fact that man is not unfolding his constitution, or developing the principles of his nature in accordance with the end of his existence. He, alas! is no stranger to deep-heaved sighs, or heavy-burdened groans and unavailing efforts.

Man must be either perfect or imperfect. If he is perfect, he is fully satisfied with his condition, wholly contented with his life, complete in the enjoyment of conscious fellowship with God, himself, and his fellows, all the powers of his nature moving in undisturbed harmony with the principles of his constitution, and all the functions of his soul sympathetic with the Divine. But the least discernment of man's present condition, or the slightest reflection on the struggles of his life, shows that such is not the case. No, the ever and anon consciousness, the universal sense of mankind, the ever striving efforts of man, tell in clearest light that he is not at ease in his life, contented with his lot, perfect in his nature.

To what, then, is all this imperfection of human life to be traced—to the design, plan, and workmanship of God, or to man's abuse of his power of choice? Surely it cannot be traced to the former, only to the latter. God, in His infinite wisdom and benevolence, would never produce a creature to be ever struggling against the Author of his existence and the conditions of his wellbeing; this would have been to have created man in conflict with the principles of his own nature, the end, and necessities of his life. It would have been to render fellowship with God possible only through the consciousness of His wrath.

Man has abused his power of choice, and in this abuse he has formed combination different from God's, and the proof of his having done so is seen in his dislike to God, and in his efforts to modify or get rid of the demands of the Divine law, that he may give himself up to the gratifications of self. And in this

his folly is apparent, for pleasure-seeking is not the end of man's being, but the propensions of his animal nature towards gratification. Man's animal instincts move, and with it they are satisfied. The search after truth in the acquisition of knowledge is not the end of man's being, but of man's rational life; towards science and philosophy his intellectual faculties move, and in the attainment of truth repose. Yet man strives to rest here. Worthiness, however, in the conscious rectitude of man's being and life, in a sense of oneness with God, is the end of his existence; for in this his soul delights, and aspires to no higher enjoyment. Man realises a fulness of an unalloyed bliss in the consciousness that his subjective and objective are one with the subjective and objective of God. But this is not the object for the attainment of which every man strives.

Man's experience proves that he is in a condition of conflict with himself and of disobedience with God; disorder within and without reigns in his life. The principles of his nature do not move in harmony, his desires are not sympathetic with the conditions of his wellbeing; he is not satisfied with his present state, he longs after a higher order of being, and strives incessantly to rise superior to the calamities of his life. Man endeavours to escape from the upbraidings of his conscience, the perplexity of his mind, the misgivings of his heart, the anxieties of his spirit—these are known to all, and do what he will he cannot surmount the evils of his present state.

Man cannot deny that he groans under the pressure

of evil; that he is existing in a state of conflict with God Himself and the conditions of his wellbeing, that he longs for a higher and a better state, a more satisfying condition of being and life. He must admit that he struggles with evils which he cannot avoid; he must allow that his body is diseased and dying; that his mind is ignorant and perplexed. He cannot deny that his conscience is ever accusing and excusing himself; nor will he refuse to acknowledge that he ofttimes desires that God's law should be different from what it is. Nor will he refuse to confess that he labours to propitiate God, and that he does so in vain. Yes, the whole being, life, and circumstances of man, prove that he is in a state of disorder and conflict, and that if his calamities are not greater, this is not traceable to himself nor to any counteracting power in his nature, but solely to the restraining grace of God, and the merciful dispensation man is placed under. Is this, then, the state in which God originally placed man, or is it one into which he has brought himself. It cannot be the one in which he was created, for, as we have seen, man's present state of existence is one of conflict with himself, with the Author and end of his existence; and to have produced man in such a state would have been to manifest weakness and wickedness which we cannot attribute to God. A nature in conflict with itself, the Author of its being, and the end of its existence, exhibits the highest possible evidence of being in a fallen condition.

The constitution of man displays a skill, power, and

benignity which, notwithstanding Mill's surmises to the contrary, we believe few reflecting men will hesitate to regard as boundless. Humanity is so constituted that it is impossible for man to act in harmony with himself, with the Author of his being, and with the end of his existence, without enjoying an elevating repose. Man is constituted in the likeness of God, and formed to find his true perfection and life in fellowship with the Divine, but he is so perverse in his dispositions, so biased in his will, so conceited in his notions, that he is ever striving to live in opposition to his highest interests, his sense of duty, his convictions of right, and hence, his burdened conscience, his suffering condition, his inner conflict, struggle, and woe. It would be the strangest of all contradictions to imagine that God has created man with capacity which can only be satisfied with the indwelling of the Divine, and has at the same time implanted within him a deep-rooted aversion to Himself.

We may discard this supposition as absolutely impossible. It is possible to conceive that, through insanity, the architect of a magnificent temple might contemplate it in a state of ruin with satisfaction and joy; that a monarch, through some hallucination, might delight in a revolution of his empire and in the rebel condition of his subjects; or that a parent, through intellectual derangement, might take pleasure in the sickness and death of his children; but daring impiety itself cannot conceive of the Holy One taking delight in the ruin of His noblest work, the anarchy and rebellion of His offspring, the death and ruin of the immortal spirit breathed from Himself. Man's present condition is traceable alone to his abuse of his power of choice, in the formation of a combination different from what God established in His creation when He breathed into him the breath of life.

CHAPTER IX.

RETRIBUTION.

GOD has created elements of being capable of endless variety in combination, and has set agents over these elements to combine them for every variety of purpose. In particular essences God has placed certain forces and faculties, to certain emotions He has attached certain sympathies, to certain ideas certain sensations, to certain convictions certain realisations; and over these He has placed will, conscience, personality, and commanded man in all his doings to obey His law, and has warned man against bringing the powers and principles of his being into conflict and discord by transgressing His law.

Original elements possess primary forces and susceptibilities which act not in themselves, nor in their individual capacity, but in combination with other powers. Primary forces are known under the designation of chemical, mechanical, and vital powers and influences. These are capable of endless variety in combination, and into whatever combination they are brought, they operate in accordance with their original nature, and the relations they sustain in the combination.

Agents are endowed with the power and responsibility of choice in forming new combinations. In the evolutions and development of nature, and in forming new combinations, they act under the conviction of doing what is right, or the apprehension of doing what is wrong. No original primary or simple power or disposition is conflictive in itself. If the forces of nature are combined in harmony, they act for God, and in acting for God they act in concord with one another; and in acting in accordance with the law of God, they develop in the most vigorous forms the powers and capabilities of their being. All power and capacity have been created to subserve the Divine purpose, but they have also been called into existence with the possibility of being brought into combinations of discord with God, and with themselves. In other words, they have been created with the capability of operating in harmony or in discord with God, and with one another.

In every combination of matter, each atom, however insignificant, tells in the whole. In every combination of sound, from the faintest whisper to the loudest thunder, whether in harmony or discord, each tone, though not discerned or even discernible in itself to the ordinary ear, has its own part in the concert or the storm; every atom or shade in the combinations of colour, although not perceptible in itself to the keenest eye, has its own part in the effect produced; every flaw or unsoundness in the material and in the construction of a machine, though not in the most careful scrutiny detected, has its influence in weakening the efficiency of the machine, and securing loss through its break down; every sensation, desire, emotion, action, whether agreeable or disagreeable, tells in the formation of the character, and in the realisation of the life. Chemical, mechanical, and vital forces acting in conflict, must ever produce disease, suffering, and destruction; intellectual faculties acting in conflict must ever produce perplexity, disappointment, confusion; spiritual powers acting in conflict must ever produce self-condemnation and despair. The chemical, mechanical, and vital forces of nature acting in harmony, produce a true cosmos; the rational and spiritual acting in concord produce a perfect human life, and secure a Divine fellowship.

In all combination of substance, mechanism, and life, every element has its position, and plays its own part; this is in accordance with the will and purpose of God, and His justice is apparent in ever securing to every element, of whatever kind, in whatever combination of relation or operation it may be brought, its own; and this holds good, no matter in what way the combination has been effected, whether blindly or with intelligence, whether intentionally or unintentionally. In combination, motive may clash with will, desire with conscience, interest with conviction, but God secures to each its own place and part; He is no respecter of things any more than of persons. His justice is not impaired, but rather the more conspicuously illustrated, in His securing calamity from discord of combination and iniquity of life. The grand end of His providence in the present state of being is to afford full scope for the formation of every possible combination, and for the full operation of every power in every combination, and to secure the natural result of all elements in the several combinations, whether they are combinations of concord or discord, or partially of both. It is the design of God, in His present government of the world, to show to principalities and powers, in heavenly and earthly "places," what endless variety of combinations may be made in human life, and what must be the inevitable results of these combinations when brought about.

No power, not misdirected, can produce disease, deformity, suffering, or death; but all powers, acting in discord with the will of God and with one another, do produce in the degree of their vigour, and in the measure of their activity, deformity, disease, suffering, and death. When the powers of nature are combined in discord, they operate in opposition to the development of their higher functions, they interfere with the wellbeing of creation, and bring destruction on whatever comes under their sway. This destruction is, however, only of the mechanism or combination of the substances in which their powers inhere. When the powers of rational life are united in harmonious combination, intelligence and godliness are the result; when they are combined in conflict, error and degradation are the result. It is a fundamental principle, an immutable law of combination, expressive of the design and determination of God, that every combination of elements and powers of life shall secure its own result; and this design is as really, though not directly, answered in the destructive effects of the one combination, as in the enjoyment and progress of the other.

The development of the capabilities of elements, and of the functions of agents in concord, is the design of God in the established order of the universe. And the deformity, suffering, and death which result from the combinations man has formed, are also designed and determined by God. The one, however, is immediately, the other mediately, determined by God. That He does not desire a conflicting combination is seen in the fact, that every conflicting combination of matter terminates sooner or later in the dissolution of the mechanism or combination itself, or in the derangement and strife of the powers of spiritual essence, which, being incapable of the dissolution of its mechanism, continues to suffer. Agents, in forming combinations of discord, usually act in opposition to their convictions of right, and thus violate the first principle of moral agency. Every agent must form some combinations, and those who will not form combinations with the Divine or with the godly, must form them with the diabolic or the selfish, and in the retributive conscience receive their reward, as did Belshazzar, Tiberius, and Charles IX. of France.

If beings entrusted with the power of choice will abuse that trust by bringing the element over which they have control into combinations of discord, God may not be expected to arrest the natural action of the several powers in their combinations and alter their relative influence. It is folly to assume that

He may cease to uphold these powers now that they are brought into a combination of conflict, and suspend their operations the moment they are brought into the relation of discord. When man violates the conditions of his wellbeing, God is not to go back in His purpose and alter the constituted order of the universe; were He capable of doing this, the consistency of His government would be at an end, and His wisdom might be questioned. God will not destroy combinations nor restrain in any way the nature of powers, or alter them in any degree in their operations of conflict, but will maintain them in the full strength of their action, until, in accordance with their nature, they exhaust their energies in the conflict, or resolve their substances into their original elements. And if the substance in which the powers in conflict act be incapable of dissolution, such, *e.g.*, as mind, then will He sustain it in the conflict of its powers throughout ceaseless ages. Influences, powers, and agencies may act upon individuals insidiously or imperceptibly in preparing them for disobedience, yet they do so none the less efficiently. Indeed, it is generally through the operation of imperceptible influences that men are prepared for acting rightfully or wrongfully. Agents may act intentionally or unintentionally, but whatever combination they form, the result of that combination must be realised, and then shall they be made to know that *they shall reap the fruit of their doings.* God will sustain the operation of every power while its strength endures, and thus justice for ever reigns, and equity holds sway in all the combinations and operations of human life.

Nor does it matter how or in what way the combination of conflict may be brought about, whether designedly or heedlessly, knowingly or unknowingly, piously or impiously, if the combination be formed, the forces of the elements combined must act. Thus, if an infant falls into a boiling caldron, and a new combination be formed, we do not suppose that God will then and there suspend the power of heat to burn or alter the capacity of the child's body to prevent its being scalded. If through carelessness a spark falls upon a magazine of powder, and a new combination of elements be formed, we do not expect that God will arrest the action of the explosive materials even though thousands of lives be endangered, and numerous families be involved in utter ruin. If in the castings of a steam engine a flaw escapes detection; if in the building of a vessel dry rot in portions of the timber be unobserved, and a combination of elements of weakness instead of strength be formed; if the machinery break down, or if the boiler burst, or the ship spring a leak, we do not expect that God is to work a miracle and suspend the action of the destroying powers to prevent the ruin of those involved in destruction. If a man by mistake swallows poison; if a medical practitioner in the discharge of his duty inhales deadly effluvia; or if a missionary in fervent zeal and self-denying devotedness incautiously exposes himself to the treachery of savages, and thus a combination of destructive powers be formed, we are not to suppose that God is necessitated to step forward and arrest the operation of these powers, or to render the sufferers invulnerable. We do not find that He interferes with any of the combinations of material substances throughout the varied forms in nature's operations, and if He does not in the combinations of matter, we can hardly imagine that He interferes with the combinations of mind and spirit. If a man through perversion forms a combination of error and prejudice, no one is simple enough to suppose that God will restrain the operations of such a combination, and rescue him from the conflict of perplexity and doubt consequent thereon. If an individual by disobedience deprives himself of the presence of God in his soul, and awakens within his breast the conviction of wrong-doing, God is not, as a matter of course, to suspend the operation of the powers of inner conflict, re-establish harmony, and secure to the guilty conscience joy and peace.

In upholding the powers of nature and securing to them their results, God displays His pleasure and displeasure, makes known His love and admiration, or His condemnation and wrath. The approbation of God is expressed in His securing to the obedient the reward of "his keeping the law of the Lord;" and "the wrath of God" is displayed in His bringing on the disobedient the penalty of their disobedience. And thus the end of God is *as really*, though not *so directly*, secured in the display of "His wrath," as in the manifestation of His admiration. Let no one, then, imagine that God will deny Himself and go back upon His work, to alter in the least degree, or weaken the force of any power brought into any combination of conflict; on the contrary, He will maintain them in the full force of their energy, until they either exhaust their strength or resolve their substances into their primitive elements. It is a false and fatal conception, and one by no means complimentary to the all-wise Creator, to suppose that the contending and destroying operations of powers in combinations of discord are not in accordance with His purpose, and that when disasters arise from any combination, they do so by accident and because they are not in accordance with His design, and that God will sooner or later interfere to mitigate the sufferings and rescue from ruin those who are involved in it. Such suppositions arise from superficial observations of God's character and designs. Disapprobation of wrong is as real a principle of God's nature as approbation of right; it exists in the subjective as really as it is manifested in the objective Divine; it is embedded in the principles of all moral being, and realised in the experience of God's rational offspring, and it is so because it has its seat in Himself. In His intercourse with man, He holds him responsible for his entire life in all his opinions and dispositions. The love of wellbeing and the hatred of illbeing is indelibly engraven on the spirit of man; and in thus creating man, God has stamped upon him His own image. If, then, He possesses such in Himself—if

He has impressed the same thing on the nature of man—is He not necessitated to uphold that law in His intercourse with man?

If, then, God has created substances with qualities, and agents with powers; if to these agents He has assigned laws for their guidance in the exercise of their power of choice, and if these laws arise out of the very nature of being; and if many, notwithstanding all God's care and attention, abuse His power of choice in the formation of new combinations —the results of these cannot possibly be the same as if he had exercised his reason in the formation of right combinations. If God has formed human bodies with sensations, minds with faculties of thought, spirits with consciousness of inner condition; if He has conferred on man the power of choice, the principle of free responsible nature; and if He has attached the reward of glory and bliss to the right use of reason, recognising its responsibility in the formation of proper combinations; and if He has affixed the penalty of conscious shame, degradation, and woe, to the neglect of reason in the formation of wrong combinations; and if He has counselled man in regard to the one, and warned him in reference to the other—then surely man alone is to blame for the degradation and suffering of humanity. If God has attached certain sensations to certain states of physical life, agreeable to healthful states and painful to diseased; if to correct thinking He has united satisfaction, and to erroneous, dissatisfaction; if He has joined dignity and delight with goodness of spirit, remorse and anguish with selfishness of soul; and if, in so doing, He has imaged in man His own perfect wisdom and life, no one surely will say that He has done wrong in so creating man in His own image. If God has given to man freedom of nature, choice of state, option of subjectivity; if He has made the consciousness of innocence the elixir of the soul, and the consciousness of guilt the anguish of the spirit, He has only acted in accordance with the nature of things. If God has entrusted to the personality of man a harmonious combination of life, to be preserved by him in the development of the constitutional relations of his existence, and if man yields to a disturbing influence, and if, in disregarding the injunctions given to him, he violates the conditions of his wellbeing and brings about a wrong combination; then the harmonious relations of his life cannot continue, and God cannot feel towards the transgressor of His law in the same way as He feels towards him who observes it.

An important and practical inquiry at this point naturally presents itself, viz., Has the possibility of derangement been unforeseen by God, or, if not unforeseen, yet unprovided for by Him? or is it in accordance with the order of existence He has established, and which He is determined to uphold? We prefer the latter alternative. This view, no doubt, represents God as capable of wrath, but gives no indication of revengefulness. Every man knows that anger is compatible with love, and wrath with mercy; indeed, the one class of feeling is the co-relation of the other. God created man so as that he should be degraded and miserable in the dislike of the Divine, in the ignorance of the true, and in the consciousness of the wrongfulness of his life, as surely as He created him to be dignified and happy in the consciousness of the rectitude of his being and life. And this is an eternal and immutable condition of man's existence, as immutable and eternal as the body of Godhead. We are anxious to direct the reader's attention to this point, and to rivet his thoughts upon the fact, that the degradation and distress is as intimately and inseparably connected with his sinning, as is his happiness dependent upon his obedience. The connection in the one case is as much the arrangement of God as it is in the other; God purposely created man, so that it is impossible that he can be other than degraded and distressed in his dislike of the Divine. But how, it may be asked, is this view of the case consistent with the goodness of God? We are under no obligation to answer this question; it might be enough to reply, that what has been advanced is true, whatever may be the inference drawn; but we may go further and say, that it is quite consistent with God's goodness, the one is in accordance with His will, the other with "the good pleasure of His will." The obedience of man is pleasing to God, and the disobedience of man displeasing to Him. God manifests Himself directly and immediately in the harmony of man's consciousness and life; He reveals Himself indirectly and mediately in the discordance of man's consciousness and life.

Man is not created to sin and to derange the order of God's combination,—to do so is not the law of his life. It is only in the abuse of his freedom that he can sin, and bring about discord with its consequent sufferings, and when he does so, God secures to him the penalty of his transgression. They greatly err who imagine that God grieves at, and mourns over, the conflict of the sinner's nature and suffering of his life; such views are common, but they display unsound judgment and mistaken conceptions in theology; they are mere sentiment. God grieves over the fact that man cherishes rebellious dispositions, but if man will sin, God is determined that while he continues in his sinful state, he shall bear the effects of his sin. The suffering of the transgressor indirectly proves the necessity of his obedience, the wisdom of the laws, and the benignity of the Lawgiver. If there was no necessity in the wellbeing of the subject of law, for his acting in accordance with the precept and spirit of the law, then would there be neither wisdom nor benignity in the imposition of the law. If all things were alike, then would there be no possibility of acting wrong, and no need of enjoining this and guarding against that, if the results of all actions were alike; then could there be no necessity in the condition and circumstances of individuals, that they should attend to this, or refrain from that mode of life. Just in the measure of the necessity of the law, must be the greatness of the ruin it guards against, and the dignity which it secures; and just in the measure of the benignity and wisdom of the law, is the necessity of obeying it. Punishment is not arbitrary, but the inevitable result of disobedience. Derangement in the physical, rational, and spiritual, will, and ever must, secure conflict and woe, and man must ever realise it to be so. It is chiefly, however, in the spiritual that God displays "His wrath," and makes "His power known." The manifestation of His wrath begins in the spiritual, proceeds from it into the rational and physical; God's wrath is muttered in the physical, whispered in the intellectual, and spoken aloud in the spiritual of man.

God has a right to be angry with the transgressor for the iniquity he has done. He has so constituted man, that, if he does what is wrong, he shall realise in the inner and outer of his being the consequences of his wrong-doing. And in so constituting man, God has acted in accordance with the nature of things; and in awakening, maintaining, and intensifying the conviction of guilt in the sinner, God makes His power known to him. He has only to draw near to the guilty spirit, in the revelation of His immaculate purity, to make its anguish intolerable in the consciousness of its guilt; and in permitting this consciousness to lull, by withdrawing Himself into "thick darkness" from the sinner's view, He manifests His longsuffering. If there be no wrath in God, why is it that He has made the consciousness of guilt the most dreadful realisation of the sinner's spirit. Or, if the conception of guilt be a delusion of the mind, as some imagine, how is it that this falsehood is the most tremendous of *realities* in the experience of human consciousness. God does not suffer the body of man to escape from the languor and pain of disease, but by its deliverance from disease; and so He will not suffer the spirit of man to escape from its restlessness, conflict, and anguish, but by its deliverance from sin. Man perceives and acts upon this principle in regard to his body; he does not wonder that his body suffers in disease, nor does he expect relief from the pain of such disease but in the restoration of the body to its healthy state. But man is slow to perceive the analogy in spiritual matters, and to act on this principle in reference to the distress of his spiritual disease. What, then, is to become of the human spirit in the conflict of nature. Its substance cannot be resolved into primary elements, for its essence is simple and indivisible. Spirits cannot moulder as bodies do into dust; the energies of spirits cannot become exhausted, for they inhere in no decaying matter, but are immortal as their essence is indestructible. While, therefore, they exist in a state of conflict, their rage must be incessant, their effort to escape unavailing, and their vexation from disappointment perpetual, "the wicked are like a troubled sea when it cannot rest, whose waters cast up mire and dirt." The lover of wellbeing contemplating his own evil-doing in the presence of immaculate purity, possessed with the clear conviction that the evil in which he is involved is the righteous consequence of his own deliberate deeds, conscious of the inner strife, and recognising the outer condemnation as the inevitable result of his acting in opposition to the conviction of conscience and the law of his Creator, and seeing the impossibility of either escape or of the mitigation of the rage of passion, seeing no end of the conflict of nature, and his deep, restless, unsatisfied craving, can he regard his condition as being anything else than a banishment into "outer darkness," an imprisonment in the burnings of "eternal fire," a perpetual realisation of the ceaseless gnawings of the "undying worm?"

CHAPTER X.

INABILITY.

It is of the gravest importance for us to know as to whether or not, Science, Philosophy, Natural religion, or Rational Christianity can point out a way whereby man can rescue himself from the state of conflict in which his nature is involved. Science and Philosophy have already accomplished so much that many look upon their domain as being practically limitless and all-embracing. Can they, then, show man how to overcome his internal difficulties; can they dispel his spiritual gloom; in a word, can they lead his soul to God?

Many have assumed, on very inadequate grounds, that man needs no external help in regard to the matter referred to; he is sufficient, they believe, for all things appertaining to his life and prospects, spiritual and physical. But they are by no means agreed as to the course which he ought to follow. Man is recommended to follow "the dictates of reason." To contemplate and follow the example of the illustrious of former times, to do penance, to repent of his former sins and give himself up to God. All very plausible; but all visionary and futile. To teach man in this manner is to trifle with the great and momentous interests of his spirit. It is only to taunt the inquiring soul. This is all that comes of "the wisdom of this world."

Philosophy and the dictates of reason can do very little to ease the burdened spirit of the transgressor; the conscience-stricken sinner cannot look upon his sins as the prejudice of an ignorant and unphilosophic mind, which the study of philosophy and the enlightenment of Science will easily dispel. It is in vain to speak of prejudice and ignorance to the man of awakened conscience, and to tell him that such convictions are but the visions of fancy, the ghosts of a heated brain, and all that he has to do to drive them away is, in the light of reason and philosophy, to look them full in the face; he knows full well, and is constrained to acknowledge, that his sense of guilt is the most tangible verity of his inner consciousness, and that he may as soon command the clouds to disperse, as by the voice of reason and the light of philosophy bid his consciousness of guilt fly away.

And what can the contemplation of innocent loveliness or of human virtue do to lift the burden of guilt from off the burdened conscience of the sinner? Those who advocate this doctrine would do well to point out how such a result can thus be realised; but this they cannot do, and the only end they could secure by the attempt, would be to show to themselves its impossibility. The murderer's conscience, while writhing under a sense of his crime, is not to be pacified by the contemplation of self-denying heroism. Ah no! it is then that he feels his guilt to be an intolerable burden, and his spirit, instead of deriving relief from the contemplation of self-denying devotedness to human wellbeing, is only the more burdened; he feels his conviction of guilt the more deepened, and himself hurried with the greater rapidity into despair.

The law of conscience is an impress of the Divine. The quickening of the sense of blameworthiness through means of the contemplation of innocence and self-denying virtue is an ultimate fact of man's nature, and is not the result of education or prejudice. It can then only tantalise the conscience-stricken sinner the more, to direct him for peace of conscience to the heroic deeds and self-denying devotedness of the illustrious of earth. To treat him after this fashion is only to mock him with delusion; to point the eye of the sinner for relief while smarting under the lash of conscience to the life and character of the self-denying One who, sooner than deviate in the least from truth and rectitude, voluntarily laid down His life, is not only to tantalise him, but to become chargeable with the absurdity of attempting to accomplish an end by means calculated only to secure the very opposite result; nay, to ignore and pervert the great end of Emmanuel's death in the very act of attempting to expound His doctrine. To endeavour to promote peace in the human heart by such an instrumentality, is to mistake both the nature and cure of man's disease. Man's deepest convictions are ever true to the principles of his nature; and, while writhing under a sense of guilt, to be told to calm his conscience and purify his life by gazing on the martyr's death is only to mock him; he feels that this is only asking him to deepen the anguish of his spirit instead of removing the wretchedness of his soul. Such doctrines may meet the wants of a fancied sinfulness, but not the deep necessities of a realised guilt. In the name, then, both of reason and philosophy we say, away with this trifling with the deepest interests both of man and God.

Such conceptions are only the dreams of fevered brain, the ebulitions of bewildering speculation. To talk to the sinner in such a style, is only to pervert the dictates of reason and the teachings of philosophy. The contemplation of immaculate purity and spotless innocence, can only show to the sinner in the clearest light the aggravations of his guilt, and thus intensify his anguish. Direct the eye of the awakened sinner to the martyr-death of Incarnate Divinity, and the only effect will be to produce an increase of his misery; the conscience is ever ready to exclaim, Whence this law of my being that condemns me to the face? and can any satisfactory reply be given to him, but that this awakening of conscious guilt is the operation of a law woven into the constitution of his being by the Author of his existence, and that it is the echo of the voice Divine. And is not the sense of guilt clear evidence to the sinner that he has incurred the displeasure of God? and if so, will the contemplation of that which arouses in the inner of man's being a sense of God's displeasure remove the conviction of that displeasure from his mind? Can the sinner, if he reasons at all, reason otherwise than thus—If my heart condemn me, must not God, who is holier than my heart, condemn me still more? If the sinner's transgression has disturbed the harmony of his life, and set in operation the reactionary laws of his nature, and awakened such feelings in his breast, the natural conclusion is that it has also awakened displeasure in God. Yes, the sinner does and must believe in the displeasure of God against sin; the sacrifices, penances, and supplications of heathendom are a witness of man's belief in this; and the anxious endeavour of the awakened sinner is not to contemplate immaculate purity, but to ascertain how God's anger can be appeased, how the dark cloud which envelops the Divine countenance can be removed, for he feels, and that deeply, that the contemplation of the heroic lives and the martyr-deaths of the excellent of the earth, instead of removing the consciousness of guilt, only arrows and deepens that conviction the more.

Again, penance can do little for the transgressor of God's law; it cannot awaken in him right conceptions of the Divine, nor draw down the spirit of God to raise the penitent into fellowship with his Father in heaven. Fasting, lacerations, &c., can never reveal God in love to man, nor afford him right conceptions of the mercy of Heaven, nor warm him with the love of the Divine. The infliction of suffering on the body cannot possibly awaken love in the heart towards Him who is conceived as demanding it, the presentation to heaven of the most endeared victims of earth cannot afford a sight gratifying to the God of compassion, nor meet the yearnings of the Father's heart. Loud supplications to heaven, deep-heaved sighs from the agonised spirit of man, cannot prevail with God to become what the blinded heathen desires Him to be; no, neither penance nor human sacrifice nor "much speaking," can present man in more acceptable form to God, nor reveal God in lovelier grace to man. The breach between God and man cannot thus be healed, such a course can only widen the gulf the more and more, and make God more tedious in the conception of man, and man more miserable in his endeavours to serve God. The history of heathenism is the corroboration of this truth; such attempts have only led man to "change the truth of God into a lie, and worship and serve the creature more than the Creator." Man, under heathenism, has sadly degenerated in his conception of God, and in his mode of worshipping Him.

Self-repentance, again, can accomplish little in the removal of the consciousness of guilt from the sinner; true repentance is not merely, nor chiefly, a change of the outer. A man may pass from all the external vices to all the outer virtues of the world, and be taken in society for a reformed man, and not be the subject of that repentance "not to be repented of," he may only be like the man out of whom went the "unclean spirits," "seeking rest and finding none," and his last state in God's sight "worse than his first." An individual may pass from one religious belief to another, till he go the round of all the creeds of the different sects of earth, and instead of being nearer the truth, he may only be further from it, like the man to whom our Lord refers when, addressing the Pharisees, He says, "Ye compass sea and land to make one proselyte, and when he is made you make him twofold more the child of hell." Again, true repentance is not merely or chiefly sorrow for sin. A man may see his sin to be so heinous that he weeps bitter tears of sorrow for his transgression, and be no better than Judas when he saw that his Master was condemned, "repented himself and brought again the thirty pieces of silver to the chief priests and elders, saying, I have sinned in that I have betrayed innocent blood. And he cast down the thirty pieces of silver in the temple, and departed, and went and hanged himself." Repentance, which is profitable to man and acceptable to God, denotes an entire change of the inner life of man through the quickening of the Spirit of God, leading the sinner to the belief of "the truth as it is in Jesus." In this change the disposition, the thoughts, the desires, and the will of man, are renewed, *i.e.*, reconciled to God and to the position and end of man's existence. By repentance, the sympathies of the soul of man are raised to God, and the movements of his will into harmony with the will of God. Repentance "not to be repented of," is a change from the love of self to the love of God; it is a change begun by the Spirit of God in the inner depths of the spirit of man, a change regulated by the Word of God and consummated in a realised likeness to Jesus. This change in some is accompanied with sorrow for sin, and involves a passing from error to truth, from ungodliness to holiness, but is in no sense a self-repentance. The subjects of this change are not the self-righteous, but sinners. Self-righteousness is the greatest hindrance in man to his undergoing this change; as long as a man clings to a shred of self-righteousness in any form he cannot truly repent, hence the declaration of Jesus, "I am not come to call the righteous but sinners to repentance." Repentance involves at least three things—the seeing transgression to be disobedience of the Divine law and ruin to the transgressor; the being convinced that God is just in maintaining the powers of the sinner's nature in their condition of conflict; and sorrowing on account of the disposition that inclined to the act, as well as over the consequences of the act. Repentance implies the seeing that God, in requiring implicit obedience, is righteous, and that He requires only what is absolutely necessary to the Spiritual life, and that God, while maintaining in the transgressor a painful sense of his wrong-doing, is holy and true. Now, can the sinner of himself thus repent? On the contrary, he is ever striving to justify himself and to merit the favour of God, and by his constant efforts to vindicate his doings he is ever trying to prevail upon God to change the manifestations which He has given of Himself.

The sinner will admit the fact of his transgression, for his conscience tells him of it, but he will not acknowledge the blameworthiness of his deeds; he will confess to the violation of the precept, but he will not consent to the righteousness of his endurance of the penalty of the law. He endeavours to persuade himself that he could not help acting as he has done, and seeks to shelter himself under the idea that the circumstances under which he was placed led to the act, and that God, who placed him in these circumstances, is more responsible than he is for the consequences of his deeds. Temptation was strong, desire urgent; if he has done wrong he should not have been created with such inclinations, and exposed to such temptations; it is, therefore, not himself, but the being who placed him in such a position that is chargeable with the responsibilities of his doings. He attempts to reason with himself, Why is human knowledge so limited? Why is not man supplied with as much light as would make it impossible for him to do wrong? Why is man made liable to sin, and not placed beyond the possibility of transgression? Why is he exposed to temptations and not raised above solicitations to do evil? Such is the light in which the transgressor seeks to view his conduct, and the manner in which he strives to rid himself of the law and authority of God. He attempts to pervert the first principles of right and wrong, the deep convictions of his own inner being; "the carnal mind is not subject to the law of God, neither indeed can be," hence it must have all things to bend to its capricious will, to fit in and square with its notions. It will have no law but its own caprice, no rule but its own inclination, no authority but its own will. If anything stands in the of way its doing whatever it pleases with impunity, it will instantly complain of injury and seek to resent its imagined wrong. The "carnal mind" strives to set itself in the very apex of being to ascend the highest summit of existence, to grasp in its Almighty fiat eternal and immutable principle, reign over all law and authority, make a god of self, worship and serve self as the end of its existence. This is the *terminus ad quem* of guilty man. Is this, then, the spirit that will repent of itself?

But although the "carnal mind" will not repent and return to God, it cannot rest in its spirit of rebellion. Man's constitution forbids this; man in every transgression he commits is furnished with sufficient light to enable him to avoid falling into the transgression; he cannot sin without acting against sufficient light—this is involved in the very nature of transgression. It is not an overpowering flood, but a sufficiency of light that involves responsibility. If man's deepest and most indestructible principle of existence be the love of wellbeing, and if sin be the doing what we doubt to be right and what we fear to be wrong, if it be the acting from any other principle than that of implicit obedience to the Divine will, and desire for any other end than the glory of God, then the transgressor acts against sufficient light in every sin which he commits. He acts against the imperative principle of his own life, the highest obligation of his own constitution, the true condition of his own wellbeing; he acts in the presence of his doubt, and in the face of his fear, and in the consciousness that he is not acting on the principle of implicit obedience to the will of God. And is not his doubt, his fear, his consciousness, that he is not acting on the principle of implicit obedience, sufficient light to deter him from acting? Would he have omniscience given to him in every moment of temptation, omnipotence to hold him back from transgression? If "whatever be not of faith is sin," surely he sins in acting in opposition to his doubt, and in the face of his fear, or whenever he acts without the consciousness of acting in implicit obedience to the will of God. No amount of temptation can make it right in man, or can justify him in doing what he is in doubt about. Nor can any force of temptation shelter him from the consequences of acting in opposition to the first principles of his nature. Man may sin against God, and by so doing disturb the principles and relations of his life; but he cannot alter his constitution, nor destroy the conditions of his wellbeing. He has been created for fellowship with his Father, and formed for the reception and preservation of the image Divine; he has been brought into existence for endless joy and delight in the study of truth; he has been endowed with the noblest powers for the investigation of the deep things of God; he has been gifted with an indestructible instinct of his lofty destiny: but by sinning he has incurred guilt, placed himself in opposition to the high conditions of his wellbeing, and stumbled on the threshold of his noble career. Still the principles of his nature are true to themselves. The guilty cannot stifle the deep cravings of his immortal spirit after God, neither can he rid himself of the desire after some sort of a god. Even sinful man feels that he must have a god to hold fellowship with, but the "carnal mind," the selfish heart of man, will not have a holy God and an absolute standard of duty. Such does not suit the "carnal mind," hence a compromise must be attempted, and thus idolatry in one form or another has universally prevailed among the nations. The "carnal mind" must have a god to its own liking, truth of its own devising, an altar of its own erection, victims of its own selecting, a heaven of its own framing, a glory of its own creating. And is this the spirit that will repent?

The fact that the first deepest principles of man's nature is the love of wellbeing, taken in connection with the fact of human transgression, sufficiently explains the present condition of mankind. The controversy which the "carnal mind" wages with the human conscience and God is not whether there be a God and an absolute right. A being created with a deep receptivity for the indwelling of the Divine, and an irradicable instinct for fellowship with God, can never rest in a disbelief of the Divine existence. Atheism is not natural to man, and never can be popular; mankind in all ages have rejected it, and never will embrace it as the popular belief. A being whose first, deepest, and most indestructible principle is the love of wellbeing, cannot repose in the disbelief of an absolute right, an imperative obligation of nature, an infallible rule of life. Man in all ages has earnestly longed for and diligently sought after a "chief good," but he has sought for it in vain because he has not grasped it "by faith," but sought after it of self.

Can, then, the transgressor repent of himself and turn to God? Look at the circumstances in which he has placed himself, and see if it be possible. Can the lover of wellbeing gaze with complacency on the fact that he has transgressed the high conditions of his wellbeing? Can he rest with satisfaction in the realisation of his own inner conflict? Can he delight in God imputing to him his sins? In the nature of things it is impossible for the sinner in and from himself to repent of his sin, and in the absence of a readjusting power to turn to God; his doing such would involve his acting in direct opposition to the cherished sentiments and the reigning effort of his rebel spirit. Is it possible, we would ask, for a creature whose deepest principle of nature is the love of wellbeing, gladly to rest in the conviction that he has deliberately acted in opposition to the first principle of his nature? is it possible for him intently to gaze with complacency on his inner strife, to listen with composure to the ever and anon upbraiding voice of conscience, to view with cordiality the opposition of desire to conscience, of will to judgment, of passion to reason? is it possible for him to delight in God's ever upholding conscience to accuse him and ever maintaining his powers of nature to act in conflict within him, ever and anon refusing to allow him to shelter himself from his distress under any or all his subterfuges of lies? Can the rebel sinner live in the belief that God is righteous in securing his degradation, just in shutting him up to listen to the accusations of his conscience, good in causing him to realise the conflict he has involved himself in by sin? No; the being that is created with the love of wellbeing as his deepest principle of life cannot look with complacency on the fact of his having acted deliberately in opposition to the deepest interests of his soul and the clear indications of the will of his God. The constituted lover of wellbeing cannot look his guilt full in the face, and gaze on his own act of self-destruction with complacency. The diseased eye of the spirit cannot admit the light of truth, it will only receive refractions of it, and only these as tinged by the medium of its own prejudice. The wounded spirit dreads the operations of its own condemning power as the most dreadful of all evils, and will prefer darkness a thousand times to the pure light of truth. "Every one that doeth evil hateth the light, and will not come to the light, lest his deeds should be reproved." The sinner will rather pervert his judgments on the great essentials of truth, of right, and wrong, shut himself in the mist of intellectual gloom, warp his mind with the maze of speculation, error, and "call evil good, and good evil;" and because "he likes not to retain God in his knowledge, God gives him over to a reprobate mind." Man might know that he cannot attempt to change the principle of his constitution without involving himself in darkness and ruin, but this is the truth the sinner will not learn. This is the conviction in which above all others he cannot dwell. Eternal ruin is so awful a thing to look full in the face, that sooner than do so, man will darken the organ of his inner vision, pervert his judgments on the first principles of morality and religion, and set the Author of his being at defiance. He will cry to the mountains and hills to fall upon him and cover him from the face of his criminator; he will at all hazards labour to escape from the conviction of guilt; and if he can in no other way, he will place himself in confirmed rebellion against God, charge the Almighty to His face of being the true Author of man's heinous guilt and the dreadful consequences of his sin—tremendous but unavoidable effect of sin when carried to its legitimate result. Can, then, man repent of himself? It is awful folly in him to make the attempt, and dire infatuation in others to urge him to make the effort.

If, then, sinful man cannot of himself repent and bring back God into his soul, can he in creation discover a power that will enable him to do so? This is equally impossible to man, for a restorative medium could never have been deposited in nature. The very nature of morality and religion forbid the possibility of any such deposit. If there could have been such in the finite, its very existence would have sapped the foundations of morality and religion. However deep it might have been deposited in the secrets of nature, man, in the onward progress of his searchings in his study of science and philosophy, would sooner or later have come upon it, and then what would have been the result? The "carnal mind" would have had the knowledge of a power which would have enabled the transgressor to readjust the disorders of his transgression, and possessing the knowledge of such a power, the sinner would have gone on in his transgressions, and in the readjusting of the disturbances of his sins, in an endless series. And thus the transgressor would have become independent of God, and superior to all authority and law—the very condition of existence the "carnal mind" so eagerly covets, and so earnestly strives to reach. The possession of such a power would have enabled the sinner to repair the evils of his transgression as soon as they were felt; nay, the existence of such a power in nature would have rendered transgression an impossibility, for if on the immediate discovery of the evils of transgression the sinner could at once repair that evil, where would have been the transgression? And would not the existence of such a power in the finite have rendered the existence of religion an impossibility? It would have rendered the sinner independent of God; it would have withdrawn him from God, confirmed him in idolatry, and created a gulf between him and God, and thus for ever separate him from his Father. Could, then, such a power have been deposited in the finite by God? does not the very idea of such a power being found in creation, and the search after it in nature, display ignorance of the first principles of religion, and afford clear evidence of a heart estranged from God?

How nobly ignoble is the philosophic search after such a power in nature, and what are the efforts of rationalism but to discover such a power? If a remedy for sin exists anywhere, it must exist in God, and only in God.

Supposing such a power to exist in God, can man by speculation discover it as lying deep in the essence of this being, or in the undisclosed movements of this life? Man does by speculation endeavour to search out the "deep things of God," but what can speculation do in the discovery of the mysteries of Godhead? What can speculation do in the revelation of the true, in the manifestation of the purpose kept in the depths of God secret from "ages and generations"? What are human speculations on the deep things of God but the reveries of darkened, prejudiced minds, the welling up of the fanciful conceptions of troubled spirits, evolutions of the tangled threads of bewildered brains? And can such disclose the things kept secret by God, and sound the inner depths of the Eternal Council, penetrate the mysteries, and reveal the unrevealed purpose of Godhead? The thing is not only impossible in regard to the impenetrable of the Absolute, but also in regard to the aim of speculation itself; for what is speculation at best but guessing, the formation of hypothesis on a mere surmise? In the very nature of speculation after such a power there can be no search, no meek inquiry by the troubled spirit, but only the new turnings up of the inner kaleidoscope of disturbed mind, the ever-fresh but ever-fanciful combinations of ideas existing in the human—a vain attempt of the disordered finite subjective to produce from its own confusion a higher order of existence than is to be found in its own objective. What else can philosophic speculation be in the deep things of God? Man in and from himself can produce no original idea; he cannot call into existence things that are not, nor can he descend into the inner depths of the Eternal Mind, and drag thence the arcana of Divine Council. In his speculations man can only combine in endless variety the ideas already existing within his scope. He can create, discover, disclose nothing of the uncreated. And what he in fancy combines may be an image the very opposite of what he imagines it to represent. How absurd, fallacious, and fatal are all human speculations regarding the mysteries of religion and the secrets of Godhead!

If man cannot by speculation discover the "deep things of God," can he by reason attain to a knowledge of them? Man has indeed gone to nature with the earnest and persevering efforts of reason, entreating her to enable him by the aid of her ladder, not only to ascend to God, but also to descend into the inner depths of Godhead and drag thence the secrets of Divine Council, but in this man has mistaken the true function of reason. Nature, even in her original perfection, could not have afforded such means and facilities, much less in her disordered and conflicting condition. Such discovery is not possible even to the unfallen intelligence of heaven, much less to fallen man, were he even surrounded by a perfect state of nature. Nature, even in her original perfection, could not have revealed the undisclosed purpose of God—God in Himself—for then she must have been God. The want of this perception underlies the speculative cogitations of man on the deep things of God, hence the pantheism which is so manifest in so many philosophic theories of the age. In this effort man perceives not that nature is no longer the exact objective of the infinite subjective. He sees not that she is no longer the unmutilated manuscript of Divine revelation she once was, the carefully-preserved parchment of that word which was written by the finger of God in the creation of all things—not this, but only the broken tablets, interpolated codices, a volume of various readings. Nor is this all. Man not only fails to perceive that his world within and without is no longer what it once was; he also fails to perceive that his spiritual eye, being diseased, cannot correctly read even this distorted revelation as it is. He sees not that the diseased eye of the spirit cannot steadily contemplate the fallen conditions of his life, but shuts itself against the light as soon as it begins to pain the unhealthy organ. But were even nature complete and entire, and could it be read by a clear and penetrating eye, it could not even then disclose to man "the deep things of God." Reason no more than speculation can create original ideas, nor disclose to itself the perfections or designs of God which He has not revealed. The province of reason is not to discover what God keeps within Himself, but meekly and teachably to inquire of nature what it has had given to it to disclose. Fallen man perceives not that in his search after God, and of a way of being just with Him, he is acting under the delusions of the "carnal mind," which is not and cannot be receptive of the pure spiritual, and subject to the law of God. "The natural man receiveth not the things of the Spirit of God: for they are foolishness unto him; neither can he know them, because they are spiritually discerned." Were man perfect, the intuitional consciousness would perceive the Divine that is in himself, but not what of God is above or beyond him; and were the God-conscious faculty of his spirit alive, it would ever perceive the manifestation of God's indwelling presence, but even then it could not discover what He kept to Himself. Neither reason nor speculation can discover "the secret things" of God. Speculation can reveal to man the conceptions of his own fancy, but nothing more. Man cannot create God in idea any more than in substance. Strive as he may, man cannot of himself conceive God. Man has not the Absolute within him, but only a capacity for the indwelling of God, and therefore cannot produce God from the womb of his conception. He can only realise fellowship with God through means of His indwelling manifestations. Reason cannot perceive God in His works; she can only trace indications of the Almighty's footprints in creation; she can draw her inferences from His works, but she cannot reveal God in Himself to the heart of man. Man cannot by speculation arrive at correct conceptions of anything. In order to knowledge he must observe correctly and deduce reasonably. He must read the facts of external nature and of internal consciousness. Let him from fancy or speculation attempt to map out the ocean bed or the planetary system, and what a different chart of the mighty deep, or of the mechanism of the heavens, would he produce from the true. Let the untutored mind of man try to form to itself an idea of anything he has neither seen nor heard described, and how different will his conceptions of the thing be from the reality. And if such be the case with his conceptions of the finite and material, how far short must they come of reaching up to the realities of God. Man without the aid of instruction cannot arrive at correct views of matter and spirit in the finite, how much less without revelation can he attain to clear and comprehensive conceptions of the being and designs of God. Man cannot, then, by the aid of reason repent and turn to God.

If, then, man cannot by any effort of his own discover a way of repentance, can he prevail upon God to manifest to him a power to reconcile his disordered condition? This, however, is not what the "natural man" desires. What he is anxious about is not a deliverance from self or selfishness, but from the consequences of sin. After a way of deliverance from this the nations have blindly wandered, but wandered in vain. In search of a favourable manifestation from heaven, man has gone to his idols with earnest entreaty, severe penances, and expensive sacrifices; but what could idolatry do in the manifestations of the Divine, or in the revelation of a readjusting, reconciling power from God? For while an idol is nothing in itself, it is, as before said, a fearful reality in the thoughts, apprehensions, and realisations of superstitious man. Man's efforts to induce God to look favourably on him have plunged him from high conceptions of God into degrading notions of the Divine, and inured him in the practice of fiendish deeds. Fallen man has conceived of God as an avenging tyrant only to be moved to compassion by the sight of mangled carcasses, bloody offerings, self-inflicted penances, and loud and long supplications. And what are such conceptions of the heart of God but caricatures of the Holy One? Man has not presented his deeds to Heaven as exponents of his deep conviction of spiritual disorder, of his eager desire to escape from the bondage of the "carnal mind," and the pledge of his resolution to deny self, but as a spectacle of wretchedness to move that Love to pity, which never has but pitied and yearned with deep emotion and earnest desire to embrace him. It is not in the faith of God's purpose to reconcile man to Himself through the manifestation of Divine self-sacrificing Love that man looks through sacrifice to God, but to propitiate a revengeful Deity, to induce Heaven to indulge him in his own desires and ways of life. He does not with earnest desire supplicate God to be merciful to him with a view to have his inner life moulded after the image of the Divine, but to induce the unchanging God to act toward him in a way suggested by his feelings, which are not heavenward. Can, then, the cherishing and expressing of such desire induce God to manifest the readjusting power of His mercy, "grace reigning through righteousness unto eternal life"? Fallen man "desires not God, nor the knowledge of His ways." The "natural man" has no desire for the truly Divine, no longing after the realisation of the melting, quickening, transforming power of infinite self-sacrificing Love. No, he only seeks to induce God to let him alone in the enjoyment of self. And is God to indulge man in such desire? That be far from Him.

Man, then, is helpless, utterly helpless in the matter of his own deliverance from the consequences of his transgression of the Divine law. He cannot by any effort of his own escape from his inner conflict. He cannot bring back God into his soul, nor can he of himself enter into reconciliation with God; and if he is to be rescued from his ruin, that rescue must be effected by a higher manifestation of Divine love than creation affords, for as in the attractions of matter, so in the allurings of spirit, the power adequate to raise a body must be greater than that which has been found insufficient to retain it in its former position. The most illustrious of the sons of philosophy and religion, from Socrates to Hamilton, have acknowledged that man is unable to deliver himself, and requires to look to a higher power than his own. "But where is wisdom to be found? and where is the place of understanding? Man knoweth not the price thereof; neither is it to be found in the land of the living. The depth saith, It is not in me: and the sea saith, It is not with me. . . . Then did He see it, and declare it; He prepared it, yea, and searched it out. And unto man He said, Behold, the fear of the Lord, that is wisdom; and to depart from evil is understanding."

CHAPTER XI.

RECONCILIATION.

RECONCILIATION between God and man is not like the formation of acquaintance between parties formerly unknown to each other, nor is it like an agreement, between individuals at variance, to sink in oblivion their matter of difference. Reconciliation is the return of those who were once at enmity to the most cordial and intimate friendship; it is the seeing the matter of former dispute in the same light, regarding it with the same sentiments, acting toward it on the same principles. Reconciliation embraces the entire life—every emotion of the heart, every thought of the mind, every movement of the will. This reconciliation is not a forcing into distasteful agreement on the one side, or the reluctant compliance with conditions of union on the other. There is indeed a drawing on the one side, and a complying with conditions on the other; but this drawing is all in harmony with the principles and requirements of spiritual and responsible life, and this compliance is all in strict accordance with the unfettered movements of free agency.

Reconciliation presupposes mutual variance—injury done on the one hand, and dissatisfaction felt on the other. If there be no wrong done, there can be no dissatisfaction felt at wrong-doing; or if wrong be done, and no dissatisfaction felt on account of it, then there can be no variance or strife. In order to variance or strife there must not only be wrong done on the one hand, but likewise dissatisfaction felt with it on the other. Reconciliation involves a change of intercourse arising out of a change of feeling; this change of feeling arises out of a change of relation, and this change of relation arises out of a change of action. And this action must be in the inverse order of the conduct producing the discord. In producing the discord, man is the first mover and chief actor; but in effecting reconciliation, God is the first mover and chief actor. In producing the discord, man disturbs the existing harmony by acting inconsistently with the rules of action and the principles of intercourse; in effecting reconciliation, God acts so as to re-establish harmony by readjusting the principles which were disturbed by the injury. In effecting this reconciliation, God cannot of course act inconsistently with Himself. He cannot violate any one principle of right, nor lose one object by attempting to gain another; He cannot gratify one class of emotions at the expense of another, nor can He maintain one set of principles by injuring another. On the other hand, we cannot suppose that God will require of man anything that would do violence to any one principle of his nature or relation of his life. He will not require of man anything that would at all injure him, or require of him what would do the least injury to another. It follows, therefore, that reconciliation must be propounded by God to man in a clear and distinct manner, in such a form as shall arrest his attention, exhibit to him the height of his offending, and the character of the Being he has injured, as also the facilities provided for his reconciliation. If, moreover, an adequate basis of reconciliation has been provided by God and propounded to man, and if man fully and cordially accepts of the terms and closes in with the basis of reconciliation, then reconciliation is complete, and the intercourse interrupted is once more restored and rendered more close and endearing, and man, learning from experience of the past, will be more circumspect in the future, and thus a friendship, deep and augmenting, will bind man to God in bonds of everlasting love and gratitude.

As long as a creature acts in accordance with the end of his being and the will of his Creator, God can have no fault to find with him; between this creature and God there can be nothing but fellowship up to the full measure of his capacity, but the moment a creature acts in opposition to the law of his life, he must injure himself and rob the Creator of His glory. From the very nature of moral being the creature, by transgressing the law of his life, deprives himself of the consciousness of innocence and the sense of the Divine approbation; he awakens within himself the consciousness of guilt, and introduces into his inner being the elements of conflict; the moral agent cannot rest in the consciousness of wrong-doing; as already indicated he will endeavour to roll over on his Creator the blame of his transgression, and try to vindicate himself at the expense of God. Now, to such conduct on the part of the sinner, God cannot be indifferent. He condemns and holds the sinner guilty because of his attempt to remove the burden from his own shoulders. In the variance that subsists between man and God, the sinner has been the first and chief actor; he has set himself in opposition to God and God to him, and if God were actuated by hatred, revenge, or any similar sentiment, reconciliation between God and the sinner would be an impossibility. If there is to be reconciliation between God and the sinner, God must be the first mover and chief actor in effecting it, for if the very ground of disputation between God and the sinner be as it is, the attempt of the sinner to justify himself by rolling the blame of his transgressions over on God, it is obvious that the sinner will not be the first to seek reconciliation; but granting for a moment that he were the first to desire reconciliation, he could do nothing in the way of procuring a basis or of propounding the terms of reconciliation, and thus, unless God desires it, there can be no reconciliation.

Further, if God desires a reconciliation with the sinner, He must provide an adequate basis, and come to the sinner with the terms of reconciliation. This basis, as already indicated, must be worthy of God, and suitable to the condition of the sinner. It must in no wise compromise any perfection of the Divine character. Nor can this basis of reconciliation require anything of the sinner that would be inconsistent with his wellbeing. It must uphold, in all their integrity, the perfections of the Divine nature, law, and government; it must afford an exhibition of God's love to humanity, and give a display of God's desire to be at peace with the sinner. It must, likewise, be adequate to meet all the sinner's wants, and able to fire him with devout love to God, to remove from him the consciousness of guilt, to unite his convictions with the eternal and immutable principles of truth and righteousness, to show to him how even sin may be made an occasion of glory to God, and of good to His creatures.

If the basis of reconciliation fail in any one of these conditions, it cannot be a means of reconciling man and God; but if it meets all these conditions, it will be sufficient for that purpose. This basis must be propounded to the sinner by God, in terms which will show to him the consequences of his continuing in enmity, and the blessedness of his being reconciled to God. And, then, if the sinner fully and cordially close in with the terms of reconciliation propounded, and take up his position on the basis provided, God will be fully satisfied with him, and he with God. The reconciliation will be complete, and the friendship one that will ever grow and prove increasingly delightful.

Any basis of reconciliation propounded by God will not be such as admits of, or in any way provides for, any alteration of the substance, or change in the constitution of the transgressor's nature; that would be to destroy the transgressor and make another creature in his stead. Nor can it admit of any alteration of the powers, or change in the faculties of the human spirit, for that would be to change the constitution of man; nor can it allow of an alteration of the circumstances, or change of the external condition of human life, for that would be equivalent to placing the transgressor in another objective world, and a virtual admission on the part of God that He was not just and benignant in the formation of the old.

Reconciliation, if effected between God and man, must be accomplished by producing a change in the inner life of man. And this change in the nature and life of the transgressor can be effected only by procuring a change in his relations to the law and demand of the Divine administration. In order to the sinner's reconciliation with God, he must be rescued from the bondage of Satan, and delivered from the condemnation of the law with its consequent apprehension of wrath, he must also be freed from false and erroneous conceptions of the Divine; and this can be accomplished in the sinner, only by leading him to see a manifestation on God's part of mercy and grace, and he can be led to see this only through means of awakening in him love to God, which may enable him to perceive the wondrous lovingkindness of the Lord in forgiving his sin, and inspiring him with longings after the likeness and friendship of God.

And this change can be effected in the sinner by no display of mere authority, for consider what the change is, viz., from enmity to love, from darkness to light, from aversion to zeal, from sympathy with self to sympathy with God. It is clear that no mere display of authority can effect such a change. Authority—the right of command belongs to God from the very nature of the case; but when authority requires to be prominently set forth and formally enjoined, the formal injunction of authority proves that there is a lack of sympathy in the subject to the sovereign—of will with duty in those over whom the authority requires to be enjoined. The inculcation of authority in such cases is not likely to awaken sympathy in the subjects of it. God, *e.g.*, is possessed of all the authority He ever had, and He always put forth His authority in its every legitimate form. He has given forth His law and enjoined His commands with all its solemn sanction, yet, notwithstanding all this, the effect has in no case been the drawing of the rebellious towards Himself. On the contrary, it has only at most made them to crouch before Him like slaves, as did the Israelites before Him at Mount Sinai. The most august sovereign on earth never yet put down a rebellion by any promulgation of his authority or mere announcement of right. No announcement of authority on earth or in hell ever has, or ever will, change a slave into a child, a rebel into a loyal subject. And he who would attempt to effect this change by such means, would manifest folly instead of wisdom; which God cannot do. Mere authority has no power to change the heart of rebel man.

Nor could this change be effected by a mere display of force; hatred cannot be expelled, nor love awakened in the human breast by any display of force, however energetic; and with reverence be it spoken, were God to attempt this change by any such means, the attempt would only produce the opposite result. It would make the sinner recoil from God and cling the more tenaciously to self. Love is a voluntary act of the soul, and can be drawn into exercise only by a display of the loveable, and no voluntary act of the free spirit can be compelled by force.

Moreover, this change from hatred to love, and love to hatred, cannot be effected by wrath, *i.e.*, the infliction of merited suffering. One of the elements in the feeling of dread and dislike which the rebellious have for Supreme power is their aversion to pain, and the pain arising from the consciousness of guilt in the operation of the reactionary powers of nature must be dreaded, and He who sustains this power in operation must be disliked.

The very dread of such infliction makes the being who is suspected of inflicting the punishment hated. Let the reader keep before his mind the fact that "the carnal mind" is enmity against God, and that the very nature of enmity from the human side is to make its possession view in the worst possible light the doings of the hated. And then let him consider what must be the effect of a display of severity by that God who is the object of the enmity of the "carnal mind." The effect in the suspicious and rebellious can only be to exasperate their enmity and confirm them in their rebellion. It is not conceivable that it should awaken love and confidence in the breasts of the haters towards the hated. A sovereign may put down a rebel force in arms against him; he may restrain the violence of the lawless; he may even convince them of the futility of their effort to disturb his government, but this will not convert their hatred into love. And even this suppression can only be of the physical, not of the spiritual. The opposition of the rebel spirit can never be put down by mere force, save in annihilation. The efforts to suppress rebellion by force has never drawn out the hearts of the rebellious in affection to the ruler. The display of severity in vengeance will never convert the rebel into a loyal subject. What, for example, has been the effect of Divine wrath on those on whom severity has fallen—on Satan and his legions? Let the temptation in paradise, in the wilderness, and the hellish assault in the hour and power of darkness declare.

We have no reason to believe that the torments of hell will allay the passions, subdue the enmity, and fire the hearts with love and gratitude of those who are shut up in chains of darkness. On the contrary, the effect is only confirmed and embittered enmity on their part. To think otherwise is to believe in opposition to the evidence of experience. If the wrath of God could lead to repentance, then would there be no need of an Atonement, there could be no eternity of punishment and little glory in the salvation of sinners. Enmity would not only exhaust itself by its own exercise, but convert itself into love.

On the other hand, clemency or mere indulgence cannot effect this change. We freely grant that the tendency of goodness on susceptible hearts is to awaken in them the feelings of love and gratitude; goodness is of the quality of loveliness. Hence, says the Apostle, "the goodness of God leadeth thee to repentance." But the goodness of which Paul speaks is the goodness of God in connection with the dispensation of mercy. Our inquiry, however, is not concerning the effects of goodness in connection with a dispensation of grace, but of goodness or favours bestowed on rebel spirits. Goodness displayed towards the fallen in connection with mercy will not of itself lead to repentance. The goodness, $i.e.$, kindness, bestowed on the young man that came to Christ inquiring what good thing he should do to inherit eternal life, did not lead him to repentance. The distinguishing favours conferred on the nation of the Jews did not bring it to repentance. The abundance of gold discovered in California and in the Australian Colonies, with their natural beauty, fertility, and salubrious climate, has not led those who most benefited by such to repentance, but have intoxicated them with vanity and forgetfulness of God. If such goodness, in connection with the proclamation of mercy, has failed to bring men to repentance, what would have been the condition of mankind if God had not cursed the ground for man's sake, but had lavished His favours in causing it to bring forth in unbounded luxuriance? What has generally been the character of those who in all ages have been nursed on the lap of fortune? Those of them that have realised repentance will be the first to declare that it was not the abundance of good things, but the grace of God, that led them to repentance. If, while restrained by a merciful dealing with them, men have been proud boasters, inventors of evil, what would have been their condition if they had been left to themselves amid the fulness of Nature's lavished gifts? The goodness of God to man in Eden's loveliness failed to retain him in friendship with God; hence we may conclude that no increased manifestations of favours bestowed through Nature's operations can draw him back into that friendship. Let a sovereign open his treasures and lavish his gifts in showing favours to rebels, and it will soon appear that this will not change them into loyal subjects. The gentleness and kindness of Louis XVI. of France is proof on this point. Lavished favours heaped on rebels is likely to lead them to reason thus with themselves: "We have brought the tyrant to his senses, and now that we know how to make him act as he ought to do, we will not lose sight of our acquired knowledge and power;" and thus they would be led to despise him the more. Divine favours lavished on sinning man would only have been received with brute indifference towards the giver, and would have led them to think in their hearts and to say, "Now that by sin we have bettered our condition in securing high and numerous advantages, we shall go on in the course we have begun, our ways are more advantageous to us than God's." Mere goodness or clemency in itself cannot lead sinners to repentance. And even were clemency capable of itself to lead men to repentance, it is a question as to whether it would have been consistent with the character of God to have bestowed such upon them. The dignity of His character, the honour of His government, the wellbeing of His creatures, might thereby have been compromised. In fact, it would have been equivalent to a destruction of the nature of things and the authority of God thus to have made the caprice and disobedience of the transgressor the principle of the highest wellbeing.

Thus we see that the mere display of authority, the mere exercise of force, the mere manifestation of clemency, could not have led sinners to repentance, nor have softened their impenitent hearts, and filled them with love and gratitude to God. On the contrary, it appears that these things would only have conferred a premium on the self-will of the creature, filling him with pride and haughtiness. How, then, we may ask, if repentance be possible, was it to be effected in the heart of the sinner? Was there anything which God could bring to bear on the heart of man which in the nature of things was fitted to effect this change in him? Let us look at the matter a little closer, and see if we can discover anything that was calculated to produce such a change.

In order to cause an intelligent being to hate what he loves, and to love what he hates, in accordance with every faculty and function of his nature, he must be convinced that what he is required to hate is of itself hateful, and what he is asked to love is in itself loveable. There must be displayed before him the hideous character and loathsome nature of the hateful, and the lovely qualities and loving character of the loveable, also the direful nature of the one, and the Divine character of the other, as bearing specially on himself. And these qualities must not only be fully displayed, but so conspicuously manifested as to arrest his observation, and fix his attention. For it should be borne in mind, that the sinner is not disposed to look on the things of God, nor to undergo the needful change. And further, this manifestation must be made so as to display the things referred to in conjunction, for it is only in their being seen together, that the effect can be produced. But how can this be accomplished? How can the tendency of sin, to increase the misery of the sinner, be displayed without subjecting him to actual suffering, and exasperating his enmity, or how can the love and loveableness of God, as bearing on the sinner, be displayed without lavishing His favours upon him, and consequently inflating him with pride and arrogance.

Repentance, the topic on which we have already dwelt, can be effected in the sinner only by a striking display of the loveableness of the Divine character, in God's love to man, in contrast with the hideous nature of sin in the sinner as displaying its enmity to God. In other words, by a manifestation of the principles of the Divine character and government, in contrast with the real nature of sin. How, then, were all these characteristics to be displayed together in such a manner as to effect repentance in the sinner. Had the King of kings adopted the method of earthly monarchs, in displaying His love of justice, and His manifestation of clemency by selecting a few of the more notorious of the rebels, with the view of making an example of them, while He extended pardon to the mass, that might have been a display of love to perhaps a large majority of the rebels, but whether it would have been a manifestation of real justice, we do not stop to inquire; we have no hesitation, however, in declaring that it would not have appeared to be just in the estimation of the condemned. Nor would the condign punishment of the few have softened the hearts of the many. Let the reader keep before his mind the fact, that it is with rebels we are dealing, and that it is of the enmity of the "carnal mind" that we are speaking. It is well known that enmity leads its subject to put the worst possible construction on the doings of the person against whom the enmity is entertained. If, then, God had manifested His favour to some, by the punishment of others, what would have been the effect of such an act on the mind of rebellious man, but to confirm him in his enmity to God? He would have looked on such a deed as mere tyranny, and would only the more have hated God. Besides this course could never have laid a basis of mercy to the whole race; those bearing the penalty, at least, must have been excluded. And if the whole race had borne the penalty, none could have been saved. Thus, then, if sinners were to be brought to repentance, it could only be through means of substitution. They cannot be brought to repentance through anything of their own doing. If a portion should suffer the penalty that portion would not only of necessity be lost, but those bearing the penalty could not exert a renewing influence on the others. If, then, a substitute could be found, whose bearing the penalty might atone for the sins of men, and at the same time convince the sinner of God's love of justice, His hatred of sin, and His gracious disposition to the sinner, then all might turn out well.

It is to this last phase of substitution that we wish particularly to point the reader's attention. We do not, at present, refer to a holy and voluntary substitute, but to the substitute whose sufferings were adequate to convince the sinner of the awful consequences of sin, of God's determination to sustain the being of the sinner, and the operation of all the powers of his nature, in whatever relation they were brought, and at the same time display such a gracious disposition and purpose of mercy towards the rebel, as was fitted to draw him out of his enmity, into love and gratitude to God. In this substitute, justice must be displayed so as to carry awe to the sinner's mind, and strike terror into his hearts, so as to alarm him about his state, and prove to him that God is the unalterable enemy of sin, and is determined to punish every transgression. Without such a conviction lodged in the breast of the sinner, he will never bestir himself about the consequences of his sin, for the effect of sin on his mind is not only to cause him to love sin and to hate God, but also to make him think that God is not so strict as He is said to be, and that, therefore, he may possibly escape the punishment of his sin. Some awful display of the fixed and unalterable determination of God to punish sin must, therefore, be afforded to the sinner. Such a display, in short, as is fitted to convince him of the real nature of sin, and its inseparable connection with suffering, for it must steadily be kept in mind that the sinner is in love with sin, and is inclined to look upon it in the most favourable light.

Had it been consistent with the principles of Divine justice, or the nature of substitution, for God to have selected any one or any number of the higher order of intelligences, to have inflicted on them the penalty of human transgression, what would have been the effect on rebel man?—men who from their enmity are prone to take the worst possible view of God's character and doings. The result on their minds would, no doubt, have been the same or similar to what it would have been had the punishment been inflicted on some or on all of themselves; their rebel hearts would only have regarded God in such a transaction as an Omnipotent Tyrant, sporting Himself with the miseries of

His creatures, taking pleasure in the sufferings of helpless and unoffending beings, and thus would only have hated Him the more. Such procedure on the part of God would not have conveyed a salutary impression to their minds; they would have looked upon the whole transaction as a capricious act of despotic power, and would have said, This is further injustice,— He has dealt harshly with us for disobeying His command, and now He delights Himself in exercising a capricious tyranny over His innocent and unoffending offspring. Or suppose it might have had the effect of striking terror into their hearts, and conviction into their minds of God's determination to punish sin, and of favour to themselves, such an impression would not have had the effect of inspiring their souls with grateful and adoring love to God; it might have alarmed but could not have allured them. If it had not have driven them from God in despair, it would only have brought them into His presence as trembling slaves. But that man may be led to repentance, he must not only be filled with hatred to sin, he must be fired with love to God, and implicit confidence in Him; and, therefore, something more than an awful manifestation of God's unalterable determination to punish sin must be afforded to the sinner. Over and above this there must be a striking and convincing proof of God's love to the sinner himself; such a proof as is not only fitted to drive him from sin, but also to draw him to God. The point now to be considered is God's power and wisdom in reference to the procuring such a substitution as could display to man this twofold manifestation, and effect a change in the inner of his being, with a view to bring him to a reconciliation with God. To the examination of this topic the following chapter is devoted.

CHAPTER XII.

POWER OF RECONCILIATION.

An effective power of reconciliation must be such as can calm man's inner discord and dispel his internal darkness. This power must make known to man how he is to rid himself of his apprehension of wrath and of his sense of blameworthiness. It must be able to readjust his relations to God, harmonise the powers, and consecrate the functions of his life to the service of God. It must be a power which will adapt the outgoings of the Divine to the conditions of the human, and open up the capacity of the human to the inflowings of the Divine, and bring back God into the soul.

Man is conscious of a deep craving of spirit after the Infinite and Eternal, but he will not believe that by his transgression he has banished God from his soul. He will allow the fact of his disobedience, but not the blameworthiness of his transgression. Were he to allow this latter, he could see no escape from the dreaded realm of despair. And in this region he will not dwell nor rest with satisfaction; and, seeing no other way of escape from this dreaded consciousness than by denying his guilt, this he is ever striving to do in one form or another, but especially by his manifold attempts to justify himself in his wrong-doing.

Hence man cannot of himself repent, nor can he cease vindicating himself and opposing God; he cannot open up the capacities of his soul to the reception of the inflowings of the Divine, and in the embrace of his heart rise to lay hold of God. And thus a readjusting or reconciling medium cannot proceed from man, or be discovered by him. If, then, man is to be justified with God, the work of readjustment must begin with God, and the power of reconciliation must proceed from the Almighty; and this power must come to man, not through the natural, but through the spiritual. Its roots are not in the likings of the carnal, but in the self-sacrificings of the Divine.

Leaving now the ground of surmise, and setting aside all antecedent inferences as to the qualifications which an adequate power of atonement, or basis of reconciliation, must possess, we proceed to observe that an atonement has been provided and manifested to the world. A new power has been introduced into the administration of the Most High, a power adequate to accomplish all that the occasion demands. This power has been manifested to the world in the person of the only-begotten of the Father, God revealing Himself in His Son Christ, the power of God and the wisdom of God, the Light of the World, the Life of Men. In Christ is revealed to sinners all that is necessary to their redemption; and all that is given to men is given to them in CHRIST CRUCIFIED. All the Divine glory converges in the Cross of Christ, and from that Cross it is reflected in bright effulgence. In connection with the Cross of Christ we have set before us the incarnation, life, death, resurrection, and ascension, of the human in union with the Divine. We have exhibited to us the design of God to glorify the human, through its union with the Divine.

Sec. I. In the Cross we have brought near to us an outlet from the realm of despair. Eternal ruin is so awful a thing to contemplate, that it cannot be looked full in the face by the sinner. It can be viewed calmly by the guilty lover of wellbeing only in the mirror of the Cross, *i.e.*, in the reflected light of God's purpose, through means of His self-sacrificing love, to make sin an occasion of glorifying Himself in the elevation of man, and of promoting the general wellbeing of His creation. The guilty lover of wellbeing must have it in his power to see how sin, by which he has insulted the majesty of heaven, degraded his humanity, and injured the creatures of God, can be made to redound to the glory of God, the highest elevation of himself, and the wellbeing of creation, ere he can calmly view sin in its enormity. Until he sees an outlet from despair and remorse, he cannot realise the fact of his sinning. Until the sinner is able to see how sin can, through means of Christ's self-sacrificing grace, glorify the Redeemer Himself and promote the general good, he cannot repose in the thought of the just suffering in the room of the unjust, nor rejoice in being a partaker in Christ's sufferings, nor joy in God through our Lord Jesus Christ.

Humanity under the power of the carnal mind is capable of the deepest degradation and meanness, but under the government of self-sacrificing love it is a noble existence, incapable of a mean consciousness. It is susceptible only of an illustrious life and honourable realisation. Hence, from the very nature of the case, man cannot accept of a humiliating deliverance, for how, then, could he become conscious of that life which only a noble, self-denying spirit can animate, and rise into fellowship with the Divine. The thing is impossible; he must be excluded from this consciousness and fellowship by the recollection of his guilt, and the conviction of the meanness of his deliverance. In deliverance from sin, the sinner must know and feel that sin is but the disease of humanity, and that his deliverance from it is a glorious work, ere he can realise the Divine life. The lover of wellbeing, ere he can realise an honourable consciousness in his deliverance from selfish meanness, must have it in his power to see that this deliverance is consistent with wellbeing in all its relations and interests; he must be enabled to perceive that sin, though essentially opposed to God, through the operation of His self-sacrificing love can be made to subserve the higher display of His glory; and that while sin is necessarily destructive of the dignity and bliss of man, it can, through means of the very fact, be made the occasion of his higher elevation and bliss. By drinking in the spirit of self-sacrificing love, the believer lives such a life as not only enables, but necessitates, his escape from all consciousness of remorse and despair. The truth disclosed in the death of Christ is the very revelation of the Divine which the sinner needs, the light alone in which he can look the awful fact of his sin full in the face, and not to be tormented by the recollection of his having sinned.

To the self-sacrificing love of God sin does afford an occasion of bringing forth and displaying, in far more conspicuous and godlike form, the highest perfections and grandest designs of Godhead. Through means of His father-love God can deliver the sinner from his prison house of despair, and bring him into the nearest possible assimilation to the Divine, fire him with purest love and holiest gratitude, and nerve him with self-sacrificing and godlike resolves. In this way the sinner attains an elevation and blessedness far beyond what he ever could otherwise have reached. But for sin, as far at least as we can see, there could have been no enmity in the human to the Divine, and no room could have been left for a display of God's love to the human in self-sacrifice. He could never have given to His creatures such a striking and conspicuous display of His divinest perfections, nor have exhibited to the sinner the fact that, by yielding himself up to God's grace, he can imitate Christ, and become a fellow-worker with Him in His glorious work. God, in bringing near His grace to the sinner, gives him the most favourable opportunity of acquiring a godlike character, and pursuing the most illustrious career possible to the finite.

And yet this display of Divine grace in no way alters the nature of sin. Sin is rebellion against God, opposition to His person, character, and government; it is loathsome in His sight, and exceedingly hateful to Him. It can in no way be countenanced, extenuated, or employed by God. If it could, to that extent, it would cease to be sin, and God's self-sacrificing love could not have been made apparent, nor have been self-sacrificing love. Nor can sin in itself be in any sense beneficial to the sinner; it is the disease, the death plague, the tormenting power of his soul. Still, because of sin, the Cross of Christ has been erected, which only the more conspicuously enables God to manifest His purpose through self-sacrificing love to make sin the *occasion* of working out the glorious design of His eternal council, and achieving the Godlike purpose of His heart. The Cross of Christ displays, in the most striking manner, the design of God, through the operation of His self-sacrificing love, to take occasion from sin to elevate man in the consciousness of the Divine life, to array him in brighter glory, and to thrill him with deeper bliss than otherwise he ever could have been made to realise. The Cross of Christ shows the purpose of God through the self-sacrifice of His love, to make sin the occasion of revealing to man the way of escape from sin, and through this deliverance rise to the highest eminence the begotten son can ever reach. The Cross reveals to man how, that by opening his heart to the love of God he is made to glow with the most Godlike flame—the very love of God itself. The manifestation of God's self-sacrificing love in the Cross shows to the sinner that by yielding up his mind to the truth as it is in Jesus, he can be made to comprehend, in the fullest manner in which they can be revealed to finite understanding, the deep things of God, and that by entering into the fellowship of the gospel of the Son of God, he is enabled to repose with Christ in the heavenly. And thus the wants of his nature are met, the restless cravings of his spirit are set at rest, and the incessant longings of his soul abundantly satisfied. The gulf between him and God annihilated, he dwells in God, and God in him; his apprehension of wrath is for ever banished; and yet, in all this, he sees that sin is the occasion only, and nothing more, of affording to the self-sacrificing love of God the opportunity of accomplishing His gracious designs.

Sec. II. But the sinner needs not only to have set before him an outlet from despair; he likewise requires to have afforded to him an insight into the character and workings of the "*carnal mind.*" The natural man does not believe that he hates God, hence his need of having an opportunity furnished to him, so that he may perceive how sin in the heart of fallen man acts towards God. He must have the opportunity of seeing that, to the extent a man is under the dominion of the "carnal mind"—he is opposed to God. The carnal mind in man is the selfish effort of the sinner to be great and happy in following the blind impulses of his godless heart, and his endeavours to vindicate himself in these efforts. Hence the sinner in acting from the carnal acts under the sway of falsehood and the dominion of "the father of lies." His notions of religion, dignity, and happiness have no agreement with the eternal and immutable principles of being and subjection to the Divine. He strives to live above the restraint of law, and is practically "without God in the world." And hence the Apostle declares that "the carnal mind is enmity against God, and is not subject to the law of God, nor indeed can be." God cannot dwell in the "carnal mind," nor can the "carnal mind" draw near to Him in the love and reception of the "Truth as it is in Jesus. God and "the carnal mind" are distant from each other by the whole diameter of being. "The carnal mind" can no more hold fellowship with God in spiritual life than the savage, with his savage habits and associations, can become the civilised gentleman, no more than the implacable foe can delight in holding friendly intercourse with his enemy; yet the mere professor of religion imagines that, by taking up a profession of the faith, displaying deeds of external morality, and consecrating a few gifts, he is presenting acceptable worship to God. Hence the necessity of affording to the world *in the light of its own doings* an unmistakable proof of the enmity of "the carnal mind" to God, and of the impossibility to man under its sway of drawing near to God, or of having any affection for him.

Now the Cross of Calvary affords to the world this insight into "the carnal mind." The Son of God, suffering by the hands of sinners, is a mirror held up by God before the eye of humanity, to enable man to perceive the essential enmity of "the carnal mind," and the bitter hatred of the sinful heart to all that is holy and Godlike. Christ, the well beloved Son of God, came into the world in the name of the Father, claiming Divine honours, living a peaceful, holy, and benevolent life, announcing Himself to be the "Sent of the Father," "the Light of the world," "the Life of men," and confirmed His claim with "signs and wonders, and divers miracles, and gifts of the Holy Ghost." He declared the Father-Heart, He revealed the sublimest truth, He disclosed the Divine purpose of God, He taught the loftiest morality, He lived a devoted, pure, beneficent life. "He went about doing good," "He did no sin, neither was guile found in His mouth." He slighted no one, He injured no one, He spake evil of no one, He harboured no grudge toward any, He never gave the least occasion of offence to any human being; He was incessant in His acts of kindness, unwearied in His efforts to benefit, and ever ready to bless men in every possible way. He never did but what was fitted to draw out the hearts of men in gratitude, and He did all that could be done to bind men to Himself, in the bonds of admiration, gratitude, and love. Yet, what was the return which He met with, for all His devotedness to the glory of God in the good of men? He was seized by the hand of violence, and wickedly condemned to the most cruel and ignominious of deaths; crucified between thieves, amid derision, scorn, and contempt; cast out of the world with all the force of its bitter malignity, as unworthy of a place among men. And what led men to this treatment of the Son of God? Simply "the carnal mind," goaded on by diabolic hatred to the Holy and Divine. This opposition arose from no want of discernment in man to perceive and appreciate Christ's deeds and benevolence; from no want of a sense of obligation to God, or a knowledge of right and wrong in their doings; from no want of a principle of gratitude in their hearts, to enable them to feel the obligations they were under to such a benefactor. No; it was the hatred of "the carnal mind" to the Spiritual and Divine, that blinded their discernment, and stirred them up "to kill the Lord of Glory."

Yet, notwithstanding the evidence thus afforded of the enmity of "the carnal mind," man is unwilling to believe, nay, very unwilling to admit, the enmity of his fallen nature to God; he positively refuses to believe in the diabolic character of "the carnal mind." On the contrary, this "carnal mind," in its vain and false delusion, is the very idol of the world, the imagined chief good which the sinner hugs to his bosom, the "stranger" he loves, and "after which" he "will go." The end which the sinner sets before him, the god which the world worships; the dreams, visions, imaginations which the vain man cherishes; the glory, honour, and immortality which the ardent of the earth pursue, these all are but the delusions of the "carnal mind."

To afford, then, the clearest evidence of the opposition and "enmity of the carnal mind" to God which man is capable of receiving, God, in mercy to the sinful race, sent His Son into the world; placed Him for the time in the power of sinful men, to let them *in the light of their own doings* see in their treatment of Him "the enmity of the carnal mind," and the utter impossibility of man, while under its influence, holding blissful fellowship with God. Yes, in the Cross the world, by its own doings, has demonstrated to itself, in the clearest possible light, the fact of the hatred of fallen man to all that is holy and godlike. No rational account, no satisfactory explanation of the treatment which the Son of God received from the world, can be given, but that which traces it to the enmity of "the carnal mind;" the hatred of the corrupt heart of fallen man to God and the godlike. "The carnal mind" in man could not, would not, endure the presence of the Son of God. His holy though silent rebuke of its ungodliness; His earnest and persevering endeavours to draw the life of man away from the fatal power under which it lies, into the power of God, was deeply offensive to it. Hence, the world rose in rebellion against the demands *of God's Son*. And *in the name of God*, in spite of all the proof He afforded it of His Divine Sonship, and in defiance of all the obligations under which He laid men, they rose up against Him and violently thrust Him out from among them. They in contempt spat upon Him, and smote Him upon the face with their hands; they mantled Him in mock robes of royalty; they bowed the knee in derision of His claims; nailed Him to the "*accursed tree*," and then, as He hung in the anguish of His atoning death on their behalf, they reviled Him, scorned Him, derided Him, and ridiculed Him in the depths of His agonies. And those who took the lead in this diabolical work, and who instigated others in this infernal transaction, were the educated, polished, and refined of the Jews, the custodians of God's truth, the very men who boasted in being the most religious of the earth, acting for the honour of the God of their fathers. And no explanation has been or can be given of this diabolical treatment of the most meek, generous, and beneficent of men, but "the enmity of the carnal mind." The crucifixion of the Son of God is a mirror hung by God before the eye of the world, to enable man to look into himself, and learn what is the true nature and character of the "carnal."

Sec. III. But man requires not only an insight into the workings of the "carnal mind," but also a clear and unmistakable demonstration of God's unalterable determination to maintain and uphold the powers of being in their full and unfettered operation, into whatever combination they may be brought, until they shall have effected the legitimate result of their combination. Man needs this, so that he may be aroused to the consideration of his latter end, and this instructive lesson is afforded to him in the Cross of Calvary.

The death of Christ, as regards its person, its principles, its manifestations, and its results, stands alone and unparalleled in the history of the world. It was the death of the Incarnate One accomplished through the malice of men and devils, and by the appointment of heaven. "Him, being delivered by the determinate council and foreknowledge of God, ye have taken, and by wicked hands have crucified and slain." The period of the death of Christ was "the hour" of the "power of darkness," the crisis of humanity, the era of a combination never to be repeated again. "The prince of this world" came to the "Son of God," assailed Him with his deadly weapons, and then a terrible conflict ensued between Satan and the Saviour. This struggle was in the Soul of Emmanuel. The Soul of Jesus was the theatre on which the great undertaking of Godhead was achieved—a deed to which all the prior acts and designs of the Almighty, with respect to man, looked forward, and from which all the after-doings of the Most High take their cast and colouring. Yes; the Soul of Emmanuel was the arena on which the grandest design of Infinite wisdom was fully accomplished, the darling purpose of the Father-heart completely achieved; a deed of Godhead veiled in mystery from the gaze of mortal eye; but a deed of Godhead in which not only the highest interests of men and the welfare of the universe, but also the glory of God, was deeply involved, and yet a mystery which will be disclosed in the clear visions of the after-manifestations of the Divine. On the Soul of Jesus the highest "principalities and powers" of being met, displayed their true nature, and accomplished their respective parts. In that wondrous combination enmity assailed love, evil encountered good, impious rebellion grappled with pious devotedness, and selfishness endeavoured to overcome self-sacrificing love. In this strange encounter the anger of God against sin was fully displayed, the principalities of darkness fully exposed, the principles of the Divine government unswervingly maintained, the manifestation of mercy given, the power of life created, and the relations of the spiritual readjusted and subordinated in a higher display of Divine perfection for the salvation of man. And in this tremendous conflict justice had her sway, for every agent, power, and influence had and did its own. In this encounter with the "powers of darkness" the Saviour stood alone; "of the people there were none with Him," and the Father stood afar from Him. The Father, who sustained the majesty of the Godhead in Himself, could not descend with the Son into the conscious abasement of that hour; for once, and only for once, the consciousness of the Son was different from the consciousness of the Father, the realisation of the Son the opposite of the realisation of the Father, the subjective of the Son the reverse of the subjective of the Father. And in this lies the deep mystery of the cry upon the Cross: "Eloi,

Eloi, lama sabachthani." The dread realities of this hour were such to the Incarnate One that even He, with agonizing recoil, shrunk back from the encounter, and persevered only because the salvation of man was possible through no other instrumentality.

Without for one moment implying that there were no other ends involved, and no other manifestations given, in this conflict, we are fully warranted in asserting that the death of Christ clearly shows that it matters not by whom, or for what purpose, a combination may be formed; yet, if it be formed, God will not go back and alter the course of things. His own well-beloved Son, for His own glory, may be brought, or rather go, into combination. He may enter into society with wicked men, and come under their power, and expose Himself to the diabolic attacks of the agents of hell, and then He may cry earnestly and repeatedly from the depths of His bloody sweat and the anguish of His lonely spirit; but the Father will not interfere with, or alter in the least, any of the powers brought into, and acting in, the combination, but will secure that each one shall work out its own legitimate result. He will not interfere in any way to weaken, restrain, or suspend any one of the powers, or alter their relations, but will secure that this, as every other combination, shall accomplish its own end.

The agony and anguish of Christ in the garden and on the Cross, the death of the Incarnate One, taken in connection with His prayer in Gethsemane, and His cry on the Cross, demonstrate in the clearest possible manner the unalterable determination of the Father to secure to every element in their combination its own, and in this way to work out the legitimate result of every combination that may be formed. The sentient or vital may dread the pain and death, the pure and holy may shrink from contact with the polluted and corrupt, the pious and devout may recoil from the assault of the impious and rebellious, the filial heart may agonise over the withdrawment of the Father's countenance, but if the resolution be formed, the choice made, and the combination gone into even by the well-beloved Son of God, for the glory of the Godhead in the redemption of the human race, and by the will of the Father, then must He meet the consequences and realise the results of going into such combination, of placing Himself within the reach of such powers, by going into the sphere of their diabolic agency. God the Father, for His own well-beloved Son, will not suspend, alter, or destroy, any one of the agents or powers in the combination. He may send His angel to animate and encourage the faithful in the hour of conflict, but deliver from the power of the combination till it shall have achieved its work He will not.

If, then, such was the display of the Father's determination in regard to combinations, and if such was the experience of the Son of God in His combination with the "powers of darkness," the dreadful realisations of His soul, when voluntarily going into combination with the principalities of evil, for the accomplishment of such an end, what must be the results and the awful experience of those who, by a life of sin, voluntarily go into combination with the powers of darkness for their own selfish and worldly ends, and who, when called upon by God in mercy to return to Him, refuse to come out of combination with such powers, to form one with love, light, and life. Such persons must be left to realise the full results of remaining in combination with the powers of evil. "If these things be done in the green tree, what shall be done in the dry?" The great end of the Father, in sending His only and well beloved Son into this tremendous encounter, was to exhibit to man that if he will, in the progress of life, ally himself in thought, feeling, association, and consciousness with the powers of darkness, then there is no possible escape from their strife and woe. God cannot go back to restrain in any degree the operation of the powers in combination; be the victim who he may, the consequences will not induce Him to interfere, however terrible these may be.

Reader, we point you not to the deluged earth, to the world submerged in the yawning billows, to the dark and dismal heavens pouring down their devouring torrents, to the nether fountains of the great deeps sending forth their gushing waters; we ask you not to listen to the loud wailings of the perishing millions of our guilty race, crying in vain for the assuaging of the waters, and as they looked to the heavens for an answer to their prayers, seeing only in the dark canopy above them the sackcloth of despair; we point you not to the cities of the plains enveloped in devouring fire; we point you not to the death of the first-born of Egypt, to the destruction of Pharaoh's hosts in the Red Sea, to the bodies of the rebel Israelites strewn thick in the sandy deserts; we point you not to the disease, suffering, and death of the entire race of man, for a proof and manifestation of God's determination to maintain in their full operation the powers of all combinations. We, in preference, direct you to Gethsemane and Calvary, while we entreat you to contemplate that solemn sight, to dwell in close and profound meditation on that scene. We ask you to consider who is there, and what He is doing. There you behold the Son of God, His heart agonised with grief and wrung with bitter pangs; His body bathed in His own blood, in the very act of honouring His Father's law, obeying His Father's will, a suppliant at His Father's footstool, entreating His Father's heart to see if it were not possible for "the cup" to pass from Him, if it were not possible for His infinite wisdom and Love to divine or discover another way of saving souls from hell, in other words, dissolve the combination formed by transgression. And yet no deliverance is found for Him. Jehovah unsheaths the sword of His justice, that He may wound and bruise the Son of His love. This solemn transaction, we need not say, was not one of Divine trifling; the Father did not sport with the agonies of His own well-beloved Son. That transaction was not a solemn mockery, on the part of the Godhead, of all that is sacred in law, just in government, and impressive in creature feeling. Was the solemnity of this scene a vain display of empty parade? Is there parade with the Almighty, is there ostentation with the Most High, is there trifling with Jehovah in the most solemn transaction of the Godhead? Does the Infinitely perfect God require to garnish His doings with unmeaning display in the view of His creatures? Why, then, did it seem good to the Father that the Son of His Eternal love should appear before men and angels in the anguish of Gethsemane? Why was the solemn stillness of midnight broken in upon by the plaintive cry of God's own Son? Why did the object of the Father's ineffable love bleed and groan on the cold damp earth of midnight? Why did He agonise in the depth of His soul, when no mortal hand was upon Him? Why did He, "with strong crying and tears, offer supplication to Him that was able to save Him, and was heard in that He feared," and yet was not rescued, only an angel was sent from heaven to strengthen Him "to drink" "the cup?" Why, but to afford to finite intelligence the most solemn and impressive manifestation it was possible for Godhead to give of the immutable determination of the Infinite Mind—to maintain the established order of the universe unimpaired. And what condescending grace in the Everlasting Father to send the Son of His love into such a combination, that He might afford transgressors a striking proof of His determination, to maintain all combinations which are formed by His creatures, whatever be their character, and thus to give them a solemn warning of the consequences of remaining in combination with the powers of darkness.

SEC. IV. But man required not only a clear and unmistakable demonstration of God's unalterable determination to maintain and uphold the powers of being in their full and unfettered operation, into whatever combination they may be brought, until they shall have effected the appropriate result of that combination, he also needed to see how his guilt is to be expiated.

Man's conscience condemns him, he dreads the anger of God, he strives to propitiate heaven, he feels that justice should be satisfied, he is the subject of remorse, he recognises and acts himself on the principle of punishing transgression; hence he inflicts penance on himself, he offers sacrifices to his gods and he cries aloud to Heaven for forgiveness. These are facts of human experience which no one acquainted with history, or conversant with the inner workings of his own heart, will question. They are, moreover, the genuine utterances of man's nature, and not the false conceptions of his superstition; for while superstition may be general in its facts, it is never universal in its characteristics. How, then, is the burden of guilt to be lifted off man's spirit?

Man's nature not only shows to him that suffering is the inevitable accompaniment of sin, but his constitution teaches him it is the necessary consequence of it. By transgression he expels God from the throne of his heart, and awakens within him the dread of Divine wrath, and the light of reason suffices to convince him that moral suffering has its origin in the very nature of spiritual being. It is inconceivable that a rational being can be conscious of wrong-doing without realising dissatisfaction with himself in the realised consciousness of his wrong. This necessary principle of spiritual being is the basis or groundwork of the condemnation of conscience, and the non-perception of a way of escape from the consciousness of guilt is the basis of remorse; suffering, then, is the necessity of the deranged condition of the sinner's nature, the indispensable requirement of his disturbed constitution. And as man was created in the image of God, man's constitution must be the reflex of the Divine, and the necessity of suffering in man's nature must have its seat in the deeper depths of the Divine. The sinner's dread of the displeasure of God is no myth, no imaginary fear arising out of an inner hallucination, but the real utterance of the condition of his nature. The sinner's deep and enduring desire, therefore, for a change in the manifestation of the Divine is not a mere dream of his relationship with God; his effort to remove the frown by replacing the smile of the Divine countenance is no groundless endeavour, it is not an effort uncalled for by the sinner's relationship with God. There is a something in the eager desire and earnest endeavour of man to effect a change in the manifestation of the Divine, something to justify this deep-heaved sigh, this universal cry of man's immortal spirit for a change in the manifestation of God. The sacrifices, penances, supplications of man to Heaven, are not uncalled for in the consciousness of his state, they are not the lie of his realised condition with God, not this, but the unsophisticated utterance of his relative state. The sinner dreads the frown and longs to see a smile on the countenance of God, because he feels from his relation to God that a change in the manifestation of the Divine is absolutely necessary to his approaching God in love. Yes, the sinner's desire for a change in the manifestation of the Divine, is the genuine utterance of the deep necessity of man's fallen condition.

But this needed change was not to be brought about by an arbitrary deed of God; if it were, we cannot conceive as to why it was ever wanting. The world would hardly have been left for centuries to suffer the dreaded consciousness of guilt if by a mere volition the Father could have changed His frown into a smile. This change in the manifestations of the Divine required more than a mere act of will in God. It required a change in the doings and realisations of the persons in the Godhead.

But is there a possibility of interchange between the persons of the Godhead? If there be not, then there are no distinctions in the Godhead; no Persons, and, consequently, no possibility of communication between the Father, Son, and Spirit; but if there is such a possibility, might not the Father, when the Son stood the Representative of fallen humanity, make known to the Son His sense of displeasure against sin? And would not the withdrawal from the Son of the sense of His Father's pleasure while He was suffering from man and devils be such a manifestation?

This, it appears to us, would be a befitting expression of the Father's displeasure, and a befitting realisation of the sinner's substitute, for it would not only be a real endurance of Divine displeasure against sin, but the nearest approach which the innocent can make to the realisation of the guilty. Is not the felt absence of God the first consciousness of the sinning, the first realisation of sinful nature, and is not the absence of the Divine in the human the source and beginning of all suffering, conflict, and struggle of fallen humanity? Such a transaction between the Father and the Son would be a deed of stupendous majesty and grace, well-fitted to appal the universe and teach the sinner the awful nature and tremendous consequence of his sin. It would also constitute an adequate basis for a change in the manifestation of the Divine to the world and cancel the guilt of sin. The belief in such a deed of Godhead is well fitted to draw the believer Godward. And nothing short of the belief in such a transaction between the Father and the Son can fully account for the cry of desertion on the Cross. There obviously was, in the sufferings of Christ, a something between the persons of the Godhead which is the ground of the forgiveness of sin and confidence of the believer. The expiatory and substitutionary sacrifice of Christ's death lay in this something, and the belief of this fact is necessary to the understanding of the cry on the Cross, and the mode in which Christ approached His death.

The propitiatory nature of Christ's death is necessary to meet the want of the guilty conscience of man, and such a death is prefigured in the rites and ceremonies of the Mosaic economy. The laws of the Mosaic dispensation clearly teach that the transgressor could escape the penal consequences of his sin only through the death of a victim which he slew, and the priest offered, as an atonement for his sin. And the same law shows us that the sins of the nation were pardoned yearly, when the High Priest entered into the Holy of Holies with the blood in his hand; not that these sacrifices in themselves possessed any inherent power with God or man— they only derived their value from their prefiguration of the sacrificial death of the Incarnate One.

There are two remarkable facts in connection with the death of Christ which arrest our attention, and which the hypothesis of His martyr suffering will not account for, viz., His cry of desertion on the Cross, and His prayer in the Garden. Christ did, certainly, in His death testify to truth, but He did more, He evolved and realised truth which otherwise could not have been made known. The cry on the Cross involves a good deal more than the mere testifying to truth; nay, the cause of this cry is altogether inconsistent with the known phenomena of the martyr's death. The one prominent peculiarity of the martyr's death is the vivid consciousness of the

Father's presence, whereas, the cry on the Cross indicates desertion. The end and characteristic of Christ's sufferings necessitated the belief of these being more than human. If they had been merely human, they must have been far less than the sufferings of many of His followers who suffered more excruciating agonies, and for a far longer period than He did, and in that case, how could He, as the patient endurer of sufferings, have been to them "a pattern of all long-suffering."

Christ's sufferings were human and divine, both in their infliction and mode of endurance. They were the sufferings of the Incarnate One, and were laid on Him directly by the hand of His Father as well as by the wrath of His enemies. Christ possessed a capacity for sufferings beyond the endurance of the human, for as the union of matter and spirit in the nature of man produces in the physical of his being a capacity for suffering, which exists not in mere matter or mere spirit, so the union of the human and divine natures in the person of Christ produced a capacity for suffering, and necessitated a keenness of anguish which neither man nor God can experience. In their infliction Christ's sufferings were human, devilish, and divine. Man assailed the Son of God with his fiercest rage; the prince of this world, in the hour and power of darkness, came upon Him with all the malice of his infernal hate, and the Father forsook Him in the extremity of His grief, and no martyr hypothesis will account for this last and bitterest element of Christ's suffering. The only rational account of this, and, indeed, of the other characteristics of His suffering is, that He died the substitute of sinners, *i.e.*, in expiation of their sin. The Father forsook Him in the manifestation of His displeasure against sin, and laid on Him the iniquity of human transgression.

Nor will the hypothesis of a mere martyr suffering account for the manner in which Christ approached His death. The only principle on which we can satisfactorily account for the trouble of His soul, and His prayer that if it were possible the cup might pass from Him, is the vicarious nature of His death. In the Garden, and on the Cross, Christ occupied the position and performed the functions of the great High Priest of the human race; and this fact not only accounts for the nature of His sufferings, but likewise for the manner in which He approached them. It is no part of a noble nature to be indifferent to suffering, nor is it any part of a holy life to be regardless of the assaults of spiritual wickedness, nor of the filial heart to be unconcerned about a father's desertion especially in the moments it is felt most desirable, and Jesus was fully sensible of the recoilings of His nature from the awful realisations of His death, and as He was acting in the room of mankind, He gives utterance to the shrinkings of His nature in order that He might impress the minds of men with an idea of the tremendous character of the sufferings He endured in their stead. In this view of the solemn transaction we see that Jesus offered this remarkable prayer, not on His own, but, as at the grave of Lazarus, "because of the people," that they might believe that the Father had sent Him.

It was not then the unconditional desire of our Lord that the cup should pass from Him. If by "*will*" we understand *fixed purpose*, unqualified resolve, then we say it could not have been Christ's will that the cup should pass from Him. But if by "*will*" we understand sentient desire, reluctance of nature to undergo repulsive and severe suffering, then we affirm it was, and could not but have been, His will that the cup should pass from Him. This twofold form of the term "*will*" employed in the prayer in the garden is not a distinction without a difference, but a distinction which is found in the nature of things, and pointed out to us in the original language of the prayer. A literal rendering of St. Luke's version would read thus: Father, if it be in accordance with Thy council ($βούλει$), remove this cup from Me; nevertheless, not My inclination ($θέλημά$), but Thy will ($βούλημά$) be done. This difference between the terms rendered "will" in this translation affords, if we mistake not, the key to the solution of the difficulties of this prayer. It was the fixed, unwavering purpose of Jesus to lay down His life in expiation of the sins of men, and thus to drink this cup in their stead. It was, indeed, the desire of His sentient nature, but it could not have been the purpose of His mind, to have the cup removed from Him. He had voluntarily undertaken to drink this cup, and for this end He had come into the world, saying: "Lo, I come to do Thy will, O God." Referring to the drinking of this cup He had said: "I have a bloody baptism to be baptized with, and how am I straightened till it be accomplished." For attempting to persuade Him from drinking "this cup" He sharply rebuked Peter, saying: "Get thee behind Me, Satan, for thou savourest not the things that be of God, but those that be of men;" and advancing to drink this cup, He steadfastly "set His face towards Jerusalem," and came up to the city for that express purpose. And that there might be a lasting memorial in His Church of His unquenchable love in drinking "*this cup*," He had but a few moments before instituted the rite of the communion feast. It was not, then, His unqualified prayer that "*this cup*" should pass from Him. No, His fixed, unalterable purpose was to drink it.

But if by "will" we understand *inclination of nature, reluctance of sentient emotion*, to undergo agonizing, awful, and repulsive suffering, then it was, and could not but have been, His will that "this cup" should pass from Him. His sufferings in drinking "this cup" were appalling, and in their very nature they must have been revolting to Him. His keen, sensitive organism could not but have shrunk from them, His pure, spotless spirit could not but have recoiled from contact with the foul spirits of darkness, and His filial heart could not but have dreaded even a momentary desertion of His Father. But it may be said, allowing that His sufferings were repulsive to Him, He ought to have considered His voluntary undertaking of them, and that it was weakness on His part to give such prominent display to His reluctance of nature, and that in doing so He showed a want of true heroism. The very reverse of this is the case. True heroism does not consist in insensibility to suffering, but in the magnanimous endurance of it. The individual who, in the view of suffering, and in the clear perception of its character and revolting nature for the accomplishment of an important end, voluntarily enters upon its endurance, displays a nobler heroism, and manifests a truer readiness to undergo such suffering, than he who, not perceiving its nature, blindly rushes upon its endurance. To display, however, this instinctive shrinking of nature when its exhibition could serve no important end, would certainly be unworthy of the character of an illustrious and generous sufferer. But when such an exhibition was necessary to, and even formed an essential part of, the work he was accomplishing, then, so far from being inconsistent with the dignity of His character, or incompatible with the principle of vicarious suffering, it was only the more worthy of Him, and necessitated by the conditions of His sufferings, and only the more strikingly displayed the true dignity of His character; for, though it laid Him open to a momentary suspicion of weakness, it only the more clearly exhibited the true readiness of His heart to comply with all that was necessary to the complete accomplishment of the high end of His undertaking.

It was necessary that the great Redeemer should

show that the sufferings He endured for the redemption of men were of an appalling and revolting character, and that it was with no stoical indifference that He bore them. It was important that it should be made clear that nothing but zeal for His Father's glory, love for the souls of men, and the ascertained conviction that the salvation of men was possible only through His suffering in their stead, that He could be induced to undergo such suffering. His sufferings were, and could from their very nature only be, known to Himself; and if He had passed through them without giving a display of His reluctance to undergo them, it might have been supposed that they were trivial in their nature, and superficial in their character, and thus the true extent of His suffering for sin, His readiness to suffer in the room of sinners, and the depth and tenderness of His Father's love in "delivering Him up" to such suffering, would have remained unknown. In dying, the "Just in the room of the unjust," it became Him to afford a striking display of the awful nature and consequences of sin, to show to the universe of intelligence that God could maintain His sway only by taking vengeance on sin, and that this vengeance must fall either upon the sinner or his substitute, and that no other substitute than the Son of God Himself could be found. The sinner imagines that he may transgress the law and yet escape the penalty of his sin, that God will not be strict to mark iniquity or to punish him for his sin, that it is the easiest possible thing with God to overlook sin and secure the sinner against the consequences of his transgression. God, on the other hand, well knows that sin and suffering are inseparably connected, and that it is not possible even for Himself to deliver the sinner from the consequences of his transgression, save only by delivering him from the love and practice of sin, and that He could do this only by laying the weight of His displeasure against sin on the Substitute of sinners. It was then incumbent on the Redeemer in suffering, "the Just in the room of the unjust," to show to the world that the sufferings He endured were of an awful and revolting character, and that the consequences of sin were indeed tremendous.

And could He have taught the world this lesson at a more suitable time, or in a more befitting manner, than by presenting this prayer to His Father as He entered upon the sufferings of His vicarious death? The period of our Lord's public ministry had now drawn to a close. In that ministry He had frequently spoken of the character and consequences of sin, and of the necessity of His death in order to the salvation of men. He had often indicated His readiness and intention to lay down His life for the life of the world, and of His Father's love in giving His Son to be the Saviour of men. But these solemn truths, even as stated by Him, made little or no impression on His age. And now that the hour appointed for the laying down of His life had arrived, as the great High Priest of the human race, He entered upon His sacerdotal work, and prepared Himself for offering the one great Sacrifice for sin. Having in the upper room prepared His disciples for the solemn event awaiting them, He retires to the Mount of Olives, not alone, as He was wont, but with His disciples, and having entered the garden, He withdrew from the disciples, and, at the distance of a stone's cast, in solemn attitude, He presents to His Father the prayer, "that if it were possible the cup might pass from Him." The well-beloved Son, the object of His Father's ineffable love and complacent delight, knowing that there was nothing that it was possible for His Father to grant that would be withheld from His asking, acting in the nature and on the behalf of men, He comes in the solemn attitude of prayer between God and man; and while His soul is wrung with bitter anguish, and His body racked with agonizing pangs, instead of suppressing the felt risings of reluctance, He gives vent to the feelings of His nature in a solemn, affectionate appeal to His Father's heart, beseeching Him, that if it was possible for His infinite wisdom and fatherly love to divine another method whereby sinners might be saved, to adopt that method, and rescue Him from the sufferings which were overwhelming His soul, yet, at the same time, declaring His readiness, if no other substitution could be found for human transgression, to suffer in the room of men. And thus, on the one hand, He affords to His Father the opportunity of publishing to the universe the momentous truth, that sin cannot go unpunished; and, on the other hand, shows the wondrous love of God to sinners, and the intense desire of His heart that they should be rescued from their sins. That this was the great object of the Saviour in presenting this prayer to His Father, and not the exhibition of a momentary weakness in shrinking back from the performance of what He had voluntarily undertaken, is manifest from the prayer itself and the manner in which it was presented. The prayer consists of two parts : the one the conditional expression of the felt desire of His sentient nature, the other the unconditional utterance of the fixed purpose of His mind, and the unalterable resolution of His heart. The conditional is uttered once, the unconditional is expressed twice. The conditional is expressed, first, in order that its conditional character may be the more apparent in its being followed by the unconditional, uttered twice, and more impressively expressed. And in order to give the prayer the greater solemnity, it is presented thrice.

The event of the Garden and of the Cross is one of great solemnity, an event which in importance rises far above any other of God's known doings to man. The scene befits the grandeur of the occasion, the period is the fulness of the times, the hour, the moments of midnight and noon. While the prayer is being offered man is sunk in sleep and buried in indifference, unable to penetrate the deep design of the solemn transaction; three, and only three, are permitted to witness the presentation of the prayer, that they afterwards may publish it to the world; but the spirits above, whose delight is the study of redemption, doubtless beheld the wondrous event as they stooped from their lofty seats to contemplate

P

the solemn transaction. One, and only one, event occurs on the mountain slope; one, and only one, voice of prayer is heard to break the solemn stillness of midnight: it is the voice of the Son of God. His soul wrung with unutterable pangs, His body bathed in its own blood, tenderly and affectionately entreating His Father, that if it was within the compass of His boundless wisdom and Almighty power to devise a method whereby sinners could be saved, and He rescued from His sufferings, to adopt that method; and what is the Father's response to that earnest and affecting petition? Is all Heaven in motion? Are its hosts astir? Do they descend in innumerable myriads and haste to the rescue of their Lord? Is there a voice heard from the most excellent glory, exclaiming, "This is my beloved Son, in whom I am well pleased." I will rescue Him, be the consequences what they may. No voice is heard from the excellent glory. One, and only one, messenger descends from the Courts above, and he is commissioned not to take the cup from the trembling hand of Emmanuel, but to strengthen Him to drink it to its dregs—thus showing that, while the prayer was neither unheard nor unheeded, the petition could not be granted if sinners were to be saved. And while the desertion of the Father is being realised by the Son, Nature, at the hour of noon-day brightness, in sympathy with her suffering Lord, attires herself in robes of darkness, the sun clothes himself in sackcloth, the earth quakes, the rocks rend, the graves open, the veil of the temple rends from top to bottom, devils exult, men blaspheme, and the Father treats the Son as He never treated Him before. This was, indeed, an appalling hour of the manifestation of the Divine. That the Father should lay on the Son, that the Son should bear the expression of the Divine displeasure against sin, that the Spirit should sustain the Son in the endurance of the load of human guilt, is the mystery of God's love to men. How great the majesty, how amazing the condescension, how wondrous the grace of the Father in giving the Son, of the Son in coming to bear the guilt of men, and of the Spirit in upholding Him while He poured out His soul unto death, that a basis might be made for a change in the manifestation of the Divine to the human, and to invite man to come near to God to receive the forgiveness of his sin. "Without controversy great is the mystery of godliness, God manifest in the flesh, justified in the Spirit, seen of Angels, preached unto the Gentiles, believed on in the world, received up into glory."

The Scriptures clearly teach the doctrine of forgiveness of sin, through the vicarious sufferings of a substitute. The disclosure of this truth to the world was the object of the ceremonial of Judaism. In the camp of Israel, the unclean were separated from the congregation for a definite time, and until a sacrifice was offered on their behalf. When an Israelite transgressed any of the laws of Moses, he was excluded from the congregation and deprived of his civil rights, until he brought the appointed sacrifice to the priest, and when the priest had atoned for his sin and pronounced it forgiven, he was then restored to his privileges again, as a member of the commonwealth. The presentation of sacrifice on behalf of the nation on the great day of atonement; the confession of the sins of the people by the High Priest, and the laying on of his hands on the head of the scape goat to be led away into the land of forgetfulness, clearly taught the Jews to look to the sacrifice of another, as the ground of the forgiveness of their sins.

Our Lord clearly taught men to view His death as a sacrifice for their sin, and His apostles did the same thing. The attempt to expunge the doctrine of substitution from the pages of revelation is altogether hopeless. This doctrine is needed to meet the deep necessities of the fallen spirit of man, and nothing short of it will allay his fear of Divine displeasure and inspire him with love to God. Man cannot be at rest in the view of wrath manifested against him; and, therefore, in every age and region of the globe, the sinner has sought to avert by sacrifice, the vengeance of Heaven. He has laboured with all his might to effect a change in God, and the idea of effecting this change, and of securing deliverance through the suffering of a substitute, has everywhere haunted the spirit of man. And why? either from an instinct of nature, or the tradition of primitive revelation.

The sacrifice of Christ, while chiefly, was not only for man, nor merely for man in this life. It is the evolution of the deepest principles of the Godhead, and discloses such grandeurs of the Uncreated Essence, such mysteries of the Infinite and Eternal, as will require the study of the everlasting ages to learn its ever brightening glories, and this study will ever occupy the attention of all the loyal intelligence of creation, and reward them with the purest and most thrilling emotions of an ever-deepening gratitude and adoring love, as they ever and anon discover more and more of the deep things of God.

Sec. V. Man further needed to have an opportunity granted him of displaying his love and gratitude to God.

Without the opportunity of displaying devotedness to the person of his sovereign, and patriotism to his country, the pardoned rebel may have ground to imagine that he is suspected of still harbouring in his breast the sentiments of disloyalty, but if an opportunity of showing loyalty and devotedness be afforded and embraced by him, then will he be deemed worthy of his pardon, and become an honour to his nation. He will win the admiration of his countrymen, and feel at ease in the confidence of his prince. And so with the pardoned sinner, he requires an opportunity of displaying his devotedness and proving his zeal.

From the fact that the love of wellbeing is the deepest principle of humanity, it follows that the desire of glory must be essential to man. And, thus, the sinner must not only perceive an honourable outlet from the region of despair, but the saint must see a glorious condition of life opening up before him ere he can be at peace with God, and satisfied with his new condition of life. As his life becomes elevated, it must have the Godlike element in higher measure to feed upon. The love of glory being innate to man, it appears in all his actions; and what the believer needs for his growth in grace, is not the annihilation of this love, but the coveting "earnestly the better gifts," pursuing "the more excellent way." To imagine that the humiliation of human nature is acceptable to God, is to misunderstand His work and His merciful design. It is the "carnal mind" in man that is to be humiliated before God. And this is done in the faith of that grace which recognises the inherent dignity of man, the glorious character of the life of God in his soul, and the lofty destiny of humanity in Christ Jesus. The great Apostle utters not one word in condemnation of the cherished desire for distinction, in reference to the competitors in the Olympic games, but exclaims: "They do it to obtain a corruptible crown, but we an incorruptible." The believer is to live in the perception that it is not in destroying, but in consecrating the love of glory that he live acceptably to God. And he must be made to understand that it is not so much in the deeds of the outer, as in the attainments of the inner life, that true glory is to be acquired; and that this glory is attained not in feeding the heart on vanities, but in securing spiritual possessions worthy of man's nature and circumstances. The believer must be made to see and feel that "he that is slow to anger is better than the mighty, and he that ruleth his own spirit than he that taketh a city." The pursuit of glory in the fellowship of the gospel is not incompatible with the humility, meekness, and gentleness of Christ, but in keeping with His character. This is clearly seen in the life of Jesus and of His great servant Paul; and when realised by the believer, will ever be found to be a present power against backsliding, and a stimulus in the progress of holiness; and in revealing to the Church the different degrees of glory in store for the redeemed, the gospel meets a real want in man. The glory of the Son at the right hand of the Father is an evidence of the approbation of the Father, and of His determination to reward the self-sacrificing devotedness of the Son. God, the Father, admires and delights in the self-sacrifice of the Son, and of this He hath given assurance, in that He hath raised Him from the dead.

Christ, in His intercourse with men in the world, has shown what humanity in union with Divinity can accomplish. And Christ in heaven, to the eye of faith, exhibits what humanity in unity with Divinity may become. Christ the Incarnate One, has gone to heaven that He might *appear in the presence of God for us*, and there secure for us all that is necessary to the believer in his upward ascent. The representative character of Christ in His work must not be lost sight of. It was in love to man that Christ became incarnate, it was in the room of man that He died upon the cross, and it is in the stead of man that He lives and reigns in heaven. And to allure man to the imitation of Himself, He makes known to us His position in glory, as the reward of His self-sacrificing life and death.

And, where amid the ranks of created beings, where, amid the various conditions of finite existence, is exaltation, glory, and bliss, equal to Christ's to be found? Where is glory so bright, honour so pure, or example so perfect? If we take our stand in the high summit of revealed truth, contemplate in the visions of faith, soar on the wings of thought through the vastness of space, and survey with rapid sweep and keen glance the numerous and varied forms of existence, we can discover no nature so receptive of the Divine, so susceptible of the indwelling of the Infinite, so near in life and likeness to God, as humanity in the person of God's Son. We behold, in Christ exalted to the right hand of God, the human in a oneness of personality and of life with the Divine; we behold on the throne of the universe, amid the splendour of the infinite majesty and the bright effulgence of uncreated light, our own humanity there; by faith we perceive the highest reward of self-sacrificing devotedness to the glory of God in the wellbeing of man; and behold the consummation of the Father's desire, the perfect achievement of the deep designs of the Eternal Council; for what do we see in the presence of the Father, in the glory of exaltation in the person of God's own Son, but our own humanity, the same human nature that we ourselves possess, and why is the Son in yonder glory and bliss of His immortal reign? Why, but to show to us what we may attain to, and to animate us to strive after a share in His glorious and satisfying fellowship with the Father. And the way we are to seek after this glory and bliss, is to yield ourselves up to the striving spirit, and to co-operate with Him in His invoking operations. It is the pursuit of the glory of the *inner* life, the experience of communion with the Son, the looking to God through Him, that leads to the deeper realisations of the Divine. It was on her, who, through sitting at Jesus' feet drinking in His wisdom, was prepared to anoint Him, that Christ pronounced the highest encomium He can utter in the ear of man, " She hath done what she could !" It is in living the life of fellowship with the Divine that we most effectually glorify God, and that we become most efficiently prepared for the distinctions above. It is working out what the Spirit works in us to will and to do, that we alone glorify God and ourselves.

SEC. VI. But man needed not only an opportunity of displaying his love and devotedness to God, but likewise to have exhibited to him wherein the energy of the Divine life consists. In the incarnation of Christ we have set before us the infinite capacity of humanity for union and communion with Divinity, and the eager desire of the Divine to possess the human. In the Incarnate One, we perceive the limitless capacity of the human, and the impossibility of its repose in anything short of the indwelling of God, hence the restless condition of humanity in any, or all the varied states of life on earth, devoid of the indwelling of God. In the Incarnate One we behold the human and Divine in a oneness of personality and life, a proof of the capacity of the human for the indwelling of the Divine. In Jesus Christ we perceive the human in the enjoyment of the highest dignity the created is capable of; in Him we perceive the infinite susceptibility of the human, for progress in its reception of the Divine; and in Him we not only behold the susceptibility of the human for glory and bliss, but its actual possession of the one personality, one subjectivity with the Divine. The incarnation thus meets and satisfies the deep yearnings and the longing aspirations of the human soul. In the fallen condition of man, sinful man cannot give up the craving of his immortal soul for union and communion with the Infinite; hence the incarnations of the East in the earlier conditions of man's existence, and the deifications of the West, in the later struggles of man to meet the felt wants of his nature and life, likewise the pantheistic tendencies of the philosophic speculations of this age. Man understands not the conditions of his peace, and the nature of his union and communion with God, as realisable only through the vital incarnation of the Divine in the human, hence arises the necessity of its being brought very near to him, and clearly disclosed in Jesus Christ, the Lord of life and glory.

But how was it that Jesus Christ possessed and

perfected humanity? This is an inquiry of great importance, and especially in the present day. The answer is that it was as the Incarnate One. He distinctly announced that He thought nothing and did nothing but what He saw with the Father. His teaching was that we must be in order to do, and not do in order to be. "A good tree cannot bring forth evil fruit; neither can a corrupt tree bring forth good fruit." "For every tree is known by his own fruit; for of thorns men do not gather figs, nor of a bramble-bush gather they grapes. A good man, out of the good treasure of his heart, bringeth forth that which is good; and an evil man, out of the evil treasure of his heart, bringeth forth that which is evil: for of the abundance of the heart the mouth speaketh." Humanity must be possessed either by the Divine, or the diabolic spirit, hence the necessity of the indwelling of God. The deep necessity of humanity lies in the direction of this indwelling. And it is only as man realises it that he glorifies God, promotes the wellbeing of creation, and attains to the true end of his existence.

It was only as the Incarnate One that Jesus Christ could overcome the wicked one, it was only as the Incarnate One that He could rise from the death of sin and ascend to glory above. By His incarnation the Lord of Glory took the human into union with the Divine. By the incarnation of His life and death He grappled with, and overcame the enemies of God; and as the Incarnate One, he triumphed over all opposition, in order that man might realise the necessity, and close in with incarnation. It is only as men believe in, realise the necessity of, and act on the conviction of incarnation, that they can live the Christian life. If they attempt to live this life on any other principle than the felt necessity of co-operating with the indwelling spirit of the Living God, they are sure to fail. It was in seeing the Father, living by the Father, and holding fellowship with the Father, that the Son realised the fact, and lived worthy of His incarnate life; He was ever present with the Father, the Father lived in Him, and He by the Father. It was because He had the Spirit of the Father, that He accomplished the object for which the Father sent Him into the world; and so it must be with the believer in Him, he must live in the Son as the Son lived in the Father, he must ever see the Son as the Son ever saw the Father, he must ever do the will and work of the Son as the Son did the will and work of the Father, he must live the life of the Son as the Son lived the life of the Father, not to the same degree of perfection, but on the same principle. Only thus can he feed on the Bread of Life. And if man is ever to ascend to that lofty condition of being and life prepared for him, it must be through the indwelling of which we speak. Behold, then, the humanity which was frail like ours, which grew in wisdom, and in favour with God and man, as ours may do now, Omniscient in the grasp of its knowledge, Omnipotent in the might of its power, eternal and inexhaustible in the resources of its life, seated on the throne of glory, conducting the immortal goverment of the Most High, and carrying into execution the grand designs of infinite wisdom and grace. Where, then, is there a nature so exalted, a character so glorious, a life so blessed, as that of "*the Son of Man,*" a nature that can ascend to such elevation of life and nearness to God—a nature which can grasp the prospect of the Infinite Mind, and live the life of God? What a noble trust, then, is the possession of humanity.

SEC. VII. But man required not only to have exhibited wherein the energy of the Divine life consisted, but also to be drawn to God by a gracious display of His love. Love draws to itself. Kindness never fails to draw the inferior animals to those who manifest it to them. In the reformatory schools of Germany, those reformers, who, while they retain their positions among their pupils, can, on befitting occasions, graciously condescend to make themselves one with their pupils, and seize the proper opportunity of placing confidence in those who have formerly betrayed, fail not to reclaim those youths to self-respect and virtue. The conduct of David, in the cave of Engedi, towards the jealous Saul who sought his life, melted the heart of his persecutor and brought the tears of self-reproach to his eyes. The treatment of Cismar, the traitor, by Augustus, wrung the enmity and treachery of the traitor from his heart, kindled in his breast fervent love and ardent devotion to his prince. And the Father, in giving His Son to die for sinners, manifests His wisdom, power, and grace, to the ruined race.

In the mission of Christ is displayed the love of God to the fallen world. It was the love of God to man that moved the Godhead to resolve on the plan of redemption. It was the yearning of Eternal self-sacrificing love to embrace humanity in Divine delight that brought the Creator of all worlds among men to create the power of atonement, and beseech men to be reconciled to God. Hence, the beloved disciple exclaims, "Herein is love, not that we loved God, but that God loved us, and sent His Son to be the propitiation for our sins." And this is in accordance with the nature of love, which is the very being of God. Love finds its purest pleasure in self-sacrificing exertions. The misery of the objects of its affection stirs it to its deepest depths. The tender mother realises her purest delight and deepest joy in her self-denial on behalf of her suffering infant. This power of love is well known to the writers of romance, who fail not to depict extraordinary displays of self-sacrificing devotedness, in order to move the passions of their readers; and they do so in the conviction of the universal acknowledgment of the readiness of love to sacrifice itself. But the highest colourings of fiction cannot reach, far less surpass, the realities of being. It is the very nature of love to be self-sacrificing. There cannot be love without self-sacrificing. Genuine love satisfies itself with nothing short of this.

The highest effort, however, of finite self-sacrificing,

is but the faintest similitude of the self-sacrificing love of God. If the genuine love of earth can display such a spirit of self-sacrificing devotedness, what is the infinite love of Heaven not capable of doing? The affection of the mother towards her sick infant; the yearnings of the aged monarch, the man after God's own heart, for the welfare of a rebel son; the fervent longings of the self-sacrificing spirit of the Apostle Paul for the salvation of his unbelieving countrymen; those, and such like, come far short of the self-sacrificing love of God. We cannot even in imagination set limits to the self-sacrificing devotedness of the love of God. It is the very nature of love to gratify itself in exerting itself to its utmost in behalf of its object. While, then, we stand amazed at the condescending grace of God, and wonder at the self-sacrificing manifestation of His mercy, may we not also be astonished that epochs and ages should have elapsed ere that love should have embraced humanity? If God gave up His well-beloved Son to death, if He gave Him up to the power of His enemies to show them that there was nothing He could give or do on their behalf but what He was ready to confer and accomplish, what more can we conceive it possible for God's self-sacrificing love to do on behalf of man?

Is it conceivable that the father of an only and well-beloved son who had bitter enemies, whose enmity tormented and degraded them, and who cherished a tender compassion for these enemies, and was desirous of doing any and everything that could be done to convince them of the groundlessness of their enmity, and of his eager desire to fire them with love to himself, that they might be recovered from their degradation and woe, and raised to dignity and bliss; could he effect this end in a more striking and impressive manner than by giving his son to death on their behalf? You enter yon cot or palace, and behold the only son of a benignant and affectionate father stretched on a couch of severe and acute suffering, the father in deep solicitude and unutterable grief is bending over his dying child, the child gazes in his countenance with tender emotions of filial love which pierces the father's heart to its quick; in his solicitations for relief what would not that father do, what would not that father part with to mitigate the sufferings, and to spare the life of his beloved child; and how intensely would his heart be set upon the accomplishment of any object to effect which, he would take that child and give him up to his malignant foes that they might have the opportunity of wreaking on him the fierceness of their enmity, and wring from him his tender life, and that to, at the very moment when the child who had never offended his father, but had only endeared himself the more to his heart, was by every possible inducement entreating his father with all the solicitude of his filial heart, with the most tender appeals that could rend the father's soul, to rescue him from his frightful anguish and terrible death; could anything on earth induce a father worthy of the name, to give up in such circumstances an only and beloved child to death?

No, we believe human devotedness can never rise to such a sublime and awful height of self-sacrificing; a father worthy of that name would himself a thousand times sooner die. Even Abraham's piety approached not within sight of this stupendous deed of the Father. It is only the self-sacrificing love of Godhead that could give to the universe such a wondrous display of self-sacrificing grace. We cannot conceive it possible, that man can imagine it possible for Eternal love itself to give a more striking and impressive proof of God's love to man, or of the desire of the Father-Heart to enter into reconciliation with man. Can the desire of Godhead, to do any and everything possible for the salvation of man, be set before the world in more impressive form than is done by the deed of the Garden and the Cross? No, it cannot.

In these manifestations of the Divine, we have the elements of an adequate power of reconciliation of man with God. We have an outlet from the region of remorse and despair, we see clearly how sin itself can be made an occasion of glory to God and of benefit to the universe of being. We also see how that the believer, in the consciousness that his sins are all forgiven him, can discern how his sin becomes an occasion of glory to God, by God glorifying Himself in forgiving him all his iniquities, and of benefit to man in his realisation of the complete forgiveness of his sins. We have a clear insight into the nature and workings of the carnal mind, we easily perceive it to be essentially satanic, and that above all things it is to be dreaded by us; that while we are animated by it we cannot but be rebels against God, enemies of our own wellbeing. We have a striking and impressive display of God's inflexible determination in regard to all combinations that may be formed, and of His purpose to maintain all combinations, that even should His own well-beloved Son, for His own glory in the salvation of sinners, go into combination with the powers of darkness, then must He meet all the consequences of that combination, so that no human being whatsoever, if he refuse to come into combination with the powers of light, but persist in remaining in combination with sin and Satan, can fail to meet and realise all the results of such combination. We have also an expiation of human guilt —the Father laying on the Son "the iniquity of us all," and accepting of the death of His Son as "the propitiation of the sins of the world." We have exhibited to us the Divine nature and results of self-sacrificing love. God's purpose to raise it above all attempts to crush it, and to glorify and bless it above all powers and principalities of life in the universe. We see the capacity of humanity for the indwelling of Divinity, and the necessity of the indwelling of the Divine in man to meet the wants and to quicken the life of humanity. We see the most wondrous display of God's love to man, His purpose to leave nothing undone, and to withold nothing He can give to save and glorify the believer in His Son. And in these phases of manifestation we have all the elements of an adequate power of reconciliation. And to effect the reconciliation of the sinner with God, all these phases of manifestation must be displayed in their true harmony, and realised in their unity; and no one of these must be thrust forward at the expense of the other.

CHAPTER XIII.

MEDIUM OF RECONCILIATION.

REGENERATION or the filiation of the Divine life in man, necessitates the manifestation of the gracious purpose and love of God, viz., the revelation of the Son of God as the son of man; and following upon regeneration, the assimilation of the life of man in his upward progress towards a perfect standard requires that a perfect example should be set before him. The native impulses of his own heart are not enough, for these are the very things which call for corrections and directions. It is beyond all things needful that the example to be copied should be a Divine personal life, with such points of human contact as shall bring it into sympathy with our lives. Hence the deep underlying want expressed in the idolatrous cry of the Israelites, "Make us gods to go before us." Mediate fellowship with God will not satisfy the cravings of the spirit of man, and immediate fellowship with God is not possible through the medium of the finite; it can only be through an incarnation of the "brightness of the Father's glory." Show us the Father, is the cry of every human spirit, and man must come into contact with incarnate life ere he can see the Father in the Son.

It is the glory of man that he is created in the image of God, and that to him belong powers which can only be adequately exercised in communion with the Almighty longings which can find their explanation and realisation in the Incarnate one. God cannot give away, even to man, the uncreated substance of His own being, but it is man's high honour that he has been made an immortal spirit capable of living God's life, and shining in the radiance of the uncreated glory.

Humanity is a trinity in unity—a oneness of personality in a threefold nature. In this trinity the one nature is subordinated to the other in a unity of life. Man is the possessor of a material, rational, and spiritual nature, and these have not only different functions to discharge in the one life, but each has qualities which we cannot think of as being possessed by the others. We find that these natures connect us with different orders of existence. The senses, *e.g.*, unite man to the material universe, and enable him to hold intercourse with it. Intelligence unites him with the world of mind, and enables him to hold fellowship with it. And his spirit unites him with the Divine, and enables him to hold fellowship with it.

We speak of the size, colour, and shape of a body, but we cannot think of the size, colour, and shape of a mind or its product, or of a spirit and its aspirations and desires. By means of the senses we receive impressions from external nature; by means of the understanding we perceive principles, &c.; and by means of conscience we perceive the right and wrong of actions, realise obligations, and approve and disapprove of conduct. By our volition we put forth energy to form new combinations which, but for our willing them to be, would have no existence. Man acts in his will, by his understanding, and through means of his senses, and while his action is one, and his own, it is distinct as regards his spirit, mind, and body.

The tripartite nature of man exists in a subordinate relationship of constitution, *i.e.*, it is a conditional union of parts. In the very nature of things, and by the Divine constitution of humanity, the body is inferior and subordinate to the mind, and the mind to the spirit; and this threefold nature of man is bound together in a oneness of individuality and unity of life. Man, amid all the changes of his threefold nature and different conditions of his individual life, possesses an indestructible consciousness of the unity and personality of his life; it is the same *ego* or I that receives impressions by means of the senses; that perceives principles, laws, &c., by means of the intelligence; that is conscious of obligations in regard to the right and wrong of action by means of the conscience; and that gives forth energy in the actions of the will. It is the same *ego* that exists in the present as existed in the past and looks forward to the future.

The knowledge of this threefold nature of man is as old as human consciousness, and the distinction between soul and body has been vividly recognised by man, since he first witnessed the mortality of the race. But the clear intimation of the distinction between mind and spirit is the gift of revelation, and chiefly communicated to us in the writings of the Apostle Paul. And this distinction is far too little attended to in the psychology and theology of our day; this distinction is clearly set before us in these words, "The very God of peace sanctify you wholly, and I pray God, your whole spirit and soul and body be presented blameless, unto the coming of our Lord Jesus Christ."

In the normal state of humanity the mind governs the body, the spirit governs the mind, and God governs the spirit, but in the abnormal state, when God does not rule in the spirit, the spirit does not rule in the mind, nor the mind in the body, and then anarchy and conflict prevail; and "the earthly, sensual, and devilish," enslave the man and reign over him. When the constitutional balance of humanity is disturbed, the liberty of man is broken in upon, the perfection of life is at an end, and satisfaction of being is rendered impossible; the dominion of man in the life, and of God in the person have ceased, the dormant state of the God-conscious faculty of the spirit is the necessary result of man's separation from God by sin, and the spirit exists in fallen man only as a capacity for the Divine, and not as energised godliness in the life.

The indwelling of the Divine, or the quickening of the spiritual in man, is needful to the perfection of his personality, and here it may be of service to consider what that is which goes by the name of personality.

The substance of my body, mind, and spirit, is mine, is my substance in a sense in which it is the substance of no other. The power which I exert is my power, and is mine in a sense in which it is the power of no other. The dispositions which I cherish are my dispositions, and they are mine in a sense peculiarly my own. The motives which influence me are my motives, and that in a sense in which they belong to no other. The volitions which I originate are my volitions, and mine in a sense in which they belong to no other. The consciousness in which I live is my consciousness, and it is my consciousness in a sense in which it is the consciousness of no other.

Substance, power, relations, disposition, motive, volition, consciousness, in the general, unite me with other rational beings, and are common to me with them; but the specific of these is that which separates me from all other individuals, and enspheres me in the region of my own *personal* existence. The immediate of substance, power, relation, &c., is that which distinguishes me from all other beings, shuts me up within myself, and constitutes my individuality. The specific of these is common to no other individual with me. The immediate of them is known to no other being, as it is known to me. The immediate of substance, power, &c., is that which is mine, constitutes me what I am, and distinguishes me from all other beings, is the region in which I dwell, exists as I exist, and would cease to exist were I to cease to exist.

I can conceive of nothing mediate between me and

my consciousness, between me and my volitions, between me and my substance, &c. The immediate of my being comes into existence with me, continues in being with me, and changes with the changes of my existence. I have a consciousness, a volition, a motive, &c., and they are mine in a sense in which they belong to no other; they depend upon me for being, they are inseparable from me. And how they are to exist in perfection is to me one of the most important questions that can be raised.

With a view to the elucidation of this matter, it is needful to bear in mind what has already been said regarding the union of three natures in a oneness of personality and life. If the union of these three natures thus produces a capacity for realisation, which in their separate state could belong to none of them singly, why, then, may not the addition of another nature produce an increased capacity, and supply the conditions of perfections of life, to an extent otherwise quite impossible? That it does supply these conditions we need hardly say the Scriptures affirm.

This fourfold union of nature, in a oneness of personality and life, already exists in its most perfect form, in the person of the Incarnate one; and it is only as we become one with Him, that we can attain to the goal of existence. It is only thus that we can see the Father, and it is only in fellowship with the Father, through the Son, and by the Spirit, that we can realise the perfections of our being and life.

Incarnation is the link of connection between the human and Divine both in personality and life; Incarnation is the ladder of the descent of the Divine into the human, and of the ascent of the human into the Divine. In the Incarnate one, the human and Divine are united in a oneness of personality; in the regenerate, the human and Divine are united in a oneness of life.

As the Logos assumed our nature and responsibilities, so must we take on His life and character. He possesses the immediate of the human, and we in Him possess the immediate of the Divine. He took upon Himself a real, perfect, complete humanity. He was "bone of our bone, flesh of our flesh," and as "the children are partakers of flesh and blood, He also Himself took part of the same." His body was liable to fatigue, hunger, and thirst; it was nourished by food, refreshed by drink, invigorated by sleep; it felt the pangs of hunger, the cravings of thirst, the exhaustion of labour; it was liable to pain and suffering in life, and to the agonies of death; it grew from infancy to childhood and youth, from youth to manhood. In regard to all these things, He was subject to the same conditions as we ourselves are subject to.

In regard to His mind, the same thing holds good; it was like our own in all sinless matters, its capacities like our own required to be developed. He increased in knowledge, and made progress in understanding. While free from error, there were things which the young mind of Jesus did not know.

Further, He possessed a spirit like our spirit, He felt as we feel, loved as we love, longed as we long, desired as we desire, aspired as we aspire.

And as Christ really took our nature into His own personality and life, in order to the actuality and perfection of His Incarnation, so must we take Him into our nature and life, in order to its perfection and enjoyment. It is only in receiving Him that we can be made "partakers of the Divine nature." As He comes into our nature to secure for us the perfection and joy of His life, so must we take Him into our life in order to realise the perfection of His life, and the benefit of His work.

The theological controversies of the last eighteen centuries are all tending to establish, with ever increasing clearness, the essential Divinity of Jesus Christ, and the reality of the Incarnation of the Son of God, in the Son of Man. But they cannot stop here, they have more to do than this; they must show that participation in the Divine nature by the human, through its union with Christ, is absolutely needful for the complete perfection and glory of the human. Humanity was erected for the indwelling of the Divine; and that this indwelling shall be a realised fact of its experience is, no doubt, the purpose of God, as expressed in the conditions of human wellbeing. Humanity being created for participation in the nature of God, as a matter of course its capacities can only be filled by God and its nature completed in Him. In order to his wellbeing, man must have all his capacities filled, all his relations harmonised, all his faculties energised, and all his powers duly exercised; and this can only be accomplished in having the God-conscious faculty of his soul quickened, and acting with delight in the "Invisible," which is alone possible through the indwelling of God. If the organ be not in a healthy state, man cannot be at rest; if it is in any way damaged, God, as He is, cannot be seen by it; ere God can be seen by man, this organ of his spirit must be quickened with love, but love to what? To self! to creature allurements however high! not with love to these, but with love to the Christlike, for if we have not the spirit of Christ, we are none of His. We may have the possessions of an Olympian deity, or the attainments of an archangel, but if "Christ be not in us the hope of glory," then must we lack the Divine Sonship, the most glorious of all possible attainments.

As truly as Christ took our nature, so truly He gives us His life, and as it was only in our nature that He could live His life, and give such a manifestation of His Father's love as was needful to our faith, so it is only in His life that we can put Him on and realise His salvation. We may abound in zeal and be abundant in labours as to rival or surpass the great Apostle. As expositors we may eclipse the labour of a Calvin, Luther, and others; yet if we have not the spirit of Christ we are none of His. I may possess the wealth of a Crœsus and devote it all to works of charity, I may have the devotedness of a Howard and spend my days and nights in visiting the wretched; I may leave the devotees of all ages in the far distance in regard to fasting and zeal, but if I have not Christ I am nothing, it is all in vain. I cannot please God, who will not acknowledge anything in the human life but what has originated in, and has proceeded from, Christ.

In the Incarnation of the Son of God in the Son of Man, the Divine and human as has been already said becomes one personality. And it is in this union that God gives the highest manifestations of Himself. It is in the human that God has accomplished His most glorious work. And it is to the believer that He reveals Himself in the most endearing fellowship. We cannot easily conceive of a nature brought into a nearer affinity to God's nature, or more capable of becoming one with it, than is man's nature. And in point of fact there is no created nature so highly exalted as is humanity, for in the person of Christ Jesus it is raised "to the right hand of the Majesty on high."

And as the humanity is necessary to the Divinity of Jesus Christ, so is the Incarnate life of the Son needful to the fulness, glory, and bliss of man, and the perfection of the humanity of the redeemed. The humanity of the redeemed is complete in the measure of the believer's reception of Christ.

The Son of Man is the only one of the race who has fully and unqualifiedly received the Son of God; therefore He alone has ever perfectly done the will of God. And this is that which constitutes the difference of the life of the Saviour from the life of the saved. In their personalities the Saviour and the saved are distinct, in their lives they are one, but the character of the life of the Saviour surpasses, as the heavens surpass in height the earth, the character of the life of the saved.

In the Incarnate one we have given to us the revelation of the Divine, both objective and subjective in its fulness. The Father desires nothing more in the manifestations of the Divine than there is in His Son, nor does He desire more of the human. And those who receive the Son by faith are of one life with Him. And to the extent of that life in a oneness of consciousness with Him, their subjective is one with the subjective of God; hence says the Apostle, "Our life is hid with Christ in God." In Him we have the revelation of the capacity of the human, the manifestation of the perfect human. Without Him the human cannot live the Divine life, nor realise the completion and perfection of its own existence.

In Christ Jesus the Divine descends into the human, fills, completes, and glorifies it. In Christ the human ascends into a oneness of spirit and life with the Divine. In Christ the Infinite comes within the limits of space, and the Eternal within the limits of time; the living comes into the dead and quickens them with His own blessed life. Who then can set limits to the revelation of the Infinite Eternal and Divine? or to the reception of the same by the human? The world has the capacity for the reception and indwelling of the Divine, but not the capability for it. The spirit of the world is the enmity of the carnal, and this is antagonistic to the Divine, hence the impossibility of the consecration of the world to the fellowship of the Divine; before this can be accomplished, the carnal must be driven out from the human by the manifestation of God, given to the world in Christ Jesus. And thus the subjugation of evil, the consecration of power, the sanctification of capacity, the fellowship of life and every excellence is attained, through the descent of the Divine, and the reception in faith of the Mediator between God and man. "The Man Christ Jesus."

In as much, then, as man was created in the image Divine, there was in him shadowed forth to finite vision, vast capacities and high possibilities. There was produced outside of the consciousness of God the embodiment of the Divine conception, the cherished idea of God. But in the Incarnation, at the fulness of the times, the conception was more perfectly disclosed. Study closely the inseparable union of the human and Divine natures in the one personality and life of the Incarnate one. Behold the human in permanent union with the Divine, see it on the throne of the universe at the Father's right hand; carried in glorious ascent to the seat of the universal empire, amid the thronging legions of attendant angels, and the exultant shouts of the heavenly host, contemplate it in majesty swaying its all embracing sceptre, and can you imagine even the possibility of God Himself raising the finite higher than this state of human exaltation and bliss; not even angelic nature may aspire to this. And to set before us what humanity in its union with Divinity can attain to, was the grand end of the Son of God becoming the Son of Man. Yes, the glorious conception of the Triune Jehovah in the Incarnation of the Son of God, was to display to universal intelligence the deep capacities, the boundless susceptibilities of the human, and its indefinite power of assimilation to the Divine.

But it was not only needful that Christ should point out to man what he might reach, it was also requisite that He should show him the way to reach his destination; and this our Lord has done. All that Christ did and said, He did and said with this end in view. Without the doctrine and example of Jesus, no son of Adam's race could ever have reached the perfections of His being and life. The Son of God, as revealer of the True, from the height of His glory might have pointed out to man the way, might have commissioned angels to guide his steps in the path of glory and bliss, but man, even with such aid, would have failed to reach his destination. It was imperatively needful that one should come to set the example, otherwise, no human being could ever have attained to life and immortality. And even the alluring attractions of Christ's example need to be supplemented with all the fascinations of Divine love to induce man to enter upon the way of life, and it needs all the skill of Infinite wisdom to keep him in it.

Behold, then, the humanity of the Glorified Incarnate One, on the seat of the empire above, crowned with the diadem of victory, honoured by the Father, worshipped by the hosts of the skies, blessed with the consciousness of the Divine, and resplendent in the radiance of uncreated light, bending from His lofty seat and beckoning you to follow in His footsteps, and to join Him in the realms of immortality. Oh, then, Eternal Spirit of the Infinite God, breathe upon us, quicken us, and fill us with Thine own fulness, that we may " see the King in His beauty, enjoy Him as He is, and reign with Him in glory." When I attempt to gaze on the orb of day in the full splendour of his noontide blaze, mine eye dims into the deep shades of night, and I am constrained to say he is too bright an object for my organ of vision; but when I look at him veiled in a dense atmosphere, I can gaze upon him with impunity; and when I contemplate him in the light of science, I can learn of him all that science can make known. So, when I attempt, by the unaided powers of reason, to grasp and comprehend the Infinite Eternal God, my mind, stunned and paralysed by the attempt, falls back upon itself in the conviction that by its own unaided efforts it can never ascend to a height so awful. But when by faith I contemplate the uncreated God through the veil of the Redeemer's humanity, I feel that my mind is expanded and elevated, in its approach to the Infinite and Divine, in such a manner as makes it impossible for me, even in imagination, to set limits to my assimilation in love, knowledge, and life, to the Eternal God. I feel myself elevated to the highest condition of my being and life, my mind becomes enlarged with the noblest and most comprehensive conceptions, and my heart is enlivened with the divinest and most God-like emotions; I feel that I have a capacity for the Divine itself, and that my spirit can contain God; I feel that by faith I can receive the Son of God. And thus, I perceive that my humanity is capable of reaching the most exalted condition of finite existence. Nor does this express the whole, for humanity in its life divine is the image of the Invisible, the heir of God, and joint-heir with the Son of God. In the possession and enjoyment of the life of God it is more than the mere finite, and higher than the mere created. It is conscious of a oneness of life with the Infinite, it is the created manifesting and enjoying the life of the uncreated. Glorious, incomprehensible, unfathomable mystery. Thus I begin to know that to lift man up to this highest height of eternal felicity, to raise humanity to this loftiest altitude of being and life, was the grand end of the medium of fellowship becoming the Mediator of Life.

CHAPTER XIV.

CONDITION OF RECONCILIATION.

THINGS which exist, and events which take place or are supposed to take place, in remote distance of space or time, can be known to men only by report. If the event has occurred in a region lying beyond the range of personal observation and outside the sphere of their consciousness, it can be known to men in no other way than as the report of it is brought to them by others. As the thought of one mind can be known to another mind through the latter's belief of the statement of the former, so the event of one place or of one age can be known to the men of another place or another age, only through their crediting the narrative brought to them of the events; and the events can only be known as they are faithfully reported, and the report simply believed. If the narrator has failed to observe correctly, or record exactly, the peculiarities of what he describes, or if in his description he has mixed up with his account of what he reports suppositions of his own, and if his narrative of the events be taken as a faithful account of the occurrence, a correct impression of it will not be received by his readers; or if the historian should transmit a faithful account of what he lays before his readers, and if they, instead of simply believing his narrative, should mix up with it notions of their own, they would not have a correct conception of the events recorded. Faithful narration, then, and simple belief are necessary to a correct knowledge of everything that lies beyond the sphere of our own experience.

If, then, the purpose of one mind can be known to another mind only as it is revealed to that other, and if the events of one age can be learned by the men of another age only as these are communicated to that other age, then the purpose of the Infinite mind can be known by the finite mind only as it is revealed, and the doings of God in one age can be read by the men of all subsequent ages only as the account of these doings is transmitted to them.

The purpose of God, therefore, to reconcile man to Himself by the death of His Son could be communicated to man only through the revelation of it in the incarnation of Christ, and this purpose could be revealed to the world only in one manifestation of it to one people in one place, and not to every man in every age and every land. The great bulk of mankind, therefore, must learn this purpose of God through the testimony of their fellows.

If the purpose of mercy to man is to be known at all by individuals who have not had the opportunity of witnessing its manifestation, it can be known to them only through their belief of the testimony of those qualified to declare the manifestation of that purpose, and by the simple belief of that testimony, all men, everywhere, to whom it is declared may become acquainted with that purpose, and by faith in it enter into reconciliation with their Father in heaven.

"Faith," says the writer of the Epistle to the Hebrews, "is the substance of things hoped for, the credence of things not seen," or, as rendered otherwise. "The realisation of the thing hoped for, the vision or conviction of things not seen," and both the Church and the world have sustained great loss by the neglect of this inspired definition of faith, and the substitution of other definitions in its stead.

Faith is the substance, or the vision of the unseen; for example, a parent entertains a purpose in reference to his child; the cherishing of this purpose on the part of the parent is a reality in the parent, but as long as it is carefully kept to himself it is unknown to his child, and while unknown, it can, of course, exert no influence upon the child; if, however, the parent reveals his purpose, say, in the form of a promise, then his purpose has an existence out of himself, it is now revealed in the statement he has made to his child, and dwells in the recollection of both parent and child. If the statement of the promise be not believed by the child, the purpose of the father has no realised existence in the heart of the child, it exists only in the heart and statement of the parent, and in the recollection of the father and son; but if the statement of the promise of the father be believed by the son, then the purpose of the father, through the belief of the child, has an existence in the heart of the son, and in the measure of the correctness of the statement of the promise made, and of the clearness of its apprehension, is the ideal of father and son the same with regard to the purpose formed. In this way the child has already an ideal possession or a spiritual realisation of the thing promised, and there is a union and communion of understanding and heart between father and son in regard to the thing promised.

There are thus two sides in faith, viz., the conception or idea of the thing promised, and the persuasion of the veracity of the person making the promise, the anticipative realisation of the thing promised; hence faith is well defined to be the thing hoped for, the realisation of the unseen.

Thus is it, spiritually, God makes promise of the life of His Son to all that believe in Him. The sinner believes, and in the measure of his apprehension of eternal life through the atoning blood of Christ, he possesses and enjoys that life, realises the forgiveness of his sins, and has the substance of the things hoped for, through the conviction of the unseen; his heart glows with the delight arising out of it, his mind is occupied with the thought of it, and his will is consecrated to the enjoyment of it. The believer in Christ, just in the clearness of his apprehension of the Gospel, has through his belief of it the possession and enjoyment of the Divine life, he has a conception of spiritual life in his mind, and a realisation of it in his heart, he has the substance of the thing hoped for, the realisation of the unseen.

As this matter is of vital importance, let us take

an illustration easy to be understood. A son, we shall suppose, disobeys his father's command, and rebels against his authority; now, while the recollection of his transgression is fresh in his mind, he is likely to dread the punishment which he knows he has merited; he dislikes, of course, the thought of his father's chastisement, and tries to avoid his presence; if he succeeds in keeping clear of his father, and gets engaged with his companions in their games, he may lose all vivid impression of his transgression and of his alarm at his father's displeasure, and, for a time, all apprehension of his transgression may be lost in the excitement of the sport. But let a quarrel arise between him and his companions, let him wander about for days uncared for by any till he is made to feel that there is no place like home, and that the way of the transgressor is hard, and at this juncture, when, perchance, his misery is deepening into despair, let him see his father approaching with tenderness and pity in his look for his miserable son, and let the father come up to him, and while he points out to him the aggravated nature of his offence, and the great trouble and expense it must entail, yet out of pity and love, and in order to free him from punishment, he has himself undertaken the whole responsibility, and declares to his son, in consequence, a full and free forgiveness, at the same time placing in his hand a striking proof of his forgiveness and love. If the son believes the word of his father, his fear will flee away, his dread will vanish, and his heart will glow with love and gratitude, delight in his father will fill his soul; he will only desire to know what it would gratify his father to see him do, and he will hasten with joy to do it. This proof of his father's love to him fills him with confidence and zeal, and thus father and son are bound to each other in sweeter bonds of affection than they felt for each other before. The father sees the filial love of the son with complacency and delight, and the son looks up to the father in the fulness of an overflowing heart, and thus their reconciliation is complete, their mutual attachment deepened and augmented.

But if, instead of freely pardoning his son, the father had sought and found him in order to upbraid him and formally banish him from his presence, never again to see him until, by the doing of some difficult work, he has merited forgiveness, what would have been the effect on this wretched son? Would this have fired him with love and gratitude? On the contrary, would it not have increased his dread and engendered dislike to his father? From fear of his father, the son might set about the doing of the prescribed work, but it would be with no love to the work, nor with pleasure in the treatment which he had received from his father, and if he felt the work to be impossible, or even difficult, he would, perhaps, give it up in disgust or despair; or, in the event of pursuing his task out to the end, it would be with a sense of degradation, and in his toil he would be a slave and not a son.

If, on the other hand, the son should fancy that in spite of his father's tender looks and fair promises, he had no intention of forgiving him his fault, but spoke to him in such a manner only the more easily to entice him home with a view to chastise him, then such a supposition would not fire his heart with love and gratitude, but only the more increase his fear and dislike. It is, therefore, only the clear announcement of forgiveness, and the implicit belief of that announcement, that can awaken love and confidence in the heart of any erring son.

Man, the child of God, has transgressed the commandments of the Father in heaven, and, in the perception of his guilt, the first feeling within him is that of fear and dread of punishment which leads him to shun the presence of God. He engages in the affairs of life, and seeks to enjoy the pleasures of the world, and as long as he is absorbed with them, he may forget his transgression, and be unconcerned about his relations to God; but if God comes to him, in the alarming events of His Providence, he becomes terrified and anxious about his spiritual state, and if, in the consciousness of guilt, he believes the gospel, then he enters into peace with God. In the light of the cross, he sees that he has grievously sinned against his Father, and has sought only to live for himself, and that, although God has left him for a time to himself, that he might the more effectually learn what he really was, that fact did not cancel his guilt, nor deliver him from its power. He sees that God, in coming to him in the mission and work of His Son, has not come to upbraid him for his sin, nor to threaten him with punishment, but to point out to him in the most tender and affectionate manner the real nature of his enmity; showing to him how great the expense, and difficult the work He has undertaken, that He might be able to forgive him his sins, and that, notwithstanding the trying nature of the work and the greatness of the expense, out of love to him He has undertaken the whole responsibility, that He might freely forgive men their sins, and bestow upon them eternal life. The perception of this great truth at once destroys the enmity of the carnal mind in the believer, fills him with love and gratitude, and inspires him with devoted zeal to the glory of his Father in heaven, and thus the reconciliation which is through our Lord Jesus Christ is effected between the Father and His erring son.

But if, instead of looking at guilt in the light of the cross, the sinner contemplates his sin through the medium of his own fears, then he naturally thinks of God as an hard taskmaster, demanding severe things of him; and, perhaps, he becomes careless and indifferent, or he begins to perform what he hopes will meet His favour, and secure His approbation, but the motive power of love is awanting in his heart, and the effort is felt to be irksome, and is either abandoned or drawled out in the deadness of formalism. There is no radical change of spirit, no life of godliness in the soul; the man is the slave of fear, performing his daily task from the dread of hell, but his efforts only the more effectually bring him under the power and punishment of sin. The very attempt thus made to merit the favour of God, shuts the divine life out of the man's soul, and plunges him into deeper degradation, and in his religious thoughts and feeling there is experienced no joy of soul.

If, again, the aroused sinner, instead of simply believing the pure gospel, clings to a mixture of gospel truth, with suppositions of his own, then does he cleave to " another gospel which is yet not another," and perplexity is the result; he is not indifferent, but restless and unsatisfied; and these feelings are greater or less in proportion as error or truth preponderate in his mind. He cannot, in such a case, realise peace with God and joy in the Holy Ghost, but only, at most, false confidence or fear.

If, further, a man in search of peace with Heaven, instead of believing the gospel, look to his own inner state, and strives by prayer, reading of God's Word, and attendance on the means of grace, all good and needful things, or, if he strives by self-mortification and righteous deeds to obtain the peace he is searching after, then disappointment must follow, for the man only labours in vain, and spends his strength for nought; he is blind to the things which belong to his peace. Jesus alone can speak peace to his labouring heart.

How much, then, depends on the preaching and believing of a pure gospel. In Christ there is a mine of inexhaustible treasure to unfold; the relation that subsists between Christ and the Father, between Christ and the sinner, between Christ and the believer, is the proper work of the pulpit, and it is a sufficient work, and profitable both to preacher and hearer. It has, however, sometimes been suggested that the pulpit might with profit be turned into a platform, and the sacred hours of public worship employed for the purpose of speculation, philosophical discussion, and literary display. Such suggestions show great ignorance and infatuation, and to encourage such things by manifesting a taste for them, and running after them, on the part of the professing Christian, is no less fearful; it is, in short, spiritual madness. We would repeat, for in these days repetition is needful, that it is only belief of the pure gospel that can give peace to the heart of man. This is the only method of Heaven to secure the wellbeing of man. It is in Christ, and in Him alone, that God hath abounded towards us in all wisdom and prudence, and in no other way can the spirit of man find peace.

It is clear, then, both from the nature of reconciliation itself, and the teaching of revelation concerning it, that faith is an essential condition to its realisation. The believer by faith receives Christ, and in this reception he receives the Divine Sonship, and enjoys fellowship with His Father. Christ is the manifestation of the Father, the *hypostasis* of His person; hence, our Lord declares "he that hath seen Me hath seen the Father also," Christ is also the "desire of all nations," for He meets the spiritual wants and cravings of our race after a divine nature; and thus faith is the substance (*hypostasis*) of the thing hoped for, the salvation long desired.

The fact that the writer of the Epistle to the

Hebrews uses the same term (*hypostasis*) to denote the substance of the Father's person and the believer's faith, is not without interest; it points out to us the union and basis of communion which subsists between the believer and God. In giving this *hypostasis*, God gives His subjective and objective to the believer, and the believer in receiving it becomes one with the Father, and thus faith is not only the condition but also the realisation of reconciliation. "With open face beholding as in a glass the glory of the Lord," the believer is thus "changed into the same image from glory to glory, even as by the Spirit of the Lord." Faith, then, we repeat, is the evidence of the thing hoped for, the conviction of the unseen, the condition of reconciliation, the measure and medium of spiritual and divine life in the soul of man.

CHAPTER XV.

AGENT OF RECONCILIATION.

The power of reconciliation requires an agent to apply it. Guilt, as we have seen, is such an awful thing, that it cannot be looked at by the sinner in itself, and as attached to him. It can calmly be viewed by him only through the medium of an atonement, *i.e.*, in the reflected light of that power which is able to rescue him from its burden. But even with the aid of this light, the difficulty in the way of the sinner contemplating his guilt is not got over, for how is this light to be admitted by his diseased organ of spiritual vision? in other words, how is the sinner to be got to contemplate his guilt, even in the light of the atoning power which God has provided? This power of reconciliation is discernible in the light of the self-sacrificing of the Divine, but how is the sinner to be brought to admire God in the manifestation of His self-sacrificing grace? This is the manifestation of the character of God which, beyond all others, is most repulsive to the "carnal mind." The admiration of the self-sacrificing love of God requires, on the part of him who would admire this, something akin to it in his own heart. This, however, the carnal mind abhors and from which it recoils. Selfishness, which is the essence of the carnal mind, cannot look with satisfaction on self-sacrificing grace.

How, then, is the diseased organ of the sinner to be brought into sympathy with the spirit of self-sacrificing love, that he may be able to repose in delightful contemplation on this wonder of redeeming grace? There is only one way conceivable in which the sinner can be brought to love, and delight himself in view of the self-sacrificing love of God, and that is by the renewing of the Holy Ghost—the bringing of the subjective of the sinner into a oneness with the subjective of God. Affinity of the subjective for the objective is needful to the discernment of the objective in its own light. Thus a subjective sentient is necessary to the discernment of the objects of sense. A subjective rational is necessary to the perception of objects which address themselves to reason, and a subjective divine is necessary to the perception of divine things. A stone, *e.g.*, cannot perceive size, colour, &c. A plant or an irrational animal cannot perceive the force of an argument. So neither can the "carnal mind" discern the glory of the self-sacrificing, nor realise the things of the Spirit. An affinity of spirit with Christ is necessary to the perception of "the truth as it is in Jesus," for the natural man receiveth not the things of the Spirit of God, neither can he know them, for they are spiritually discerned."

If there be disease instead of health in the eye, it will neither receive the rays of light, nor look at objects in the light. It matters not how lovely the objects may be which are presented to it, the pain produced by the light will force it to shut up itself in darkness. Ere the diseased eye can be made to look upon objects in the light, there must be such an operation performed upon it as shall not only alleviate its pain, but also make it pleasant to look at the objects presented to it. Similarly there must be such an operation performed on the spiritual organ of the sinner's vision, as shall rescue him from pain in the contemplation of the self-sacrificing, and make the beholding of God's face in righteousness the joy and rejoicing of his heart.

What, then, is this operation, and how is it to be effected? It is the quickening of the heart of man with the love of the self-sacrificing.

Fallen man does not possess the love of "the truth as it is in Jesus," he, on the contrary, hates the light and avoids it because his deeds are evil. He does not, indeed, hate truth in the abstract, he rather delights in speculative knowledge, nor would he hate the Divine self-sacrificing on his behalf could he clearly see it in its own radiance; but this is just what he is unable to do, for this is only to be seen through the medium of the consciousness of his own inexcusable guilt. It is only as guilty that he can accept of forgiveness, and it is only as he sees himself inexcusably guilty that he can feel truly grateful for such self-sacrifice on his behalf. But the consciousness of such guilt is that which is most abhorrent to the carnal mind; hence to imbibe the spirit of the self-sacrificing, and delight in its deeds, is not possible to the carnal mind.

The "carnal mind" rises in indignation at the idea of God coming to it in the imputation of sin, and thus the "law worketh wrath." This is, in fact, the inevitable result of sin in the experience of the natural man when the law brings home to him the conviction of guilt. Under the influence of divine truth the carnal mind cannot but prove rebellious, and it does so in accordance with the analogy referred to, viz., that as the clear light shining into the weak or diseased eye gives pain, and causes it to close itself against the light, so the light of the radiance that streams from the self-sacrificing love of God pains the guilty spirit, and causes it to rise in rebellion against it and prefer its own inner darkness.

Ere the truth which necessarily discloses the sinner's character to himself can be received into the heart of fallen man, the love of it must be implanted within him, for if he hates the light, no exhibition of light, however clear, will prevail upon him to receive it. Even the merciful tempering of the truth by the work of the Saviour will not prevail upon the sinner to embrace it in the love of it, for even the loveliness of this manifestation of the Divine must be apprehended through the conviction of guilt, and this is the conviction which above all others the sinner dislikes. In order, therefore, to the sinner's reconciliation, there must not only be the creation of truth adapted to his state and character, but there must also be the quickening of his heart with the love of that truth.

How, then, is this state of matters to be brought about in the life of the sinner? We believe that this is only possible through the implantation of a new principle of life, a new Christ-like disposition, a new bias or bent being given to our whole spiritual nature. In the change which thus takes place, and with a view to it, God comes to us by His Spirit and awakens within us holy emotions, God-like desires, as He works faith in us leading us to endorse and act out these inner risings, as He works in us to will and to do of His own good pleasure.

The Spirit of God, the agent of man's regeneration, comes to him with "the truth as it is in Jesus," and holds it up before the gaze of the human spirit while by His own immediate act He touches the organ of God-consciousness, and quickens the springs of vitality in the soul with the love of the Divine. In this work let it be borne in mind the Spirit of God does not act irrespective of, or in opposition to, man's nature, but through means of it, and in entire accordance with the free agency of man. God will in no way overlook these things in any of His dealings with man, for, as man fell in the exercise of his free responsible nature, so must he rise in full accordance of the same thing.

The consciousness of man bears out the doctrine of God's Word on this important matter, for consciousness reveals to man both the facts and the extent of the Spirit's working in him, and, although he may not be very quick to discern these facts now, he shall afterwards be made fully aware of them. All who have ever lived under the preaching of the gospel are aware of the fact, that there has been in them at one time or another the feeling after a better state of being and condition of life, the awakening within them of conviction of sin, and the stirring up of holy dispositions. Now, whence came these inner risings? Not surely of Satan, the world, or the corrupt heart of man. Certainly not of the sinner himself, in any sense, for this inspiration of heavenly thought and desire is in direct opposition to the natural tendencies of his heart, and as like produce like, these cannot be the product of the "carnal mind." These risings are the beginnings of the most precious possession which the finite can ever hold, and in comparison with them the whole world is but as a trifle to man. They are the beginnings of the greatest work God Himself can accomplish, and with a view to produce them, the Spirit submits to resistance and grief; and to supply the Spirit with the power of awakening these risings, the Son of God shed His blood; and to die the death, the Father sent the Son into the world.

And every man is conscious of how he treats these inner risings of the heavenly and Divine, he knows whether he neglects, pays little or no attention to them, resists, or cherishes them in his heart. If we cherish and strengthen these inner risings in our hearts, then do we yield ourselves up to the Spirit of God, who works in us thus to will and to do of God's good pleasure. He takes up His abode in us, and we become, through His indwelling, temples of the living God. But if, instead of fostering these risings, the sinner strives to rid himself of them, then does he resist and grieve, and, perhaps, finally quench the Spirit, and in the end it happens in his case, that these awful words are applicable to him, "Whosoever speaketh against the Holy Ghost, it shall not be forgiven him, neither in this world, nor in the world to come."

In resisting the inner risings of the Spirit, the sinner refuses to repent and be converted, he prefers his own way to the righteousness of God, and tries to vindicate himself by an endeavour to roll the odium of his state over on God, and in doing so he insults the Almighty to His face. In refusing to believe on the Son of God, the unbeliever commits the most heinous sin that can be committed by any creature; a sin which goes beyond anything in the power of demon or devil to do; he disobeys the highest mandate of his Father in heaven, he treats lightly the most striking display of Divine authority, resists the persuasive influence of the Holy Ghost, and despises the compassion and mercy of God.

To be guilty of all this is to commit the sin which is unto death, which those who are born of God cannot commit. The inability to commit this sin is one of the differences that exist between the regenerate and the unregenerate. The unregenerate ever strive to justify themselves by attempting to make God the real author of sin, whereas the regenerate, whensoever they detect themselves in sin, instead of striving to justify themselves, confess and bewail their sin. "I acknowledge my sin unto Thee, and mine iniquity have I not hid. I said I will confess my transgression unto the Lord, and Thou forgavest the iniquity of my sin." This is the view of sin and its guilt, so far as we can see, that alone can sustain the consistency of St. John, and, indeed, the unity of revelation. John writes, "If we say that we have not sinned, we make Him a liar, and His word is not in us." And again in another place, "Whosoever is born of God doth not commit sin, for His seed remaineth in him, and he cannot sin because he is born of God.

The method, above indicated, of dealing with these texts removes their apparent contradiction. There is sin in the believer which is forgiven, and there is sin in the impenitent which is never forgiven. And, we may ask, how can the sin against the Holy Ghost be forgiven? This, in the very nature of things, is impossible; the Holy Ghost is sinned against only by stifling the inner risings of the heavenly and divine which He awakens within the sinner, and it is only through these that He can calm the inner discord, and secure reconciliation with the Father of spirits. If, therefore, the sinner persists in keeping down these risings, how can he realise the divine life within him? And, if he persists in quenching them until he has steeled his heart against all impressions of the Divine, there is no power in the universe of God that can rescue his soul from hell.

All life has, as our readers know, its beginning in the embryo state, and is at first very feeble. If the embryo be cherished, it develops itself into the vigour of maturity; but if it be neglected or crushed, it perishes. How important, then, that the sinner's attention should be clearly directed to this fact in its spiritual bearings. Man has not the power to create, he can only indirectly produce life; and in no way can he produce his own life in any of its departments, sentient, intellectual, or spiritual. But while he cannot produce his life, he may ruin or destroy it as truly as he can ruin or destroy the lives of others; and here he wields a tremendous power, and incurs a proportionate responsibility. To this corresponds the doctrine of Scripture—"this," says Jesus, "is the condemnation, that light is come into the world, and men loved darkness rather than light, because their deeds were evil." And herein lies the dread responsibility of the sinner; he cannot atone for his sins, nor discover the truth which is to enlighten his mind in regard to the mercy of God, nor procure the influence of the Spirit of all grace; but he can quench the risings of the Spirit in his heart.

In this fact the preacher has a powerful hold on the conscience, for he can convict the sinner of quenching the inner risings of the Divine, and clearly show to him that he is committing a grievous form of sin. He can drive him out of his refuge of lies, in connection with abstract questions about Divine decrees, &c., and show him that in the consciousness of these inner risings he has the evidence that God is dealing with him personally in the matter of his salvation, and that, if he continues to resist God in His gracious work, he not only commits an awful sin, but will carry in his own bosom to the Judgment Seat a witness that will rise to condemn him.

But to proceed. In vision, there must be the object to be seen, the light in which it is to be viewed, and the eye which is to look upon it in the light. If there be no object, there can be no vision; or, if there be an object and no light, there can be no vision; or, if there be no eye, or an eye diseased, there will be no vision, or at best a distorted one. If the diseased eye is to be brought into a healthy state, it must be healed in accordance with the laws of health, and not in opposition to these; and if it is to see clearly, it must be led to look at the object in the light, in accordance with the laws or principles of human vision. This point may be illustrated by a reference to photography, in which art the image of the human face is conveyed to a sensitive sheet. First of all, the image is transferred to a prepared plate, and then from that to the prepared sheet. Here we have, then, the countenance, the image of which is to be transcribed, then the prepared plate which is to receive the image, and further, the light which is to transfer the image, and finally, the agent who is to bring the countenance into such a relation to the sensitive plate as that the light shall transfer the image correctly. If there be no countenance, there can be no image to transcribe; if there be no light, there can be no transcription of an image; if there be no prepared plate to record and retain the image, there can be no likeness obtained and preserved; or, finally, if there be no agent to bring the prepared plate into the proper focus for receiving the image, there can be no photograph.

Thus is it, spiritually, in order to faith in the mercy of God, there must be the manifestation of His self-sacrificing love, the record of that manifestation, a heart also in a state of sufficient preparation to receive the truth as it is in Jesus, and, in addition, an agent to bring the heart into the state in which it shall be willing to receive the truth in the love of it. If the heart be not prepared with a view to the reception of the truth, then in vain may you look for an attentive listening to it. Disposition to attend to the truth, and an inclination to receive it, is a primary element of faith in Jesus, hence it is written of those who perish, that they perish because they "received not the love of the truth, that they must be saved," and thus the Saviour addresses those that rejected Him. "Ye will not come unto Me, that ye might have life." "The truth as it is in Jesus" can be received into the heart only where there is love to it, and the producing of this love is the work of the Holy Ghost. In brief, the Word of God everywhere teaches the doctrine that the Holy Spirit is the Author of everything gracious and holy in man; and that through His operation alone, are we reconciled to God by the death of His Son.

CHAPTER XVI.

CAPACITY OF THE HUMAN FOR THE INDWELLING OF THE DIVINE.

GOD fills immensity, but neither immensity nor the material universe which space contains have any capacity for the indwelling of God. God can only impart Himself to, and dwell in, those who have been made in His own image, for example, His offspring, man. God is the Father of our spirits, and to prove Himself to be such, is the one great end of all His doings.

A father, as such, cannot impart himself to the locality in which he dwells, the time in which he lives, the goods and chattels which he possesses, the servants he employs, or the friends with whom he associates; these have no receptivity for him in his outgoings as a father. A father can only impart himself to his children, realise in them his paternal delight, and be fully satisfied in his intercourse with them. And to beget children in his own image, and to delight himself in them, has been the profound thought and cherished purpose of Godhead from unbeginning ages.

Immensity and duration have nothing of God in

them, the countless worlds that are spread out in the fields of space have nothing of the Divine in their constitution. The various orders of sentient and animated tribes have nothing of the spiritual in them. The angelic hosts have nothing of the redeemed filial in them. These have no divine capacity such as man, no receptivity nor filial instincts like his. God can look abroad with admiration on the work of His hands, and meditate on the purpose of His mind, but it is only in His child, man, created in His own image, that His heart can rest satisfied. On man alone He lingers with Divine complacency, while He calls this portion of His work "very good."

Vast and immeasurable as are space and eternity, God cannot stamp Himself upon them. Great and glorious as irrational creation is, God cannot impart His life to it. High and holy as the heavenly hosts are, God cannot create them anew in the image of His Son. Acting in accordance with the nature of things, God fills immensity with His presence, and dwells in eternity, calls creation into being, and employs His angels as "ministering spirits," but He inbreathes the breath of life only into man, and begets in the renewed spirit His own life. Space is His chamber, Eternity the measure of His days, Creation the manifestation of His power and goodness, but humanity is His offspring, the true image of Himself. He holds no fellowship with space and eternity, nor can these be filled with all the fulness of God. The heaven of heavens cannot contain Him, and yet the finite spirit of man can. He dwells incarnate in the temple of humanity. He reigns in the hearts of His children, and rests in the love of the redeemed. Beyond this He has no desire, "This is My rest for ever, here will I dwell for I have desired it."

But God dwells not in the heart of all humanity. Fallen humanity has a capacity, but not a receptivity for God. The capabilities of fallen man are guarded against the entrance of God by the demon spirit and corrupt passions of sin, and his intellect is closed by prejudice against the entrance of the truth. The life of fallen man is consecrated to the service of self, and thus it happens that the nature which is nearest to God's own, is at the same time at the farthest possible distance from Him; and in its fallen condition all the glorious possibilities of which it is capable are lost. We may, therefore, well exclaim, "Oh, what a spectacle to the eye of Omniscience is rebel humanity!" A child of immortality, an heir of God, created in the likeness of the Father of spirits, gifted with capacity for the indwelling of the Divine, and capable of entering into fellowship with God, absorbed in self, in love with the carnal, and governed by a spirit defiant of God, engrossed with the cares of a purely earthly life, and alone anxious to satisfy itself with the things of sense and the efforts of vain glorying.

But all this was foreseen, and a purpose formed for the casting out of Satan from the heart, and for the entire regeneration of the spirit of man into the life of God. With this end in view the incarnation in the fulness of the time was resolved upon in order to overcome the powers of darkness ere man was brought into existence, and to exhibit what humanity in union with divinity was capable of becoming. The sacrificial death of the Son of God was determined on, and the striving of the Holy Ghost secured, to overcome the rebellious disposition.

That a spirit created for the indwelling of God should be the subject of aversion and dislike to the Godlike, and the abode of demons, is certainly a deep mystery and matter of amazement. Yet the awful fact is patent to the observation of all, and cannot be denied. But that, on the other hand, a father should mourn over the disobedience of a child, and desire the recovery of a lost son, and earnestly exert himself with a view to his recovery; that a father should display the highest perfections of his being in the reclaiming of his lost child, and rejoice with his most sacred joy over his recovery; this at least should be no matter of amazement to the possessor of humanity, while it is a matter of the highest encouragement to the sinner.

And that the life of one reclaimed from sin, and restored to his father's favour, should be more grateful, and watchful, and fervent in devotion, is quite in accordance with the nature and experience of man; but the perversion of sin prevents even the renewed son from altogether acting upon this confidence, as becomes him, in the present state.

The spirit of pride must be broken and crushed, banished from the heart ere God can dwell in it, or work in it by love. God cannot dwell where there is unrighteousness, or a spirit which cherishes mean grovelling dispositions. The spirit in which these dwell is more distant from God than even material being or sentient life. But all that is needed to save the sinner, and raise his soul to the loftiest condition of finite existence, is simply to expel the rebel spirit from the soul, and enthrone God on the heart. "Blessed are the poor in spirit, for theirs is the kingdom of heaven." Yes, this rebel disposition, now that Christ has ascended, and the Holy Spirit descended, is the only obstacle, the one grand impediment, to the salvation of every soul of man unsaved. Everything that the nature of the case requires is present, and has been provided for; there is in every human spirit a capacity deep as the Infinite, and abiding as the Eternal. There is in the heart of the Father a desire gracious as His own self-sacrificing love, restrained in its operation only by the limits imposed by the individual capacity of man; there is in the Son a boundless sufficiency; and there is in the Spirit an infinite readiness. But in opposition to this, the capacity of the human is filled with a spirit of antagonism to God, which guards its every avenue against the entrance of the Spirit of God; and to expel this usurper from the throne of the human heart, requires all the skill, prudence, and omnipotence of the God of grace. For as man freely drank in the spirit of darkness, and willingly entered into an alliance with the enemy of God, so must he also freely drink in the spirit of holiness, and as willingly "kiss the Son" in his return to the Father, and in yielding himself up to the reigning powers of God's grace.

A physician has a satisfaction pure and deep in restoring his patient to health; a teacher has a like satisfaction in aiding the progress of his pupil in education; but the father's joy surpasses them all in seeing his child grow up in health and happiness; and so of the Heavenly Physician, Teacher, and Father. The physician knows that his patient is sick, and treats him not as convalescent. The teacher knows that his pupil has only made some progress in learning, and so he treats him not as an accomplished scholar. The father understands the inexperience of childhood and youth, and with tenderness guides his son not as an adult, but as a child; and on this principle acts the Heavenly Father, Teacher, and Spiritual Physician.

There are to be overcome in the believer, the weakness, awkwardness, and inexperience of an imperfect sanctification, for these chiefly stand in the way of his constant and unqualified reception of the Divine. Hence Christ will always have to say to His disciples to the end of the age, "I have many things to say unto you, but you cannot bear them now."

The disciples of every age have manifested a greater readiness to bring Christ over to their notions, than an eagerness implicitly to drink in His spirit, and to be conformed to Him in all their ways. To yield unqualifiedly the spirit and life, to the reception of the Divine, is all that the quickened spirit needs to its complete glory and joy, but the disciples on earth have not yet learned how to comply with the simple and important necessity of their wellbeing, hence there is no truth more important for us to realise than this, viz., that God is possessed of all the influence and instrumentality necessary for the complete salvation of every believer; that He has perfectly formed His plan; that He kindly cherishes His purpose, and that He works by His Spirit in the heart of every believer, to will and to do of His good pleasure; and that all that is now needed on the part of His children, is their hearty co-working with Him, in His carrying out into completion the gracious and glorious design of His heart, to fill them "with all the fulness of God."

God, in the transformation of the spirit, and renewal of the life of man, is working out the high problems of His grace, to the admiration and delight of "the principalities and powers in heavenly places." He does not look upon His redeemed offspring as slaves to be treated as property, nor as subjects to be reigned over, nor as friends to be occasionally visited, but as children, part of His own household, to whose education and training He consecrates Himself. To renew the life and raise the spirit of man to more than its pristine purity; to impress on the human soul divine perfection, in higher measure than He has impressed it on angel nature, and to quicken the human with His own divine life, is the great end He has in view in all His doings.

In all this, the Heavenly Father in the midst of His family is not an imperial ruler, He is simply the Father in all His infinite tenderness, unfolding to them His divine perfections, and imparting to them His inmost life. He not only causes streams of light from His outer works to illuminate their understanding, but He also pours forth emanations of His own blessed life into them up to the measure of their capacity of reception. He not only transcribes on the spirit the lineaments of His life, but He also fills them with His own indwelling person.

No thoughtful father is satisfied merely with the birth and embrace of a son, his desire and aim is to raise that son to the closest and fullest enjoyment of his own life, and he would be pained in the highest degree were he to see him rising into a life of rebellion against him. Nor is the desire of the Divine Father, in reference to His children, different from the desire of the genuine affections of an earthly parent. And of this fact, God has given the most ample proof in all that appertains to the redemption of the world by Jesus Christ.

Who, then, can fully estimate the grandeur and importance of the sinner's conversion to God? It is the commencement of the ascent of the immortal spirit of man through the descent of the Eternal Son of God into this region of dead souls; it is the realisation of spiritual poverty, through the action of the quickening Spirit; the return of the prodigal son to his gracious Father, through the drawing near of the love of God; it is the yielding up of the life to God through a perception and reception of "the truth as it is in Jesus."

How great, then, is the capacity of the human for the Divine! and how lofty the dignity of the inner life of man, as quickened and led by the Spirit of God! How ravishing the fellowship of the filial circle, drawn around the Father in His house of "many mansions!" and what is there that the sons of God can be denied, if it is at all consistent with their well-being?

The filial heart is the best of all blessings which man can possess; let him acquire what he may, and attain to whatever he may set his heart upon, if he is without the filial heart he is an imperfect, restless, dissatisfied being. The production of this heart, however, is the work of the Holy Ghost striving with the sinner, quickening his spirit, and energising his risen life. And this work of the Spirit in the spirit of man is the most God-like production of the Godhead,—the work of God, travelling in the greatness of His strength, mighty to save; and not without good reason might the Saviour ask, "What is a man profited if he should gain the whole world and lose his own soul? and what shall a man give in exchange for his soul?"

The filial heart of man is that alone of all finite being which can give the full response to God as the Father. And it is that which God values most. His

Father-heart can rest in nothing short of the perfection of the filial heart in His children, and the reason it can be satisfied with nothing short of this, is to be found in the nature of the Father's heart, and in that alone.

CHAPTER XVII.

RECEPTION OF CHRIST.

IF the human spirit is ushered into conscious life in a state of aversion to the Godlike, and if the man grows up in a state of error, and in conflict with the manifestations of the Divine, with which mankind has been favoured, then must he descend in the scale of life, and become the subject of torment to himself and a power of injury to others. If, however, the foundation of a new course of life is laid within him, if he becomes the possessor of new biasses in the direction of holiness by the implantation of a new principle of life, then must he rise in the scale of being; and this state man realises and attains to in yielding himself up to the Spirit of God, in his acceptance of Christ through belief " of the truth as it is in Jesus."

In all cases, as is well known, the reception of anything is determined by the nature of the thing received. Our reception of a friend is conditioned by the laws or usages of friendship. Our reception of wealth is among other things conditioned on our steady application to business, &c. Our acceptance of health is conditioned on our attendance to the laws of health. And a similar statement may be made relative to all the things we are capable of receiving and enjoying.

And as it is socially so is it spiritually. Our reception of Christ is also conditioned, and, according to the point of view from which we regard Him, is the condition of the reception which is accorded. As is well known, Christ may be received historically, ecclesiastically, and spiritually. Holding the gospel narratives as true accounts, is the condition of receiving Christ historically. Regarding Christ as the founder of the Church, and professing belief in His doctrines, is the condition of receiving Him ecclesiastically. And believing Him to be the Son of God to the saving of the soul, is the condition of receiving Him spiritually. This latter, of course, overlaps the two former modes of viewing Him.

The careful observer of human life can have no doubt of the fact that some men change in the spirit of their lives, become the subjects of new dispositions, and are influenced and actuated by different principles from those which formerly governed them. Some profane persons become pious, some infidels become believing, some implacable become merciful, some licentious become pure, some intemperate become temperate, some vicious become virtuous, and some slothful become energetic. And this change in their lives is affected, not merely or chiefly by a resolve or an idea taking possession of them, but by a new disposition, a new spirit produced in them by the Holy Ghost in leading them to receive the Son of God. The changes usually effected in men's lives by means of new ideas are transient; whereas, the change accomplished in receiving a new spirit is permanent, and this is realised through means of a man's acceptance of Christ.

To receive Christ spiritually as already indicated, we must receive Him as the Son of God, and yield ourselves up to the influence of this truth plied by the Holy Spirit. Receiving Christ thus, we receive Him in His Spirit, and become one with Him, " He that is joined to the Lord is one Spirit."

When Christ ascended on high He received gifts for men, even for the rebellious; and the first gift which He received was the great Agent of man's salvation, viz., the Holy Ghost, and the first great manifestation of this gift was on the first Pentecost after His Ascension. And the work of this great Agent is to bring sinners to the faith of the Gospel, and then to take up His abode in the believer's heart with a view to enlighten him, and satisfy him with the joys of salvation. Hence, when the Spirit works in the believer the good-will of God, he bears witness with his Spirit that he is a child of God, and seals him to the day of redemption. And, until a man has this Spirit of Christ, he is none of His, he has no spiritual life in him, but in receiving the Spirit he becomes alive from the dead, and lives unto God in newness of life.

By receiving Christ in his spirit, the believer receives Him in his mind. It is the function of the Spirit to take the things which are Christ's, and show them unto the believer. "He shall glorify me," says Jesus, "for he shall receive of Mine, and shall show it unto you."

We receive the mind of Christ, not by speculation, nor by vain dreaming, nor by human tradition, nor by the study of nature, but by the Holy Ghost working faith in us. The Spirit imparts to us a love of the truth, and produces within us a disposition to search the Scriptures with a teachable heart. He gives us a relish for the things of God, and kindles in us a desire after the knowledge of God, which is in Christ Jesus. He inclines us to wait on the ordinances which are of Divine appointment, helps us in our supplications, and affords us glimpses of the things which are unspeakable and full of glory.

In thus receiving Christ, we become identified with Him in His perceptions of truth. We receive His view of the Father, Son, and Spirit, in all that these are to us, and in all that they have done for us. Hence, Paul prays on behalf of the Ephesian saints, "that the God of our Lord Jesus Christ may give you the Spirit of wisdom and revelation in the knowledge of Him, the eyes of your understanding being enlightened that ye may know what is the hope of His calling, and what the riches of the glory of His inheritance in the saints." And again, in another epistle, he prays that believers might be "filled with the knowledge of His will, in all wisdom and spiritual understanding," but on this point, it is needless to multiply quotations.

When the believer receives Christ in his spirit and

mind, he also receives Him into his life. They live for Him, they live in Him, and they live by Him. The source and motive power of their whole life is Christ, "because as He is, so are we in the world." They love what He loves, and hate what He hates, and pursue what He pursues. They do not live unto themselves, but unto their Saviour; and the law of their life is laid down in these words, "For whether we live, we live unto the Lord, and whether we die, we die unto the Lord: whether we live, therefore, or die, we are the Lord's."

Paul tells us that we are quickened together with Christ, even when we were dead in sins, hence he can say, "I live, yet not I, but Christ liveth in me." And in another place, he says, "When Christ, who is our life, shall appear, then shall ye also appear with Him in glory." And yet again, "For we which live, are always delivered unto death, for Jesus' sake."

When the believer receives Jesus in his spirit, mind, and life, he receives Him also in his righteousness. Christ in Himself has always stood in right relation to His Father. And in His work, in His people, and on their behalf, He occupies a righted relation to the law, and justice, and God, and thus the believer through Him receives a readjusted standing before God and man. All the capacities of his being are now open to the reception of the outgoings of the Divine, and to the inflowings of the Christian into his soul, and hence all the powers and functions of his life are exerted in accordance with the conditions and obligations of his wellbeing.

The foregoing is just what sinful man needs. Man, in a sinful state, is like a plant out of the ground, and, therefore, not in a right relation to the soil on which its life necessarily depends. The sinner is not in a state of union and communion with God, and, therefore, cannot consecrate the functions of his life to the glory of God, in the promotion of his own well-being, and that of others. In his reception of Christ, however, he is brought into that relation to God, in which the capacities of his soul are opened up to the inflowing of the Divine, and the energies of his spirit are all consecrated to the service of God. And in this way his sanctification is carried forward, by the power of the Holy Ghost working within him the good-will and pleasure of God.

In receiving Christ and that righteousness which He wrought for man, and which is imputed to him by faith alone, the sinner undergoes a thorough radical change, in reference to God and His holy law. "Such," says the apostle to believers, "were some of you, but ye are washed, but ye are sanctified, but ye are justified in the name of our Lord Jesus Christ, and by the Spirit of our God," and thus it is that "God is in Christ, reconciling the world unto Himself, not imputing their trespasses unto them," but, on the contrary, imputing "the righteousness of God, which is by faith in Jesus Christ unto all and upon all them that believe."

God, in bringing men into the faith of the Gospel of His Son, is bringing them into readjusted relations with Himself, and with the conditions of their own wellbeing, hence Christ is our righteousness, and we are righteous in Him.

The believer is identified with Christ, regarded by God as one with Him, hence the apostle's expressed wish to "be found in Him, not having mine own righteousness which is by the law, but that which is through the faith of Christ, the righteousness which is of God by faith."

Moreover, in receiving Christ in his mind, spirit, life, and righteousness, the believer receives Him also in His glory. If the believer stands before the boundless riches of sovereign grace with all the avenues of his being open to its inflow, then must he receive Christ in His glory. This glory arises out of the beauty of righteousness and the radiance of character which, through Christ, the believer is led to assume; hence our blessed Lord, in addressing His Father on behalf of His disciples, says, "The glory which Thou hast given Me I have given unto them," and Paul says that "when Christ who is our life shall appear, then shall we also appear with Him in glory." And He shall at His coming change our vile body, that it may be fashioned like unto His glorious body, and we shall be changed; even now we are changing from glory to glory. As the light falling upon the camera transcribes the image to the prepared plate, so does the light of the glorious gospel of the grace of God shining into the heart of the believer transcribe to his life the glorious image of the ever blessed Jesus.

And when the believer receives the Redeemer in

the manner above indicated, he also receives Him in His joy. The consciousness of union and communion with Christ, in the various elements of spiritual life indicated, must awaken within the believer "the joy of the Lord," having Christ in him the hope of glory, he must have Him also at the same time the wellspring of his joy. From this point of view the Saviour stood and cried on the great day of one of the Jewish festivals, "If any man thirst, let him come unto Me and drink. He that believeth on Me, as the scriptures hath said, out of his belly shall flow rivers of living water."

As the mighty oak, when shaken by the violence of the tempest, darts its roots more firmly into the soil, so the disciples, when their creature sources of joy and comfort fail them, when persecuted by men and devils, fall back on Christ Himself, and evermore realise the opening up of the well-springs of the Divine in the inner depths of their spirits, hence Christ said to them, "These things have I spoken unto you, that in me ye might have peace; in the world ye shall have tribulation, but be of good cheer, I have overcome the world;" and on behalf of His disciples He thus prays to His Father: "And now I come unto Thee, and these things I speak in the world, that they might have my joy fulfilled in themselves."

Such, then, is the reception of God's Son by the believer, and what, we may ask, is so conducive and even necessary to human wellbeing as is this reception? Without Christ, fallen man is a longing, perplexed, and suffering creature, struggling after an escape from his woes, but by his very efforts to better his state only plunging himself more deeply into misery. Christ is, indeed, the greatest gift God can bestow upon man, no other acquisition can meet his necessities or alleviate his distress in any permanent shape. What infatuation, then, in the sinner to refuse, or delay, his reception of Christ! And what condescension on the part of the Father to give up the Son of His love, and of the Son to come into the world to take up His abode in man, and also of the Holy Spirit to apply Christ to the sinner!

This reception, however, of Christ is by no means perfect and complete in its first beginnings on earth. The work of sanctification is progressive. The reception of Christ begins with the quickening of the spirit of man with the Divine life, and is completed in the full manifestation of the Godhead in the glory of the perfect state above, when, seeing Him as He is, "we shall be like Him." Blessed consummation of Divine grace!

CHAPTER XVIII.

THE INDWELLING OF THE DIVINE IN THE HUMAN.

By indwelling we mean residing in and operating through means of another. Of the possibility of this, or rather of the fact itself, we have clear proof. The soul dwells in the body and acts through it, and this indwelling of the soul makes all the difference between a dead body and a living man. Knowledge dwells in, and operates through means of, the faculties of the mind. This is realised by all intelligent persons in the experience of daily life. The difference between the ignorant and the learned, is the indwelling of knowledge in the understanding of the one, and the absence of it from the mind of the other. Disposition, again, resides in the heart of man, and reveals itself in all the acts of his daily life; this is recognised by all men everywhere, and they form their judgments and frame their intercourse accordingly.

Now, as really as the soul dwells in the body and acts through it, as really as knowledge dwells in the mind and reveals itself by means of the mental faculties, and as surely as disposition dwells in the heart and manifests itself in the conduct, so surely do Father, Son, and Holy Spirit dwell in the believer's spirit, and act through his life. Hence, says the apostle in pregnant words which can bear frequent repetition, "I live, yet not I, but Christ liveth in me," and Jesus Himself referring to the same thing says, "I in them, and Thou in Me." And God. even, long before, had said of humanity in far more emphatic terms than He ever said of Zion, "This is My rest for ever: here will I dwell, for I have desired it."

Creation indicates the necessity of the indwelling of the Divine in the human, and Incarnation proves the fact itself. Look at Jehovah, if we may dare so to speak, toiling up the heights of creation, through the dreary waste of ages from the first formation of chaos to the completion of His great and beneficent work, and what do we see but God preparing an abode for Himself in the spirit of His child, man. The crowning act of creation was, when God formed man out of the dust of the ground, and, into His own image thus formed, breathed the breath of life, His own living Spirit. Creation and Redemption are preparatory to the indwelling of the Divine in the human, and the completion of salvation will exhibit God taking up His full and everlasting abode in, and along with, His redeemed children.

The indwelling of the Divine in the human might be argued in the following manner: All finite existence is dependent on God, but all finite existence does not realise alike its dependence. The nature which is nearest in the scale of being to God is that which, in one sense, is most dependent upon Him, which certainly most of all is capable of realising its dependence, and so must be the first and closest link of connection between God and creation. Now, as far as known to us, man is of all finite existence the nearest to God, being created in His own image, and, therefore, is the best suited to His indwelling.

If, then, man's nature be nearest to God's nature in the scale of being, and through which He operates on creation; the fall of man may not only have deeply affected Himself, but the whole creation on which God thus operates; and that such seems really to be the case, is borne out by these words, viz., "The whole creation groaneth and travaileth together in pain."

But whatever may be thought of the foregoing view of the case, the indwelling of God is not left to the discovery of reason, for nothing is more forcibly insisted on in Scripture, "Ye are the temple of the living God; as God hath said, I will dwell in them." "Whoever will confess that Jesus is the Christ, God dwelleth in him." "If a man love me," says Jesus, "he will keep My words, and My Father will love him, and we will come unto him and make our abode with him." Scripture to this effect might be indefinitely multiplied, but it were needless to advance anything further, in order to show what the teaching of God's Word is, in regard to the doctrine in hand.

It is very true that we know nothing of the *how* of this indwelling, it is the profound mystery of existence. But the how of all indwelling is to us unknown and mysterious. What, *e.g.*, do we know of *how* the soul dwells in the body? yet the fact of its indwelling is clear and patent to all. Mystery is connected with every sphere of human knowledge, and many of these mysteries are beyond the ken of mortals, and this ought to be matter of gratitude to us, for it shows us that no limit can be set to our progress in knowledge. But because a theme of contemplation may be closely allied with the unknown, or a high phase of truth with the mysterious, it is none the less real or important on that account, but only the more so. And it is our imperative duty not to let it alone, but to approach the study of it with the greater caution and meekness. Mystery is not contradiction nor absurdity, but the deep relation of things undisclosed, unperceived links of being, or uncomprehended operations of existence. Mystery is profound truth, and what is mysterious to us now, may be known to an angel, and what is mysterious to an angel, is known to God. This indwelling of which we speak, is, indeed, mysterious to the intellect of man, but not unknown to the heart, nor unrealised in the life of the believer. And as we advance in the life of faith, into the visions of the unseen, we shall know more and more of the glorious indwelling, for the realisation of which creation itself was called into being, the Son of God Incarnated, and for which the Spirit of God has energised from age to age.

And what is there in the constitution of the universe, in as far as our knowledge of it extends, more natural than is the indwelling of the soul in the body, an indwelling which constitutes the physical life of man. This indwelling is in accordance with the original constitution of things, for it is not natural for man to die. Death is an abnormal state from which we naturally shrink back, it is only a possibility of our being, and is the result of violence done to the human constitution. It is the separating of the component parts of his existence and the result of sin. By sin death entered into the world, and death along with it, and so "death passed upon all men, for that all have sinned."

And why has the body received its present constitution, its skin, flesh, muscles, &c.? Just that it might be the fit abode of the soul; it has been created purposely for the indwelling of the soul; therefore, when the soul is removed from the body, the body returns to the dust again. It is this indwelling soul that imparts constitutional form, graceful and free action to the body; it does not coerce the limbs of the body, nor enslave it in any of its functions, but only affords to it and secures for it free unfettered constitutional action. A body from which the soul has departed may be made to move by the application of an electric battery, but such motion is not free constitutional action.

What, again, is more natural in the rational order of being, than that knowledge should dwell in the human mind, act in the understanding, and reign in the intellect; for the human mind has been created with the faculties of perception, comparison, inference, &c., in order to contemplate, receive, and enjoy truth, and truth has been revealed in its manifold forms, and through its numerous channels, in order that the mind of man should be increased in knowledge, cultivated and enlarged. Ignorance and error enslave the understanding and hold the mind in bondage; but truth known enlightens the mind, energises the faculties, and sets free the intellect.

But, further, nothing is more natural in the sphere of the spiritual than that meek, gentle, and generous dispositions should hold sway in the spirit of man. The spirit of man has been called into existence with capacity, and endowed with receptivity for the indwelling of meek, gentle, and generous dispositions; and to be moved by such dispositions into vigorous action constitutes the life and liberty of the spirit of man, whereas, selfish, wrathful, and revengeful dispositions, enslave the soul and hold the spirit of man in direful bondage.

Advancing now beyond these things, there is nothing within the range of finite existence more natural to humanity than that God should dwell in the spirit, reign in the life, and act in the soul of man, and be ever present in pure and blissful fellowship with the believer. God cannot, indeed, dwell in sinful humanity; this would be the most unnatural of all things. God can draw near to sinful humanity only in the sense of awakening and intensifying the consciousness of guilt, showing the man his sin, and thus shutting him up in the prison-house of remorse and despair. After this fashion God dealt with the world when in the exercise of His longsuffering kindness He withdrew Himself into thick darkness on the first entrance of sin into the world. But God can dwell in sanctified humanity;

indeed, this is His chief delight, His supreme joy. Redeemed humanity is the chosen temple of the Lord God, "This people have I formed for Myself."

How preposterous, then, is it to talk of religion or Christian life degrading humanity, enslaving the soul, and tormenting the spirit of man. Life, health, and energy do not enslave the body; truth, knowledge, and understanding do not enslave the mind; meek, gentle, and unselfish dispositions do not enslave the spirit. Why, then, should the indwelling of God, which is as natural as any of these, enslave the soul? Rather, it is the indwelling of God alone that emancipates the spirit and secures true liberty. It is the indwelling of God that imparts energy to the faculties, light to the understanding, and direction to the will; therefore, it is written, "Where the Spirit of the Lord is there is liberty," and "If the Son shall make you free, ye shall be free indeed." This is at once true, and richly philosophical.

Reader, this overwhelming theme is as true as it is grand and mysterious! Yes, blessed be God, it is the most natural of all things that the Lord Almighty should dwell in sanctified humanity; and this is the pledge and the actuality of all true and abiding liberty to man. And how great is the beauty which this indwelling imparts to the soul of man! There is no natural thing so beautiful as the human body indwelt by a pure spirit. When God completed His work of creation, in the formation of man, He pronounced it "very good."

In the persons of our first parents, during their

INDWELLING OF THE DIVINE.

innocence, the human body presented to the discerning eye the loveliest object on which it could gaze. And when the body of man shall be raised, like unto the "glorious body" of the Son of God, then shall be seen again the highest perfection of material beauty. And all this loveliness shall be the result of a pure spirit, possessing a perfect body, the perfected work of the indwelling of the Divine.

There is nothing within the sphere of intellectual existence so beautiful as the mind of man indwelt by truth; in comparison with this, material beauty, however great, is poor indeed; in fact, the loveliest displays of material beauty are those which indicate intellectual greatness. The mind of man, irradiated with the light of truth, shines in the loveliness of the Divine. The outflowings from the human lips of sanctified intellect, whether poetic, scientific, philosophical, or theological, is a pure and elevating enjoyment indeed.

The human soul also is very beautiful when possessed of meek, godlike dispositions. Such a soul is, above all others, the resting place, the chosen habitation of God; in it Jehovah delights to manifest the glory of His infinite perfection.

But more beautiful than all is the human spirit filled with all the fulness of God. Within the boundless range of the All-seeing eye, there is nothing so gratifying to the heart of God as is the soul in which He himself thus dwells, nothing on which His eye can rest with such complacency and delight.

The necessity of the indwelling of God in man, to

his glory and bliss, is seen in the majesty displayed in the great facts of the Incarnation and Ascension to glory of the Son of God. And when the pure soul shall dwell in the glorified body, when the cloudless light of truth shall fill the vast capacities of the human mind, when divine, and only divine, emotions shall fully possess the heart, when God—Father, Son, and Spirit—shall dwell in and fill the redeemed with all the fulness of God, oh what shall be the unspeakable joy which shall then ravish the heart and delight the human spirit? What shall then be the felicity of the perfect eternal indwelling of God? The joys of a first love are sweet; sweet the soul's first embrace of truth, and the first awaking consciousness of peace with God. This, however, is but a faint tasting—the infant spirit obtaining but a glimpse of its future manhood, the heir arriving at a feeble conception of his after inheritance.

Of the full and perfect bliss of the Divine indwelling, we can here speak only in the broken accents of infancy. "We see through a glass darkly," but then shall we "see face to face," and "know even as we are known," and the full tide of light, with the full swell of bliss, shall flow into and fill the soul. The eternal realisation of fellowship with God, in the knowledge and enjoyment of the godlike designs of His infinite love, shall all thrill the spirit with purest felicity. Glorious consummation of immortal life and fellowship Divine, how great shall be thy bliss and joy!

CHAPTER XIX.

UNION OF THE HUMAN WITH THE DIVINE.

As the indwelling of the Divine in the human arises out of the reception of the Divine by the human, so the union of the human with the Divine arises out of the indwelling of the Divine in the human. In the contemplation of this all-important and glorious theme, extremes, prevalent even at the present day, are to be guarded against. These extremes are the dreams of mysticism on the one hand, and the speculations of rationalism on the other.

This union of which we speak is not one of a pantheistic character, *i.e.*, a union of identification of the several departments of nature, in which God is all, and all is God; a union in which there is no distinction of essence and personality between the Creator and the creature. The union for which we contend in nowise interferes with the personalities, or confounds the individualities, of the natures united. It is not a union like that of a spark in a flame, or of a drop in the ocean, where the one is lost in the other; but such a union as preserves the Divinity of the one nature unimpaired, and the free agency of the other unfettered.

Nor, on the other hand, is this a mere rational union, *i.e.*, a union of Divine and human natures only in views of mind, feeling, and principles of action. If this union of idea and will were the only one possible between the human and Divine, then, however possible in the nature of being itself, it could hardly ever be realised in the actuality of life, inasmuch as fallen man is not only devoid of the one essential principle of such a union with God, but is also antagonistic in spirit to a union of will with God. If, therefore, a union of the human and Divine wills is possible only through a union of the human and Divine minds, how is a merely rational union to be attained? Fallen man, as we have seen, hates the light, and nothing can lead him to welcome the light. No mere revelation of the truth of God will ever prevail upon the man who dislikes it to receive it, and rejoice in the light of it. A union, therefore, meditated only through the truth itself, from the nature of things, cannot be realised between God and man.

This rationalistic view of the union between God and man, however scientific the dress in which it is set forth, and with whatsoever philosophic authority it is backed up, is yet most unscientific and unphilosophic; for a union with God, through the medium of truth, is possible to the sinner only through means of a prior union of the spirit of man with the Spirit of God.

Contemplate the world lying under the wicked one, at enmity with God, in opposition to the light of His saving holiness, though diffused in the purest radiance of the Divine effulgence, *i.e.*, in Him who is the "brightness of the Father's Glory." This radiant effulgence poured on the diseased organ of the sinner's vision, only causes him to nerve his every effort, to exclude it the more effectually from his heart. The softening, melting influence of Heaven's mercy, falling upon the corrupt heart of man, is thus seen only to arouse it to more confirmed rejection of God.

Ere, then, there can be a union between the sinner and God through means of saving truth, there must be an experience on man's part of quickening grace. The Spirit of God must touch the heart of the sinner with His own immediate power, firing it with love of the Divine; otherwise, the truth cannot be received in the love of it. It is only when the Spirit works faith in a man, warming his heart with the love of the true as He unveils to him the beauties of sovereign grace, that he will yield himself up to God in the reception of "the truth as it is in Jesus," and, receiving the truth in the love of it, he will enjoy fellowship with God through our Lord Jesus Christ, and enter into the realisation of union with the Father, through the Son, and by the Spirit.

This union, as we have indicated, is not a blending or confounding of the united personalities or lives; nor is it an absorbing of the one by the other, so that the one is in any way injured or lost in regard to anything that appertains to it. There is nothing, *e.g.*, of blending or confounding together of mind and truth in man's grasp of the truth. After a man has laid hold of the truth, his mind is as perfect as when he was ignorant of it; in point of fact, it is more perfect; nor is the truth grasped in any way injured or changed in its nature through being understood. The body in its union with the soul is in no way injured, blended and confounded with the soul. The body is as material in its union with the soul in life, as were the particles of which it is composed before the body was made. And the soul is, in its essence and all its essentials, the same as it shall be when it parts company with its present body. The humanity also of the Incarnate One is as real and perfect in its condition of inseparable union with the Divine, as it is in any of the human race. And, in like manner, the Divinity of the Man Christ Jesus is as perfect now, as it was when in the beginning the "Word was with God, and the Word was God." Similarly the Godhead in the indwelling of the Divine in the spirit of man, is as essentially Divine as was Jehovah, ere the silence of eternity was broken by the obtrusion of created being. And the spirit of man is as really human while enjoying the life of union and communion with God, as when it was "without God in the world."

This union of nature in no way degrades the higher, but it unspeakably exalts the inferior. Truth, *e.g.*, is in no way degraded by its indwelling and influence in the understanding of man, but through it the mind of man is greatly raised, especially by the apprehension of "the truth as it is in Jesus." The soul of man is in no way degraded by its dwelling in the body, but the body is highly dignified by means of the indwelling of the soul. And, blessed be God, Jehovah is not dishonoured by His dwelling in the Faithful, for it is in His manifestations in connection with this indwelling that He has displayed in purest radiance the glory of His infinite perfections; but human nature in the redeemed is mightily exalted on account of this indwelling of Father, Son, and Spirit; they are able in consequence to prove to the world that they are sons and daughters of the Almighty.

This union of the human and Divine is spiritual and enduring. The Spirit of God unites Himself with the spirit of man, and quickens it by manifesting Christ to the heart, and working faith in the obedient. In this way the believer is "renewed in the spirit of his mind," that he "may put on the new man which, after God, is created in righteousness and true holiness," the "deep things of God" are revealed to him, and the work of sanctification is carried forward in his nature.

Hence the union of the human and Divine is a vital one; in fact, it is impossible for the Spirit of God, the Author of life, to come into contact thus with the soul and spirit of man, and not produce life, and quicken all the powers and capacities of human nature. This spirit has been sent by the Son to regenerate souls "dead in trespasses and sins," and coming into the spirit of man, He produces and sustains the life of God in it. This is the point of view occupied by the apostle when he says, "If Christ be in you, the body is dead because of sin, but the spirit is life because of righteousness," and in another place, "If the Spirit of Him that raised up Jesus from the dead dwell in you, He that raised up Christ from the dead shall also quicken your mortal bodies by His Spirit that dwelleth in you."

This union, moreover, is a growing one, ever developing itself in the heart and life of the believer. It is not perfected in its first beginnings; there is such an infinite capacity in the spirit of man, and there is such an infinitude of grace in God, that the soul cannot be "filled with all the fulness of God" in its first receptions of "the grace that is in Christ Jesus." There are too many obstacles in man, standing in the way of his reception of the Divine, to be overcome even by the Holy Spirit in His first approaches to the soul. The slaying of the antagonism of the self-righteous spirit in man, the quickening of his heart with the life of God, is not all that is needed in order to the salvation of man. The ignorance, error, and prejudice of the believer have to give way before "the truth as it is in Jesus," in the process of sanctification; and the remains of the corruptions of self-love have to give way before the "spirit of a sound understanding" in perfecting the life and godliness which are in Christ Jesus; and thus the union is ever advancing and consolidating in the continual assimilation of the believer to the Spirit of God. The spirit of man is ever enlarging in its capacity through its reception of the Divine, and God is ever unfolding fresh manifestations of Himself to the believer's soul.

Finally, this union is an indestructible one. All

other unions existing on earth are dissolved sooner or later; however closely we may cement our earthly unions, however eagerly we may desire to perpetuate them, they must break up and perish one and all. The heir of many lands must soon bid them a lasting adieu; the possessor of numerous titles, vast wealth, and earthly glory, must ere long be torn from them all. Crowns must fall from the most dignified head, and sceptres from the most tenacious grasp; but this union shall never be impaired, it is in its very nature imperishable, augmenting, and consolidating. It shall survive when all things else decay. It shall spring forth in full and deathless bloom when all other buds of promise shall have withered and fallen to the ground.

Such, then, is this union of God with man, the most glorious and blessed that can be entertained even in the loftiest imaginings of man. Yet in the pursuit of earthly gain and human acquisitions, how greatly is it overlooked and neglected! Surely folly is ingrained in the heart of the man who strains every nerve to gain what this world can afford, and yet never spends a single earnest thought on the transcendantly-glorious prospects which this union opens up before him. But happy, thrice happy, are those who have already entered upon it; they alone know what true life is here below, life which they shall enjoy in ever-increasing sweetness while the ceaseless ages of eternity revolve.

CHAPTER XX.

THE UNION AND UNITY OF BELIEVERS WITH ONE ANOTHER, IN THEIR UNION AND UNITY WITH CHRIST.

THIS union consists of a union of co-ordinate lives with one another, in their subordination to a higher life. It is the union of believers with one another in their union with Christ. This matter may be better understood if we look at it in its twofold aspect, viz., the union of believers with Christ, and the union of believers with one another, as arising out of their union with Christ.

The union of believers is effected through means of the union of humanity with Divinity, in the union of the son of man with the Son of God, in the person of Jesus Christ. This union of the two natures exists in its highest form in the Incarnate One, and as God and man are united in one person in Him, so God and man are united in one life in the believer, and just as in the hypostatical union there is no blending of natures, so in the union with Christ, of which all believers are partakers, there is no confounding of the lives.

This union of believers with one another is close

and endearing, and would be found by them in their experience to be so, if they would only realise its true nature and godlike privileges.

As children of God, believers have no union or communion with one another save in and through Christ their head. The emblem of this union is beautifully set before us by Christ Himself in His simile of the vine with its branches. The branches of the vine have no union with one another but through their union with the stem. In their union with the stem, however, they form one vine, and the same sap with its life-giving energy which rises from the root circulates in them all.

The limbs of the human body have no vital union and communion with one another save through their union with the one body; but in virtue of this union the same blood circulates in them all, and the same life energises them all, and, as a consequence, if one member suffers, the others suffer along with it, but if on the contrary one member rejoices, the others rejoice with it. And thus is it with believers; they have union and communion with one another through their union with Christ. Having received Him they become with Him one in spirit, mind, and life. And the one grace of Christ thus flows into them individually, and constitutes them one with Himself, and unites them all into one body of which He is the Head.

If a dead branch be allowed to remain on the stem of the vine, it has no vital union with it nor with the other branches. Or if a paralysed limb remains on the body, it has no fellowship with the other limbs in the health, vigour, and activity of the body. Similarly, if another spirit than the Spirit of Christ dwells in any professed member of Christ, such an one can have no union with Him, and must be separated from Christ and His brethren by the whole difference of mind, spirit, and aim which animate him, from the mind, spirit, and aim which animate believers. Is it, then, a matter of wonder that the Church of Christ has been so inconsistent, inefficient, and even dead, when we consider how much the spirit of self has divided the visible organisation and enfeebled its members?

The stem, roots, and branches of the vine, however numerous, make but one plant. The parts of the body, however varied, make but one body, and the members of a family, however few or many, near or remote, united or scattered, make only one family. The nature of man, consisting of body, mind, and spirit, form but one man. So, in like manner, the whole company of believers of all ages, of all dispositions and peoples and tongues, make but one household of God, one spiritual theocracy. This brotherhood or body of Christ is one in all its essential conditions, it is the same humanity that is redeemed in its every member, and every member of this family is redeemed by the same blood, called with the same calling, quickened by the same Spirit, fired by the same love, taken to the same heaven, and brought near to the same Father.

It is the same humanity that is possessed by every member of the human race; what is peculiar in the individual mode of possessing it constitutes the individuality of the person. It is the same truth that dwells in the minds of all believers; what is peculiar in the individual mode of apprehending it, is what constitutes the specialty of that believer's mind. It is the same love which is shed abroad in the hearts of all God's children; what is peculiar in the individual's mode of cherishing it, is what determines the peculiarity of each believer's heart and life. It is the same God that dwells in the redeemed; what is peculiar in the individual mode of fellowship, is what constitutes the individuality of the life of the believer, and determines the degree of nearness or distance between him and God.

Out of this union arises the unity of the Church, a unity which binds together into one the several members with Christ the Head. They are all "begotten of God," and made "partakers of the Divine nature." As Christ is the incarnation of the Divine, so they are the embodiment of the Divine. "Of His will begat He us." "We are members of His flesh, of His body, and of His bones." The Church is His body, "the fulness of Him who filleth all in all."

This unity includes a great variety of things—a few of which we here enumerate, in order that the subject may be set forth with some little approach to the fulness which it deserves. These things, therefore, this unity includes, viz., a oneness of relationship, believers are all born into the family of God, and constitute His household. They are all, therefore, brethren. They have all a oneness of spirit, of mind, of heart, and of life. They have a oneness of love, of interest, of righteousness, of glory, of joy, and of destination. These privileges, and they might be greatly increased in number, indicate merely lines of thought which might be followed out at length with much profit, rather than constitute a setting forth of the subject. We leave it to the reader to follow out this matter for himself, assuring him that in doing so he will be richly rewarded for his labour.

The Church of Christ, as before said, is essentially one, consisting of the regenerated of all ages and lands. Her members on earth are separated by time and space, and distinguished by different degrees of attainments in the Divine life, but in Christ Jesus they are all one. In her present state the Church is unhappily divided into sects, in which condition the formal is more apparent than the real, the divisions than the unity, which is her normal state.

In consequence of her position and compound elements, the Church must realise more or less conflict on earth, opposition from without, and imperfection within. The powers of light and darkness, of truth and error, of the love of God, and love of self, must contend with each other. The light and love of the Divine in the Church must provoke the opposition of the darkness and enmity which are in the world, and contend with them. And the light and love of the Divine, which are in the believer, must provoke the carnal to opposition, and contend with the ignorance and love of self which still remain in him.

In view, then, of these things, a perfect Church,

however desirable, is not to be looked for on earth; this can only be attained to in heaven. And the one grand distinction between the Church militant and the Church triumphant is, that the latter is perfect in light and love, the former is imperfect in both. Hence, however much it is to be regretted and guarded against, there will be found in all the ecclesiastical organisations of the Church of Christ on earth imperfections of a twofold kind, viz., the existence of unregenerate within the pale of the denomination, and shortcomings on the part of the regenerate belonging to all the sections of the Church; and in guarding against the intrusion of the one, and in endeavouring to purge out the evils of the other, the bearers of office in the Church should be careful lest they root out the wheat with the tares. They ought to strive to present to the world not a perfect Church, but a purifying Church. Not members that have already attained, or are already perfect, but brethren pressing "toward the mark for the prize of the high calling of God in Christ Jesus." A Church, in short, which values her spiritual life far more than her rational acquirement and her formal progress. The spiritual is the first in the order of being and importance, and ought ever to be supremely desired by the children of God; it has, however, been one of the besetting sins of the Church that she has looked rather to her unity in the formal, than in the real and spiritual.

In the New Testament, while formal unity is indubitably enjoined, yet the great stress is laid on spiritual unity, *e.g.*, "If any man have not the Spirit of Christ he is none of His," "hereby we know that He abideth in us, by the Spirit which He hath given us." Indeed, the Church can enjoy a similarity of form only in as far as she possesses a oneness of spirit; formal unity arising from any other source is misleading and mischievous.

The position, then, assumed is this, viz., that the great essential in the Church is the spiritual—that the Church on earth is not a perfect but a purifying institution. Through conversion, the Church receives out of the world those who are to be made "meet for the inheritance of the saints in light." Perfection, however desirable, is not to be looked for in the members of the Church; it is that, however, which is placed before us as our standard of duty, and towards which we are enjoined to press with all our might.

Viewed in this light, the Church is to be regarded as an hospital, established by Christ, for the cure of souls; or, it may be regarded as a seminary, designed for the instruction of those who are ignorant in the things of God. The Church, therefore, can only consistently refuse to acknowledge as Christians those whose wounds are incurable. As long as any exhibit signs of spiritual life, however faint, the Church ought not to exclude them from her pale; and as long as a denomination maintains the essential truths of Christianity, it is not to be anathematised by the others; nor are they to refuse to hold intercourse with it, unless Christian principle in any case should be imperilled by so doing.

If the sections into which the Church of Christ is divided are not prepared to look upon one another as essentially corrupt, however much they may differ and bewail the corruptions of one another, they are bound to recognise one another as sections of the one great family of God in Christ, and to "seek the things which make for peace." They should feel it to be their duty to work together, and to pray that, in due time, God may lead them to see in the same light the things on which they differ at the present moment.

If the sects were deeply impressed with the conviction, that perfection was in the agencies, influences, &c., given to the Church, and not to be sought for in the minor points about which they differ, and over which they are so ready to wrangle and fight that one would almost suppose salvation depended on them; were they to realise the fact that it is their duty to hold lightly minor points of difference, in comparison with the grasp with which they lay hold upon the great essentials in regard to which they are all at one; then would there be less difficulty in the way of eventually effecting even an incorporate unity, which in present circumstances must be pronounced an impossibility.

The continuance of divisions in the Church is a standing memorial of the inattention of His disciples to the object of Christ's prayer. And the divisions themselves are a striking proof to the world that His disciples are not so affectionate to one another, and so devoted to Him as He desires they should be.

Were the Church in all its sections earnestly to cooperate with Him that His prayer might be answered, we would no doubt soon see the realisation of the thing prayed for.

The denomination that refuses to co-operate with other denominations, in so far as it is one with them, proves itself schismatic, inasmuch as it manifests a greater love for the accidental than for the essential; and unless it is prepared to say that the things on which it differs from the other denominations are of more importance to Christianity than the things on which it is at one with them, it must be chargeable with showing more love for the less than it shows for the greater. It sets itself in opposition to the Saviour in His prayer for unity, in thus giving chief prominence to the very grounds of the difference which divides it from other sections of the Church; and in doing so it also shows a greater regard for what is accidental than for that which is essential in the Divine life.

Are we, then, to be understood as pleading for a rash and inconsiderate laying aside of all our minor differences, and rushing into a formal oneness; this would be to conceive of our advocating the very thing here protested against, viz., the placing of the formal before the spiritual, the less before the greater, and the accidental before the essential. What we wish, is to turn the attention of the denominations to the fact that they are one on the great essentials of Christianity, and that this aspect of the case should ever be vividly realised by them and set in the foreground. Our oneness ought to occupy a deeper place in our hearts, and in our views of Divine truth, than the points on which we are divided. And we ought ever to be impressed with the fact, that by so doing, we shall far more efficiently promote the glory of God, the honour of the Church, and the conversion of the world than is now possible. Let us, therefore, drink more into "the one spirit," and have more of the mind of Christ; let us cherish, more ardently than we do, love for the great essentials of spiritual life; and in thus drawing near to the great centre of attraction, we will draw near to one another, our minor differences will fall into their proper place, and perchance, finally, be lost sight of in the oneness of light, and loveliness of the Divine brotherhood.

O Thou Eternal Spirit of the One Jehovah, breathe upon us, quicken us, and come down upon us in all the plenitude of Thine own grace, fill us with Thine own fulness and life, and make us one Church, the honoured instrument of accomplishing Thine own glorious work!

CHAPTER XXI.

EXALTATION OF THE HUMAN IN THE SONSHIP OF BELIEVERS.

IN the reception of Christ believers are "raised up and made to sit together with Him in heavenly places." In this reception they are necessarily raised into the realm of the spiritual, and enabled to repose in the calm fellowship of Heaven itself. In the measure in which believers receive Christ they rise in the consciousness of the Divine, and live in the visions of the unseen. "As many as received Him, to them gave He power to become the Sons of God, even to them that believe in His name." In the reception of Christ believers necessarily receive the power to realise the Sonship. In the very act of receiving Him they become possessors of the germ of the Divine life in their souls, and set out on an upward progress toward perfection which is limited only by the perfection of the Eternal Himself.

God in giving the germ of a reality necessarily gives the right, title, and privileges of that reality. In giving to a creature the germ of sentient life, He gives that creature the right, title, and privilege to him to enjoy a sentient life; in giving to humanity the germ of rational life, He gives to the possession of humanity the right, title, and privilege of living a rational life; and in giving to the believer the germ of the Divine life in His Son, He gives him the right, title, and privilege of living that life up to the full measure of his capacity, means, and opportunities of living that life. Hence, the believer, through believing in Christ, receives the power of the Sonship, and in the consciousness of this life realises the Sonship; in the reception of Christ the believer receives the right of the Sonship, and in the measure of his life in Christ is he conscious of the satisfaction of the righteousness of Sonship. But who can adequately conceive of the power of the reception of Christ? What is there in being, life, and destiny, that Christ has not the title to a right over? What is there among the possibilities of honour, glory, and bliss, that He has not the ability for? And what is there amid these possibilities that the Father will not give with Him? "He that spared not His own Son, but delivered Him up for us all, how shall He not with Him also freely give us all things?"

And who will dispute the believer's right and title to the benefits of the Sonship, to the consciousness and delights of the filial, to the glorious and blissful realisations of the oneness of the subjective human with the subjective Divine? This cannot be disputed; for, in the measure of the believer's conscious life in Christ, he realises the possession of that life. The believer's Father in heaven who glories in His Son and in all who bear His image, who has done so much to produce the filial heart in the believer, He certainly will not dispute the believer's right and title. Were He to deny this right and title, then would He have to repudiate His own Son, nay, His Son's work in the believer, and all the manifestations He has given of Himself in His Son. And will the Father do this? Can we believe it possible that He could do any such thing? Will the Son deny, or refuse to acknowledge, the Sonship of the believers?—the Son who delights in His brethren, who exults in the work He has accomplished in and for them, who glories in their fellowship with His Father, with Himself, and with the Spirit—then would He require to deny Himself, to discard His Sonship, to repudiate His work, and thus tarnish His glory and mar His own bliss. And is this the object for which He sits at His Father's right hand, for which He received the gift of all power in heaven and earth, and for the completion of which He is to come again at the end of the world in the glory of His Father and His holy angels? Or will the Holy Spirit deny the Sonship of the believer in Christ, and refuse to acknowledge his right and title to the privileges of the Sonship?—the Spirit who produces in the believer all that is peculiar to the Sonship, the Spirit who rejoices in perfecting in the believer the Sonship, and who is yet to present him faultless in the presence of God's glory with exceeding joy—will He deny the Sonship of believers then? Must He discard His own doings, repudiate the

very work He has achieved in the face of so much
resistance and so much grief? Will He reject His
own doings, deny Himself, resist, grieve, and quench
in His turn the very Divine emotions He Himself
has produced in the hearts of the believers? Is it
possible for us to conceive that the Spirit will do
any such thing?

Will the heavenly hosts, the sager students of
God's redemptive work, the principalities and powers
in heavenly places, to whom God displays His
manifold wisdom by His doings in the Church,
and who not only with earnest expectation wait
for the manifestation of the Sons of God, but even
delight in aiding the believer in his working out
what the Spirit works in him to will and to do of
God's good pleasure—will they who thus minister
to the heirs of salvation refuse to acknowledge the
Sonship of believers? Impossible! for then would
these holy ones be guilty of rebellion against God,
treason towards the sovereign Lord of the universe,
and, consequently, traitors to their own best interests.
Or will the believer himself, who rejoices in God
through our Lord Jesus Christ, and who delights
in having Christ in him the hope of glory, will he
deny his own Sonship? If he does, then must he
fail to recognise his own consciousness, and misunderstand the movements of the Divine in the
realisations of his own inner life. And this, un-
fortunately, he frequently does in consequence of
his present imperfect condition, and the co-minglings
of the Divine and self in his inner life, the conflicts

between the new and the old man; he not unfrequently mistakes the deeds of the one for the doings of the other, the fiery darts of Satan for the risings of the renewed heart, and often walks in gloom and dejection when he ought to be rejoicing in the visions of the unseen, in the blissful realisations of the risen life.

But this warfare between the powers of light and darkness, and consequent confusion of mind in the believer, will not always last, or be his experience for ever.

The world and the devil may deny the Sonship of the believer, and strive to retard his progress in the Divine life; this, however, is only what the believer is to expect, for he is warned to that effect, and for his encouragement he is told that greater is He that is for him than all they that are against him, and that all this opposition will be overruled for his highest good, "for all things work together for good to them that love God, the called according to His purpose;" "at the name of Jesus every knee shall bow, of things in heaven, and things in earth, and things under the earth, and every tongue shall confess that Jesus Christ is Lord, to the glory of God the Father." And in this acknowledgment of the Son, there will and must be the recognition of the Sonship of His brethren.

The Church of the first-born in heaven; the general assembly of the just made perfect, the great cloud of witnesses, the gathering together of all that is in the heavens above, and in the earth beneath, and under the earth, will these deny the Sonship of believers in Christ, or refuse to acknowledge the manifestation of any of the Sons of God? Surely not; they sympathise with them in their groanings, and aid them in their travailing in pain; they anxiously wait for the full display of the mystery, kept secret from the foundation of the world, to be given to all intelligences, and anticipate with joy the period when they shall behold the perfected Sonship of believers in the manifestation of the Sons of God.

But how can the Sonship of the believer in Christ be denied? Will it be disputed that the love, spirit, mind, and life of Christ are the true and unfailing elements of the Sonship; or will it be maintained that he who, by faith, has received Christ, and has Him in him the hope of glory, and who in the possession of Christ possesses these elements of the Sonship, has not the right and title to the Sonship? There is no denying of the Sonship in the consciousness of the Divine, in the consecration of all that is in the Father, Son, and Spirit; of all that is in the principalities and powers in heavenly places for the full development of the Sonship, for the bringing out into highest manifestation the glorious and blissful realisations of the Sonship.

What, then, is this Sonship of believers, this Sonship of which they only now receive the foretaste in its right, title, and privilege, by believing in Christ. What can it be but the oneness of love, spirit, mind, life, righteousness, glory, and joy with God's own

Son, the appearing with Him in glory, the reigning with Him in light, the realising with Him the consciousness of the Divine, the having the subjective human in a oneness with the subjective Divine. And what higher Sonship can the believer desire? What more illustrious condition of existence can he aspire to? To what nobler state of conscious being will he ever hope to ascend? What purer, more satisfying bliss is it possible for him to realise than the clear, deep, and uninterrupted consciousness of a oneness of love, spirit, mind, life, righteousness, glory, and joy with God's own Son in the completed manifestation of the Divine, the fullest disclosures of the subjective in God?

Is there in the possibilities of renewed humanity, capacity, and receptivity, for the full and complete indwelling of the Divine, is there in the renewed nature of man a susceptibility of his entering into a oneness with the Infinite and Eternal in the deep things of God? There is in the designs of Godhead a purpose of arraying the deathless spirit of humanity with the meekness and gentleness of Christ, of adorning the life of man with the dispositions, motives, and principles of the Incarnate One. The spirit of humanity can be made to glow with the same love which has fired the bosom of God Himself. There is in man's rational nature the possibility of his receiving the very ideas which have occupied the Infinite Mind itself; there is in the illimitable compass of the human soul a possibility of its being quickened with the very life of Him who is the

Living One who hath life in Himself, who only hath life and immortality; there is within the vast and interminable range of man's immortal spirit, the possibility of his being brought into such righted or readjusted relations as that his righteousness shall be one with that of the Son of God. There is the possibility of the regenerated life shining in the glory of Him who is the brightness of His Father's glory, in the splendour of Him whose effulgence dazzles created vision and lights up the coruscations of suns and systems. There is in the once agonised spirit in the sorrowing heart of the believer the possibility of His being gladdened with the joys of Him who has in Himself the well-springs of infinite and eternal bliss. And there is a desire cherished in the Father-heart, to animate the redeemed spirit with the consciousness of the Divine nature, the perfect life, the inexhaustible bliss of the subjective Divine. In the mysterious union with the Son, the believing soul can become one with Him in His conscious possession of all the fulness of God.

Here our philosophy and our faith diverge, and appear to be in contradiction, but this contradiction is only seeming; the explanation is, that faith rises into regions into which philosophy cannot ascend; love can comprehend what intellect cannot conceive of, ascending in the flight of fancy even within the sphere of reason. I can mount to illimitable heights, I can set no bounds to my onward progress in the future, I can conceive of no terminus to my advance in knowledge, to the development of my faculties, to the enlargement of my powers, to my reception of the Divine, to my assimilation to God. Neither reason nor philosophy can tell me how I may be filled with all the fulness of God, but faith assures me that in the Incarnation of the Son of God, the very Divine, the very Infinite, the very Eternal God is united with the very human in a oneness of personality, dwells in the very human in a oneness of life, and fills the very human with itself. In this fact—a fact indisputable to the believer—faith announces to me an infinite capacity in the human for the indwelling of the Divine, a boundless receptivity for the reception of the Infinite. Revelation declares to me that in Christ dwells the fulness of the Godhead bodily; revelation also assures me that the Spirit of God takes up His abode in man; and Christ Himself told His disciples that He and the Father will come and manifest Themselves in them that love Him.

Before these disclosures of revelation my mind falls in deepest prostration, and exclaims with the great apostle of the Gentiles: "O the depth of the riches both of the wisdom and knowledge of God! How unsearchable are His designs, and His ways past finding out! For who hath known the mind of the Lord? or who hath been His counsellor? Or who hath first given to Him, and it shall be recompensed to him again? For of Him, and through Him, and to Him, are all things: to whom be glory for ever and ever. Amen."

One torch communicates to another the same flame that burns in itself, and the very same idea dwells in the mind that receives it as dwells in the mind that imparts it; the parent begets the very same nature and life in the child that he possesses in himself. A believer in Christ can hardly be so sceptical as to reject the teachings of revelation because of the mysteries that are in them, or refuse to acknowledge the fact that there are mysteries in the Scripture; and no true believer can be so vain as to imagine that he can, in the brief period of his present state, comprehend the deeper depths of the things of God. Glory be to God because of the mysteries of His Word, and for the unfathomable depths of His redemption! The keenest analysis cannot detect the full life of the oak in the acorn; still it is there. Who, therefore, in opposition to the express testimony of Scripture, can maintain that believers cannot be made partakers of the "Divine Nature," or imagine that they can realise the fulness of the Divine life in the first quickenings of the Holy Ghost.

Well may it be said of the "Sons of God," that it doth not yet appear what we shall be, but we know that when He appears we shall be like Him, for "we shall see Him as He is." And well may the believer exclaim, "Eye hath not seen nor ear heard; neither can it enter into the heart of man to conceive the things that are laid up for them that love Him." For the believer has not yet already attained, neither is he already perfect, but he has the germ, the foretaste, the seal, the promise, and it is "the Father's good pleasure" to give him the kingdom; it is the determination of God that all His children shall be one in the fulness of their heavenly inheritance.

The time is approaching, all things are preparing, creation from her inner depths is heaving her inmost sigh of expectation, all nature is travailing in pain, together waiting for "the manifestation of the Sons of God." When Christ, the Infinite God, shall appear in the bright effulgence of His uncreated light, in the full splendour of His infinite majesty, then shall His brethren also appear with Him in glory, and they shall be like Him, for they shall see Him as He is; and then shall be exhibited a scene for which time might well prepare, for which also eternity might wait, and for which angels might hope and saints tarry, for which the Spirit of God Himself might make ready, and the Redeemer travail in the greatness of His strength, mighty to save; for then the deep mysteries of God will be clearly disclosed, and the unsearchable depths of sovereign grace fully displayed.

Now the Church is militant, then shall she be triumphant; now and here her salvation is but begun, then and there it will be complete; now on earth we have to hold fast the beginning of our confidence, then in heaven we shall receive the fulness of our inheritance; below, we see "but through a glass darkly;" above, "face to face;" on earth, we know but "in part;" in heaven, "we shall know" even as we are "known." In all this the disciple is as His Lord. Here He appeared as a humble, dying man;

there He shall be seen as the "great God" in glorious majesty; and when He shall appear in His glory, then shall the Sons of God be manifested with Him.

The revelation of the perfected project of the Infinite Mind shall then be displayed, and the conception of the Eternal Council which was devised before worlds began, made known. And then shall this redemption song of Jubilee be chanted with joyous hearts. And they sung as it were a new song, the song of Moses the servant of God, and the song of the Lamb, saying: "Great and marvellous are Thy works, Lord God Almighty; just and true are Thy ways, Thou King of Saints. Thou art worthy to take the book and to open the seals thereof, for Thou wast slain, and hast redeemed us to God by Thy blood, out of every kindred, and tongue, and people, and nation, and hast made us unto our God kings and priests. We give Thee thanks, Lord God Almighty, which art, and wast, and art to come, because Thou hast taken Thee Thy great power, and hast reigned. Even so, come, Lord God Almighty. Hallelujah, for the Lord God Omnipotent reigneth!"

CHAPTER XXII.

PERFECTION.

THE Saints of God have ever devoutly longed for perfection; and yet the most advanced among them are sadly conscious that they have not attained to it, that, on the contrary, they are very far from reaching it. Christ Jesus alone presents to us the model perfection of the Sonship, or pattern of Divine life in man. In Him alone we have a perfect example; and it is only in our endeavours perfectly to copy this example that we make any approach to the perfection for which we long, and which we see embodied in Him.

The perfection of Christ Himself consists in the reality of the incarnation, the fulness of the Divine indwelling, and the correspondence of His life, and being with the subjective and objective of His Father. And the perfection of His people can only be realised in their experience through their oneness with Him in spirit and life.

The Scripture doctrine on this point is clear and explicit. The Father and Son are indifferently set before believers as the goal towards which they are to press, and they are warned against being content with any lesser attainment. As for example, when Christ Himself says, "Be ye perfect even as your Father in heaven is perfect." And the apostle, after referring to Christ as a pattern, speaks of Him as being holy, harmless, and undefiled; and to the same purpose Paul exhorts believers to be followers of Christ as dear children. To the mind of the sacred penmen Christ Jesus is the perfection of all excellence, and in setting Him before us for our imitation, they show as clearly as it is in the power of language to do, that it is in following Him our chiefest excellence is to be realised.

The Father perfects humanity through coming into it in His Son. The Son perfects, glorifies, and blesses humanity in proportion as He is received by it; and for this He requires entire conformity to Himself. Were He to demand anything short of this, He would simply sanction defect in the disciple and do dishonour to Himself. The world spurns with contempt the demand of unqualified reception and complete conformity to the Son of God, and were it left to itself with all the grace of God in its view, it would not be benefited by His salvation. But the Spirit comes with the things that are Christ's, quickens the sinner, and prevails with him to yield himself up to God in the embrace of His Son. And as the sinner submits to God, he is "raised up into newness of life," and in proportion as he receives the spirit and mind of Christ is he perfect with Him in the Spiritual and Divine.

In yielding up to the strivings of the Spirit there

must be no halting between two opinions. In the fellowship of life with Christ there must be no dallying with temptation, no tampering with conscience, no conformity to the world. If there be not this unqualified reception of Christ, and entire surrender to Him, there *cannot* be perfection in the fellowship of Divine life. The believer realises perfection only *as* and in *the degree* in which he works out what the Spirit works in him, to will and to do of God's good pleasure.

In order, however, to this unqualified reception of Christ and complete conformity to Him, there must be supreme love felt for Him; He must be the greatest of all in the heart, the understanding, and the life. When Christ is thus embraced, the inner life is calm, consistent, and blissful, whatever may be the state of the outer. It was thus that Paul apprehended Christ, and herein lies the secret of his sublime Christian career. When arrested in his mad attempt to stifle the infant cause of Christianity, the apostle saw the glory of God and felt the power of His grace to such an extent as thoroughly to convince him of the supreme excellence of the person and work of Christ; from henceforth ardent love for the Risen Saviour sprung up within him; and through the grace thus shown to him, he became one of the pillars of the cause which he formerly sought to destroy. And he is to this day renowned as one of the greatest champions of Christianity.

Supreme love to Christ is, indeed, the one principle of Christian life, and until this is realised in the experience of the Church and the individual believer, there can be no perfection. Wheresoever there is felt any love superior to the love borne to Christ, there is an obstacle to the reception of Him.

This demand of Christ, however, of complete surrender to Himself, is not only necessary, it is also the wisest requirement which He could have made. It is not on His own account that the demand is made, but for the sake of His people. He asks of them the surrender of their entire life, that He may return it to them purer, loftier, and sweeter than when it is yielded up to Him. His own words are: "Verily I say unto you, there is no man that hath left house, or brethren, or sisters, or father, or mother, or wife, or children, or lands, for My sake and the Gospel's, but he shall receive an hundredfold now in this time houses, and brethren, and sisters, and mother, and children, and lands, with persecutions; and in the world to come, eternal life."

Whatever affection of our own rivals the love of Christ; whatever temper of our own restrains His Spirit; whatever notions of our own mingle with "the truth as it is in Jesus;" whatever motives of our own enter into the life; whatever joy is sought not in Christ; whatever relation is sustained unconsecrated in Him: these all tend to destroy fellowship with the Divine, they indicate imperfection in the life of the believer, and are defects in his faith. There must be, as has already been indicated, no holding back, but a complete self-surrender. The Holy Ghost must fill and consecrate every part of a believer's life, for whatever is assimilated in the inner life that is not of the Spirit of Christ, mars its beauty and hinders its perfection.

How glorious, then, is the perfection that awaits the believer; how godlike his destination, and where are the fancied incarnations, apotheosis or pantheistic conceptions (granting for a moment their reality), that can compare in grandeur and importance with this perfection of the human in the Divine. And yet this is the glorious consummation of humanity in the family of the Redeemed. With a view to this lofty exaltation, humanity was created in the image of God, gifted with its vast capacities, and favoured with its Divine susceptibilities; for this high perfection it has been preserved during the long career of its rebellious opposition to God; and to realise this wondrous indwelling, the Creator of all worlds condescended to become incarnate, lived among men on earth and died the accursed death of the cross, and ascended to the right hand of majesty on high; and for the perfect consummation of this indwelling God enters into the life, and thus the perfection of the being of man is secured.

The indwelling, however, which thus secures the perfection of humanity does not dim the glory of the Infinite Indweller, it only affords the fit opportunity to Jehovah to display the purest radiance of Divine perfection to created intelligence, and it furnishes at the same time the richest manifestation of eternal sovereign grace.

For this indwelling creation began in the remote epochs of eternity past, for this perfection providence

has evolved itself in the flight of ages, and for this
consummation redemption has displayed its surpassing
wonders. Let faith, then, in rapid flight, wing her way
back to the moment when first eternity recognised the
beginning of time, let her dwell in meditation on the
evolution of matter from its primeval chaos to its
bright and shining orbs, let her listen to the Almighty's
fiat, commanding light to spring out of darkness ; let
her view the Spirit brooding over chaos and putting
forth His forming skill, till paradise is beheld in all
the loveliness of its new-born charms, with its tenant
man, the crown and glory of creation; and what is
the wondrous majesty displayed to her view, but the
fit residence, the glorious temple of Divine majesty?
And from this vision let faith descend the stream of
time in the contemplation of the designs of infinite
wisdom, as manifested in the different dispensations
of God's providence, till arrested by the mysterious
Incarnation in the fulness of the times. And what
does she behold, but the brightest possible manifestation of God dwelling in man! Let her, then, look at
the sublime life of "God manifest in the flesh," and
gaze with reverence and awe on the dark scenes of
Gethsemane and Calvary, and then let her ascend in
wrapt contemplation of the glorious ascension on high,
and let her behold humanity in union with Divinity
array itself in the splendour of never-fading light,
lifting up the sceptre of universal dominion, and seat-
ing Himself at the right hand of Power, amid the
acclamations of the hosts of heaven ; then let her
return to earth with the descending Spirit at Pentecost

and witness His entrance into the eleven, filling them with grace and power; and, through their preaching of the everlasting Gospel, striving with sinners, converting them into saints and making them temples of God. Finally, let faith anticipate the end of the age, and fly with the speed of thought over the ages of millennial bliss, till arrested by the trump of the Archangel, she beholds the flame of the universal conflagration, the destruction of the sinful earth, the rolling together the scroll of the heavens, polluted by their gaze on a sinful world; let her witness the rising of the resurrection body in likeness to the glorious body of the Son of God; let her anticipate the events of the judgment of the world, and see the "house of many mansions," the final and complete display of the Divine to created vision in "the manifestation of the Sons of God," the presentation of the redeemed "in the presence of God's glory with exceeding joy; and what will faith, in giving place to sight, see but the glory of the redeemed "made perfect in One," the unity of the general assembly and Church of the firstborn, the oneness of the family of God in Christ, the completed indwelling of God in man.

Then, and then only, shall be known the meaning of that profound and mysterious utterance, "I in them, and Thou in Me, that they may be perfect in One."

How mysterious a being is man! how momentous the interest of the soul, and how awful the guilt of degrading human nature, and neglecting the privileges conferred on us by God; and how inconceivable the infatuation of rejecting Christ! Reader, beware! The tiny threads of the spider's web twined around the bud withstands nature's power to free it; thus imprisoned there is neither blossom nor fruit. In like manner, simple neglect of the Gospel will for ever ruin the soul!

CHAPTER XXIII.

DUTY AND RATIONALE OF PRAYER.

As already indicated, the main condition under which man is quickened with the Divine life is the yielding up of himself to the Spirit of God working faith in him. And having attained to this, the condition of his after progress in the Divine life, is his praying "always with all prayer and supplication in the Spirit." Our Lord says, "If ye abide in Me, and My words abide in you, ye shall ask what ye will and it shall be done unto you."

Prayer is the hunger of the soul after God, a craving brought about by the Holy Spirit. It is the coming in desire to God. The opening up of the capacities of the soul for the reception of the gracious communication of the Divine. It is the coming to God the Father through the Son and by the Spirit in the fellowship of the manifestations which He has given of Himself. It is the asking for the grace necessary to this assimilation in the assurance that if we ask we shall receive; hence the earnestness with which Christ enjoins the duty of prayer on His disciples, "I say unto you, Ask, and it shall be given you; seek, and ye shall find; knock, and it shall be opened unto you: for every one that asketh receiveth, and he that seeketh findeth, and to him that knocketh it shall be opened;" hence, also, the powerful argument with which He enforces the duty, "If a son ask bread of any of you that is a father, will he give him a stone? or if he ask a fish, will he for a fish give him a serpent? or if he ask an egg, will he offer him a scorpion? If ye then, being evil, know how to give good gifts unto your children, how much more shall your Heavenly Father give the Holy Spirit to them that ask Him."

Absolute independence belongs to the Infinite God alone. All creatures are dependent directly or indirectly on God. "In Him we live, move, and have our being," and the more complex the nature, the more clearly can we trace its dependence. The animate needs more than the inanimate, rational life more than mere animal existence, and spiritual being needs most of all. Hence man stands in need of aid in every department of his tripart nature, but needs most for his spiritual life, as being the nearest approach of the finite life to the Infinite. Other lives may be maintained by God indirectly, for anything we know to the contrary, but spiritual life must be upheld by Him directly, for spiritual life is that which constitutes its possessor, the proper subject of union and communion with God, and it is that through which God communicates Himself to, and holds fellowship with, His offspring.

The immutability of the Creator is the ground of

the creature's entire confidence in Him. Were the Almighty capricious or changeable, He could not be the proper object of confidence to His creatures. This immutability consists in the unchangeableness of His nature, purposes, and principles of combination, but not in the unchangeableness of His manifestations, modes of operation, or forms of combination. If there were no diversity in the manifestations of the Divine, and the operations of the Godhead, there would be no sphere for the display of Infinite wisdom; and if there were no unity in the principle of Divine action, there could be no ground for the exercise of trust in God, on the part of the creature.

Every species of life is sustained by its own proper kind of nourishment, and is never sustained or preserved in a state of health by anything else. Animal life is sustained by material food, rational life by an intellectual diet, and spiritual life by "the bread of life" which came down from above. Animal life cannot be sustained on intellectual food, rational life cannot be sustained by animal food, nor spiritual life by rational food; each in order to health and vigour must have its own proper mother aliment.

In the fertility of the soil, God has furnished man with the means of procuring for himself an abundance of food for his bodily life; in the facts and operations of nature there is an inexhaustible store of food for the rational life of man; and in God Himself, as brought near to us in His grace, there is supplied to us a boundless store of provision for the soul. To obtain a proper supply of food for the sustenance of his body, man must cultivate the soil; to obtain a supply of food for the support of his rational life, he must acquaint himself with the principles of truth as set before him in the works and Word of God; and to obtain a proper supply of food for the life of God in the soul, he must wait on God in the contemplation of His grace, "praying always, with all prayer and supplication in the spirit." In these several departments we must diligently use the appointed means, or go without the requisite supply of nourishment, and in consequence languish and ultimately perish from starvation. Others may obtain food for us, but they cannot eat for us our portion of it; this we must do for ourselves. Others may collect information for us, but it must be comprehended by ourselves. Others may by supplication and prayer obtain for us the blessing of God, but they cannot appropriate for us our portion of " the Bread of Life."

Man is taught by nature, revelation, and experience to pray. If he understands the constitution of his being, he will not only perceive that prayer is in perfect accordance with that constitution, and the condition of the Divine life in his soul, but he will also find that in certain circumstances he cannot but pray. In these circumstances, in which nature utters her own voice, he will learn from his own experience that he cannot but pray. Let a man by any sudden emergency be thrown into a danger that threatens to engulf him in ruin, and whether he be atheist, infidel, or Christian, he will feel impelled by the instincts of his nature to pray; his soul, constrained by her inner convictions, will irresistibly rise in supplication to God.

Man is also taught by revelation, Christ by His example teaches him to pray, the Father by promise and entreaty urges him to pray, and the experiences of Spiritual life lead him in the same direction. When the soul in the outgoings of faith and love rises in desire after God, and opens the deep cavities of his inner being to the reception of the Divine that she may enjoy closer fellowship with God, then does the believer realise that there is a power in prayer; that God by His Spirit, in answer to his longing desire, descends into the soul and fills it with the joys of His salvation as He ravishes it with the bliss of His indwelling presence. And when we carefully study the events of God's providence in the movements of our lives, we clearly perceive that there is a power in prayer, and feel constrained with the disciples to say, "Lord, teach us how to pray."

Yet some men are reluctant, and refuse to pray, on the ground that they can see no connection between prayer and the events of everyday life. Nay, some even go further, and deny that there can be any connection between these things. But in doing so, they display an amazing amount of ignorance, not to speak of impiety. All men grant that there is a connection between the cultivation of the soil and an abundant harvest, and, therefore, they till the ground. All men admit that there is a connection between the study of nature and the growth of the human mind in knowledge. But because they do not see the connection between prayer and its answer, they deny that there is any such connection. Now were it even so that we could see no connection between prayer and its answer, and could at the same time see clearly every link in the connection of cause and effect in the physical and mental progress of man, this would be no solid objection to prayer. Much less would it justify us in refusing to do what, as we have seen, Nature herself prompts us to, what God Himself expressly commands us to do, and what the experience of spiritual life urges and encourages us to do.

It would seem, therefore, that in this objection to prayer, there is both too much expected on the one hand, and too much assumed on the other. The truth is, that in natural causation, the connection is no more seen than is the connection in Divine causation; strictly speaking, the connection in both is one, and in urging upon men the duty of prayer, much might be urged on the plea that prayer is the language of faith and not of sight, and much might be made of the fact that we are commanded by God to pray, and that, therefore, on the simple principle of recognising the authority of God, "men ought always to pray," and further, that it is irrational and impious, because we see no connection between prayer and its answer, to refuse to pray. But waiving these grounds, let us look at the objection more closely, and see if it be really as valid as its supporters would have us to believe.

Nature, as is well known, has not as yet revealed

to us every link in the chain of cause and effect. Science cannot explain to us the nexus which binds the cause to its effect; it has not as yet conducted us through all the departments of Nature's workshop, nor shown to us the entire process of all her fabrications, nor led us into the knowledge of all the qualities of every element of matter, and all the relations which do subsist, or may subsist, among them, and how she combines her forces in bringing about this or that result. Science cannot throw all the light we desiderate on the connection which subsists between means and end, nor can it show us the bond which binds together the different atoms of matter, nor tell us what are the simple elements or elementary forces of matter, and how they operate in harmonious or discordant combinations. It cannot lay bare the connection which subsists between mind and matter—how matter influences mind, and mind acts on matter, or how spirit acts on spirit, and operates in mind.

If the physical laws, about the immutability of which we hear so much now-a-days, be such as to preclude the very possibility of answer to prayer, and make it absurd for us to pray with any prospect of receiving an answer, will those who thus speak explain to us the cause of the variations which are ever taking place in the lives of individual men, or in the movements of Divine providence?

If all events happen in accordance with an eternal law of matter, how is it that no two results in chemical experiment, in the operations of nature, or in the actions of man, turn out alike? We would not thus deny the existence of eternal and immutable principles, by no means; and here, if we mistake not, lies the solution of the difficulty which presses in connection with material laws.

Law is nothing more than the mode or invariable manner in which certain forces, in certain combinations, act. And as forces are dependent on atoms, and the relations in which the atoms stand to each other severally, the mode in which the forces act cannot be eternal, but the principle of their operation is, and must be, eternal, viz., that the exact same forces, in the exact same relation to each other, or in the exact same combination, will ever be found to produce the exact same result.

It is involved in the very idea of cause and effect that the effect depends on the cause, the end on the operation of the powers in combination, the action on the will of the actor. It is one of the first teachings of reason that an end cannot be looked for but through the employment of the means, that effect cannot proceed but from an adequate cause, and that like causes must ever produce like effects. Whence, then, the variety which we find all around us in the operations of nature, and in mind and spirit? Philosophy cannot explain these varieties on its principle of immutable law, nor can philosophers, by clinging to this doctrine, ever reach an adequate explanation of the variety referred to. Can, however, the principle involved in the doctrine of prayer throw any light on this important subject? Let us humbly inquire if it can.

The object chiefly sought in prayer is the progress of the kingdom of God in the hearts of men individually and in the world. Prayer is the asking of God to regulate the events of His providence by the operations of His Spirit, so that the soul of the petitioner may be assimilated to God; it is the asking of God to conform all lives to the pattern of His Son's life, and to regulate the movements of His providence and the operations of nature, so as to subserve this end. This request involves two things, viz., God's agency in combination, or His control over the operations of nature; and the giving of His Spirit to influence subordinate agents, so as to lead them to co-operate with Himself. And in this there is nothing inconsistent with the character of God, the co-operation of subordinate agency, or the operations of nature.

We speak of forces and of agents, we speak of particles of matter as possessed of energy and capacity, and thus we conceive of the negative and positive forces. If one atom is brought into contact with another, the energy in the one will unite with the energy in the other, or repel it; and thus there will be an increase of force, or a decrease, as the case may be. And thus, power in matter is not uncontrolled, but dependent on the combination of atoms in which it resides; and every combination of atoms requires the action of one or more agents, and a plurality of agents involves a subordination, and, as a result, a supreme actor or ultimate combinator. These we may postulate as primary beliefs.

The forces inherent in elements continue ever the same, and differ only in their mode of operation; but this difference in the mode of operation is the result of difference of their combination, and is no alteration of their nature. The proper idea, then, of causation, is the order observed in combination, and the immutable law of physical nature is merely the necessity of the forces combined, to act in accordance with the principle of their combination. Combine so many elements possessed of certain characteristics, and you will have, as often as you make the combination, the same result. Alter in the least the mode of the combination, either in the number of the elements or in the order of their arrangement, and you have a corresponding alteration in the result. Combine so many agencies of the same nature to act in the same manner, and you will have the same result as often as you make the combination. Alter the combination in the number or order of the agents, and to that extent you will have a change in the result.

We know of nothing on which to ground the idea that the Almighty has subjected Himself to any principle or law of combination which excludes Him from the free exercise of His function as Supreme Combinator, and if He has reserved to Himself, as doubtless He has, the right of the free exercise of the power of combination in connection with all His creatures, has He not done this in perfect harmony with the nature He has given to them, and the principles of His righteous administration? And it is surely conceivable that whenever He pleases He may make any combination to bring about whatever result in nature, providence, or redemption which may seem good to Him, whether in answer to prayer or otherwise. It is surely not a wild idea to suppose that God has so arranged the principles of His government, that prayer shall form an element of power in the combinations of causation. As already indicated it is clear from the nature of man that he is formed to pray, and as all Christians hold, experience shows that God does answer prayer. It is, moreover, demonstrable—we hold from the entire history of mankind—that God has in His providence over man constituted prayer an element in causation. All history, in fact, proves that asking is a means to an end; every page that records the deeds of men or nations shows that the most important events, which have taken place in the providence of God, have been brought about through the instrumentality of asking. Yes, events the most unlikely to occur in the ordinary course of nature have been brought about through the power of asking. What, *e.g.*, secured the deliverance of Rome, when every other means failed, but the urgent prayer of the mother and wife of Coriolanus! What rescued the Jewish nation from the destruction which the crafty malice of Haman had prepared for it, but the petitioning of Esther! What, again, was the prevailing element in bringing about the death of our Lord when Pilate was anxious to let

Him go, but the urgent request of the rulers, and the loud cries of the Jewish mob.

Volumes might be written on the things which have taken place in answer to requests made. The principle of petition we maintain enters largely into, and acts powerfully among, the elements of causation; indeed, it would be difficult to find another so general in the relations, and influential in the movements of human life. What we are to guard against is, not the idea that prayer acts in the movements of life, but the supposition that the principle of petition acts alone irrespective of or in opposition to the other elements of causation, a means necessary to an end.

Now, if God has assigned so prominent a position and influence to the principle of petition among the doings of His creatures, is it not unreasonable to affirm that He has reserved to Himself no power of being influenced thereby. It would, indeed, be strange if God has constituted man so that in certain circumstances he must pray to his Father, but that his Father has so tied up His own hands by physical laws that He cannot hear and answer the cry of His dutiful child. There is something almost monstrous in the thought that the power of petition moves man in every sphere and circumstance of his life, but that it can have no influence with God. If God has reserved to Himself the supreme power in every combination, and has constituted prayer an element of causation, it will take far weightier reasons than have yet been advanced to persuade the unprejudiced mind that when man acts in accordance with the promptings of his nature and the command of God, God can in no wise act so as to secure an answer to that prayer; and all because, forsooth! certain philosophers will have it that physical law is unalterable. Surely the unbelief that, on this ground, refuses to see how prayer can be answered is far more credulous than is the most unassuming of all those who believe and pray, because in their simplicity they expect that God will hear and answer their cry.

Physical law, as already indicated, is nothing else than the necessity that like combinations shall produce like effects. Now, is this any obstacle to the answering of prayer? On the contrary, it is rather a guarantee that prayer can be answered. If every effect in physical science be what it is by the presence or absence of this, that, or the other element of combination, then the presence or absence of an element must affect the result. And, in point of fact, the history of man illustrates the truth of this position, for the most trivial as well as the mightiest and most important events in human history have been influenced by petition, and have been brought to pass at the same time, in entire accordance with the operations of universal law.

Reader, acquaint yourself with all the results of petition. Go to the selfish, parsimonious, and grudging creature, man; get from him by petition what otherwise you would not receive, and obtain it in perfect accordance with the law of his nature, and the ordinary principles of his conduct. And, then, realise the deep promptings of your own inner being, beckoning your desires Godward, forget not the commands and encouragements He has given you to pray, but, ah! request not anything of Him, lest you grieve and vex His Spirit, by reminding Him of the folly and weakness of interlacing Himself with immutable laws to such an extent that He cannot take any notice of the requests addressed to Him, in compliance with His own commands. Oh, spare the tenderness of His heart, the melting compassion of His love, lest you cause Him to repent that He has so interlaced Himself with immutable physical laws, that, although His children cry unto Him, and His own bowels yearn over them because of their wretchedness, He is yet wholly helpless to aid them in the very least, or to move in accordance with the desire of His heart.

But it would appear that we are mistaken in attributing care and minute attention to God, for the all-important discovery of the new philosophy is, that "God does not take up His attention with small, but only with great matters." The Great God not taking up His attention with small matters! What, we ask, are small or great matters to Him? Does He not from the minute advance to the vast? His conceptions of small and great are not like ours. Is He not every day proving to us that we can form no proper estimate of small and great? He is ever showing us that what we suppose to be small or trivial often turns out to be that which has folded up in it the most important and lasting results, which affect deeply the entire lives of those connected with it;

the wellbeing of communities and the destiny of nations. How conspicuously is this truth seen in what are regarded as small sins. And, on the other hand, how often do we find that what we have looked forward to as of great importance, passes away as a shadow of a dream! We dare not thus limit God, who is found to be equally present and careful in the formation of the insect's wing and in the creation of a planet or an entire solar system.

And this wonderful announcement that "God does not take up His attention with the small but only with great matters," is pompously given forth as the great discovery of the enlightened wisdom of the age. But every tyro knows that such nonsense is only the resurrection of the epicurean dream, the dictum of ancient sceptics found in the writings of the sophists, and as old as the delusions of Satan. We have only to study the record of the ancient schools to meet with this very doctrine, which in these days is given forth with the most oracular assurance to the youth assembled for the study of that volume—every page of which teaches them to pray. Not to speak of the intelligence, wisdom, and piety, where, we would ask, is the kindness of the professor to his students, or of the minister to his people, who would perplex and harass them by teaching such views to the youth or the congregation, convened for the study of the doctrines of Him who taught that the providence of God extended even to the numbering of the hairs of our head, and to the observing of the fall of a sparrow; and who taught that if man, even though selfish, knows how to give good gifts unto his children, our heavenly Father is much more inclined to give good things to them that ask Him; and who not only taught His disciples to pray, but Himself spent whole nights in prayer on the cold mountain slopes.

In comparison with the dogma referred to, it is not only more scriptural, but also far more philosophical, to instruct students of theology and congregations of worshippers that God is everywhere present through all His works, and that while His nature is unchangeable, His modes of operation are ever so changing that no two of His acts are precisely alike, and from this to teach them that there is nothing so variable as the phenomena of Divine Providence, or the operations of physical law, but that these variations in the phenomena of physical law do not happen from any change in the principles of the Divine administration, but simply from a difference in the nature, number, or order of the elements in combination. It is both scriptural and philosophical to believe that Jehovah, sitting on the circle of the universe, can at any time send forth an influence through all the ranks of being, and thereby affect the elements and agents of His government in such a way as to secure in perfect harmony with the nature of His creatures any event He may desire to bring about. Or, if there be no existing power to accomplish His end, He can when He chooses create such a power.

If God has established a subordinate order of

agencies and powers, it takes no great stretch of imagination to regard Him as accomplishing through them whatever He pleases, and also as doing this in answer to the prayers of His dutiful children.

There are more things in nature than philosophy has ever dreamed of; and the great vice of the disciples of unbending physical law is the assumption, that because physical nature does not lay God bare before their eyes in His being and working, therefore, it is questionable as to whether He exists at all; or, if He does exist, whether He has anything to do with the affairs of men; and as they deal with God, so they also deal with all matters in any way supposed to be connected with Him. The Spiritual is relegated into the background, and the physical set prominently forward.

It is an easy matter for such persons, though not very philosophical, to deny what believers have always affirmed, viz., that matter and mind are wholly different substances though compatible substances, and that the former is subordinate to the latter. It is also easy to deny all Satanic as well as Divine influence. As, for example, when it is said that Satan brought about the ruin that overtook the patriarch Job, it is easy we say to deny this, because that it is all explicable on natural grounds, but it is not, therefore, an evidence of wisdom. Our position is that mind, angelic, human, or demoniac, has power over matter, and, God permitting, can form new combinations, and bring about new results good and bad. It is neither so foolish nor unphilosophical as the disciples of physical law seem to fancy the assertion, viz., that the angel of death may blow in the face of the enemy as he passes through their midst, and that the angel of the Lord encamps round about them that fear Him, and that all is done in accordance with the principles of universal law.

The utmost efforts of the ablest and most consistent advocates of immutable physical law fail to satisfy us that the different prohibitions and commands of God to these different orders of spiritual agents have no connection with the prayers of His people. Or, that the prayers of one individual have no influence on the destiny of another. Nothing which they have to advance can shake intelligent confidence in the belief that the petitions of one age have a bearing on the condition of another. The upholders of invariable physical law cannot show us that trivial matters in themselves, but mighty in their results, may not have had some connection with prayer. Such, *e.g.*, as the glance of Bruce's eye to the repeated efforts of the spider when his case seemed hopeless, the awakening of Luther's desire in his cell to turn over the pages of his Bible; or the impression on the mind of Columbus that a continent lay embedded in the western waters.

But, still, it is urged that the particular answer to prayer involves a miracle, and what if it should? Miracles are not impossible to the Hearer of Prayer. If the Gospels are trustworthy records, apart even from inspiration, miracles occurred in answer to the prayers addressed to Christ. But let those who make the assertion show that what they say is true, and how a miracle is involved in bringing about the particular event supposed to happen in answer to prayer. Are not events happening every moment that would never have happened but for the asking of them? And does the occurrence of these involve a miracle? No one will assert that it does. If, then, God has granted to His creatures the power of answering the requests of one another without the working of miracles, or the infringement of any physical law, why are we so strongly urged to believe that He cannot Himself answer the petitions of His children without working miracles and infringing laws? Surely it is a strange delusion to suppose that God is more restricted than man is—a hallucination that can only be explained on the ground that men do not like to retain God in their thoughts.

Still men will cling to the idea that miracles are necessarily involved in answering prayer, and we must try to meet them on their own ground. Such persons, we fear, have not formed to themselves clear conceptions of what a miracle is; probably some of them regard a miracle as an impossibility, inasmuch as it in some way involves a contradiction. Then, if the answering of prayer necessitated anything of this sort, we would join with them in the belief that prayer cannot be answered. Probably others among them look upon a miracle as an infringement of the laws of nature, which are the laws of God; then do we also agree with these, that if the answering of prayer necessitated any such infringement, it could not be answered. If, however, a miracle be regarded as the communicating of an additional power to the functions of nature, or even the creating of a new power to effect a new and hitherto unheard-of result, then one or other, or both of them, are possible, and have in point of fact occurred, *e.g.*, in the incarnation of the Son of God, and the regeneration of the soul of man. But these also are denied by some men who are not ashamed to call themselves Christian.

The existence of sin, however, we think, will not be denied; if not, then, let all such persons look into its nature, and they will perceive that it is an infringement of law; for it is "the transgression of the law," the derangement of moral harmony and physical function. The sinfulness of man is a grievous discord introduced among the principles of his spiritual being and life, and this fact of sin is stronger than any miracle known to us in its violation of all law and order. In the sense indicated, viz., the violation of law, sin is one of the most dreadful of all possible miracles, and does it become a creature, who in his every-day life experiences the sad effects of sin, to object to prayer on the ground that its answer involves an infringement of physical law!

The conclusion, then, at which we arrive is this, viz., that it enters into the original constitution of things, that God should give certain blessings when these are asked for in prayer, and withhold them when not sought thus; further, that an instinct has been implanted in man which prompts him to make his wants known in prayer to his Father in heaven.

A difficulty, no doubt, here arises, inasmuch as God is the Supreme Judge of right and wrong; and as we have broken His laws, and stand before Him as rebellious sons, it is needful in some way that this matter should be met, and the difficulty overcome. With this object in view, a new power has been introduced into the government of God, and as we have seen, this new power is the atonement of Christ which harmonises the manifestations of God with the wants of men and the requirements of law. And, now, in order to lead man to pray, the Holy Ghost has been sent to plead with him, and the gospel of the grace of God in Christ has been published abroad, in which gospel men are entreated and commanded to pray, and the most precious promises are held out with a view to encourage men to engage in the exercise.

Am I, therefore, not to pray, because some men are disposed to imagine that the answering of prayer involves a miracle, a some wonderful infringement of physical law? Am I really to believe that by sinning, I can derange the functions of my whole nature, and disturb the harmony of Divine government, and refuse to pray, because certain philosophers have a vague idea in their minds about the infringement of physical laws? Am I not rather to believe that it is the will of God that I should pray? Am I to believe that He has so ordered matters in connection with my salvation that the very first step in my return to God shall be the utterance of prayer? Am I, we say, to believe all this, and yet be deterred from praying to God because of a vague inference drawn by some men that an answer to my prayer violates physical law? Good God! on what are the hearts of men bent in their idolatrous worship and insane jealousy on behalf of physical law?

Scriptural views of prayer do not lead us to imagine that physical law is plastic in the hands of men, by no means; but they do lead us to the belief that by means of these very laws in all their rigidity and invariableness, God works out the good pleasure of His will in harmony with the nature of His creatures, and the principles of His administration.

Another objection to prayer is, that it is presumptuous for a creature like man to think that God will listen to his requests, or interfere with the movements of nature on his behalf. This objection, like most others, arises out of mistaken notions about the nature and purpose of God, and His doings in connection with man. From His omniscience, He cannot but listen to the requests of every man, and observe the motions of every soul. And it is just as easy for Him to arrange the movements and guide the operations of nature so as to answer the petitions of His children, as it is delightful to Him to listen to their prayers.

God is not a being of limited resources, dealing out His gifts with a grudging, or even sparing hand; but the Father of Spirits, glad to impart of His own fulness to His offspring, man. And in all the plenitude of His being He has made Himself the treasure of their soul, He has created humanity receptive of Himself, the temple of His holy habitation; and it is His delight to bestow, with all the generosity of His being, His fulness on man; and His gifts in no degree impoverish Himself. Look at His unspeakable gift, the Son of His love, the brightness of His glory, and the express image of His person. And is it presumption on the part of those who profess to have received this gift to ask for anything else the Father hath to bestow? To all such persons no argument comes home with greater force than that used by Paul, when, with irresistible power, he urges: "He that spared not His own Son, but gave Him up to the death for us all, how shall He not with Him also freely give us all things."

The end of all God's dealings in creation, providence, and redemption, is to produce the filial heart in man; and if so, can there be anything too great for the Son to ask, or for the Father to bestow?

CHAPTER XXIV.

CONCLUSION.

THE whole of God's dealing with man from first to last has been, as indicated, with a view to impart to him the highest nature, and to place within his reach the highest development which finite existence is capable of reaching. And in the carrying out of this purpose man's relation of being and life are indefinitely multiplying, and his capacities are being unfolded in the most glorious manner. God is begetting sons in His own image, and revealing Himself to them as their "Father in heaven."

In all creation's work there is nothing grander than man. The mechanism of his body is perfect, more perfect than any machine ever devised, and nothing can transcend his rational and spiritual existence; humanity of all natures known to us has entered into a oneness of life, and even personality with the Divine. And in the redemption of man God is not only displaying the highest perfection of His own being, but developing the capacities and powers of humanity, and is calling man into the Sonship, and leading him into the inner circle of His own immediate fellowship.

Man, however, in order to the attainment of this end, must work out what God works in him. The function of the body is to work out what the soul works in it, nothing more and nothing less; and the Spirit's function is to work out what the Spirit of God works in it, nothing more and nothing less. In this outworking the perfection of being and the harmony of life is realised. Man is blessed only in fellowship with God, and the work of bringing him into this fellowship is the work which God has emphatically made His own, and in the accomplishment of it He is showing forth His glory.

In everything, however, that appertains to this work, the believer should carefully bear in mind that he is only an under builder, working out what God by His Spirit works in him. He should never lose sight of the fact, that it is the prerogative of the Holy Ghost to work within him, "both to will and to do of God's good pleasure." The great mistake of the disciple in all ages, has been to loose sight of this one fundamental principle. One of the first public blunders which the twelve fell into was the forbidding of one to cast out devils because he followed not with them; a regard to formal ends, and a leaning to human opinions and authority, has been an error of the disciples all along, instead of sitting at the feet of Jesus, and learning the law from His lips, and desiring above all things to be conformed to Him. The first twelve were ever clinging to their own notions, and endeavouring to bring Christ over to their likings, ideas, and ends. The undivided looking to the

Saviour, the unqualified reception of Him, and the depending upon Him alone for salvation, has been the one difficulty of the quickened, and partially sanctified on earth, and this is still the folly and weakness of the Church below.

It shall not, however, be thus in heaven, for there the disciple shall be raised far above such folly, the saint, both in his external circumstances and internal condition, shall then be perfect in knowledge, in purity, and in strength; here he sees but "through a glass darkly," "he knows but in part," but there "he shall see face to face, and know even as he is known." Revelation, here, unlike the noonday sun, which completely chases away the darkness of the night, is rather like the midnight star, which, while it discloses itself, tends only to make the surrounding darkness the more palpable. Revelation not only tells us of a darkness within it, but also makes known to us a darkness without; it tells us of things which lie beyond the reach of reason's discovery, and far remote from the sphere of our present power of investigation. It also tells us of truths, which, while beyond the reach of our present comprehension, are truths in the knowledge of which our highest interest are deeply involved, and truths which, while we remain in our present state, can never be adequately known by us.

But in the world to come our present limitations shall cease to clog our powers, the clouds and darkness which now surround us shall all be dispelled in the light of God's countenance, and we shall be perfect in love and knowledge; for, possessed of a capacity for knowledge boundless as space, and of powers capable of indefinite expansion, the believer will be able to contain in his comprehensive grasp not only adequate ideas of all worlds, but a complete acquaintance with all created essences, and, scanning not only the surface but penetrating into the inmost recesses of things, the glorified son shall be acquainted with all the possibilities of creation, as well as with all the actualities, and shall rise to the perfect knowledge of the divine wisdom and goodness of God as displayed in the works of His all-creating hand. And most of all, interested in redemption's glorious achievement, the son will surpass the angels in his knowledge of the things which they even now earnestly desire to look into, and advancing to all but absolute knowledge of the being and perfections of the Eternal God, as displayed in the highest of all His works, beholding the divine love in all but the infinitude of its grace, the divine mercy in the boundless riches of its majesty and grandeur; nor resting here, but in the full consciousness of the filial heart admitted into the immediate presence of the "Father of Spirits," holding uninterrupted communion with the Eternal Jehovah, and standing in the nearest relation to the unveiled Three, the son in glory will obtain the highest knowledge of the divine essence, perfection, and work to which created nature can attain.

And what shall be the bliss of that vision? If, even here, amid the imperfections of the present state, the perception of divine wisdom and goodness is found to impart a pure delight, and the knowledge of God in Christ, to afford a transporting joy, what must be the emotion produced by the cloudless vision of Jehovah's glory, and the untainted purities of the perfect state? What must be the ravishing ecstasy of the redeemed soul perfected in the image of God, when, all but absolute in his grasp, he shall survey the entire fabric of creation, and comprehend the beauty of God's perfect and complete design, and when, worshipping in the temple not made with hands, he shall behold the Father enthroned on the necessity of His own existence, and radiant in the glory of His own uncreated essence?

Yet, desirable and blessed as knowledge is, it is only after all a means to an end, and this end is holiness, the perfection of nature and life. There are attainments in heaven on which the heart of the glorified son shall be more intent than even knowledge. The son knows that beyond the grave he shall no longer bewail his imperfect purity, for there he shall be bright with the transcript of the Divine Image, and pure as the spotless resemblance of God. The son knows he shall then be no longer the subject of contending passions, torn and distracted with the motions of sin. No longer exposed to the disturbing influences of the wicked one; no longer surrounded by objects which withdraw his attention from the divine, and lead him to forgetfulness of God; no longer within the reach of diabolic hate, but in heaven itself, the region of perfection and bliss.

The son shall then realise obedience to be as spontaneous as the perennial spring, and delightsome as the overflowing of gratitude. Fully delivered from evil of every kind, washed with all the cleansing efficacy of redeeming blood, and wholly sanctified by the Spirit of God, he shall dwell in the immediate presence of the Father, and bask for ever in the smile of His love.

If even on earth amid the remains of imperfection the son realises the joys of holiness to be delightful, and if the anticipation of its full realisation above thrills the soul, and wafts the spirit of the believer in transports of joy to the realms of bliss, what shall be the ravishing ecstasy of the believer's delight when completely delivered from all imperfections, from sin and all its consequences, he shall behold the face of God in righteous bless?

In heaven the saint shall be strong in "the grace that is in Christ Jesus," "strengthened with all strength in the inner" and outer man he shall for ever reign with imperial power over all evil. Here the saint is feeble and frail, he halts too often in moments of temptation, and hesitates at times between self and God; but in heaven he shall be strong in the possession of a renewed and wholly sanctified nature. Perceiving the possibilities and results of all actions, and acting in entire harmony with the ends, and in perfect concord with the agencies appointed by God in the full energy of the conscious rectitude of his doing, in bringing about new combinations, the son shall accomplish glorious results and send thrills of delight to creation's utmost bounds. Immortal in his nature, all-discerning in his knowledge, all-righteous in his principles, all-beneficent in his designs, all-divine in his volitions, there can be no conflict or restraint in his acting. What, then, must be the conscious delight of the son in the full enjoyment of his strength above?

The believer may be unknown to the world and disregarded by it in the glorious work of assimilating his life to the divine. As his Lord was so is he in the world. But in the kingdom of God, as a prince in the court of his Father, the son shall occupy the loftiest position, and shall be fully appreciated as one of those for whose sake the universe was called into being, and on whose behalf the highest powers and perfections of Godhead have been displayed. As a King and Priest unto God, the believer shall closely resemble his Elder Brother, the Incarnate One, the King of Glory.

While on earth the believer is often denied the society of the illustrious and learned, from whom he could learn many things; but in heaven he shall mingle with the most illustrious, and occupy a position higher than the angelic host; he shall meet with the virtuous of all ages, and hold intercourse with the loftiest orders of existence; he shall company with all the great and good who have gone before him, and may yet follow after him; he shall enjoy their society and commune with them on all that can occupy their thoughts and delight their hearts; and above all, he shall enjoy uninterrupted communion with Father, Son, and Holy Ghost.

If, then, the love of distinction and the consciousness of dignity be natural to man's immortal being, what shall be the pure satisfaction and delight of the son when he becomes fully conscious of his true dignity and high distinction in His Father's house above? No heart on earth can comprehend the joy and delight of such a realisation. Oh, then, what shall be the emotions of the ransomed soul when first it awakens to the consciousness of the felicities of the life above, and finds itself in the immediate presence of the Eternal God, beholding His unveiled glories, and sharing in the full participation of that glory which the Eternal Son has received from His Everlasting Father, as the reward of His obedience unto death, ever worshipping with extasy and delight, ever studying with adoring wonder the mysteries of redeeming love, and conscious that all is of free sovereign grace! What must be the enrapturing beatitude of the immortal soul, as ever and anon, in adoring gratitude, it casts its crown before the throne, ascribing "blessing, and honour, and glory, and power, unto Him that sitteth upon the throne," as they all with one united heart and voice exclaim, "Not unto us, but unto Thy name, be the glory."

> "A word reached me stealthily,
> And my ear heard a whisper thereof
> In the play of thought: in the visions of the night,
> When deep sleep falleth on men,
> Fear came upon me, and, trembling,
> And it caused the multitude of my bones to quake with fear,
> And a breathing passed over my face,
> The hair of my flesh stood up.

It stood there and I discerned not its appearance,
An image was before mine eyes,
A gentle murmur and I heard a voice :
Is mortal man just before Eloah,
Or a man pure before his Maker ?'

" Thou hast gone up on high,
Thou hast captivated captivity,
Thou hast acquired gifts for men,
Yea, even rebels may become the dwelling of Jehovah God."

"I in them and Thou in Me, that they may be made perfect in one, and that the world may know that Thou hast sent Me, and hast loved them, as Thou hast loved Me."

THE END.

Catalogues of American and Foreign Books Publish'd or Imported by MESSRS. SAMPSON LOW & CO. can be had on application.

CROWN BUILDINGS, 188, FLEET STREET, LONDON,
October, 1876.

A List of Books

PUBLISHING BY

SAMPSON LOW, MARSTON, SEARLE, & RIVINGTON.

ALPHABETICAL LIST.

Ablett (H.) Reminiscences of an Old Draper. 1 vol. small post 8vo, cloth, 2s. 6d.

Abney (Captain W. de W., R.E., F.R.S.) Thebes and its Five Greater Temples. 40 large permanent Photographs of Egypt, with descriptive Letterpress. Super royal 4to, cloth extra, 3l. 3s.

About in the World. See The Gentle Life Series.

Adventures in New Guinea. The Narrative of the Captivity of Louis Trégane, a French Sailor, for Nine Years among the Savages in the Interior. Small post 8vo, with Illustrations and Map, cloth gilt, 6s.

Adventures of Captain Mago. A Phœnician's Explorations 1000 years B.C. By LEON CAHUN. Numerous Illustrations. Crown 8vo, 10s. 6d.

Adventures of a Young Naturalist. By LUCIEN BIART, with 117 beautiful Illustrations on Wood. Edited and adapted by PARKER GILLMORE. Post 8vo, cloth extra, gilt edges, new edition, 7s. 6d.

Adventures on the Great Hunting-Grounds of the World, translated from the French of VICTOR MEUNIER, with Engravings, 2nd edition, 5s.

Alcott (Louisa M.) Aunt Jo's Scrap-Bag. Square 16mo, 2s. 6d. (Rose Library, 1s.)

—— *Cupid and Chow-Chow.* Small post 8vo, 3s. 6d.

—— *Little Men: Life at Plumfield with Jo's Boys.* Small post 8vo, cloth, gilt edges, 2s. 6d. (Rose Library, 1s.)

—— *Little Women.* 2 vols., 2s. 6d. each. (Rose Library, 2 vols., 1s. each.)

—— *Old Fashioned Girl,* best edition, small post 8vo, cloth extra, gilt edges, 3s. 6d. (Rose Library, 2s. 6d. and 1s.)

—— *Work. A Story of Experience.* New Edition. 1 vol., small post 8vo, cloth extra, 6s. Several Illustrations. (Rose Library, 1s.)

—— *Beginning Again.* A Sequel to "Work." 1s.

—— *Shawl Straps.* Small post 8vo, cloth gilt, 3s. 6d.

—— *Eight Cousins, or the Aunt Hill.* Small post 8vo, with Illustrations, 5s.

—— *Silver Pitchers, and other Stories.* 1 vol., crown 8vo, 10s. 6d. Smaller and cheaper edition in the press.

A

Alexander (Sir James E.) Bush Fighting. Illustrated by Remarkable Actions and Incidents of the Maori War. With a Map, Plans, and Woodcuts. 1 vol., demy 8vo, pp. 328, cloth extra, 16s.

All the Way Round. What a Boy saw and heard on his Way round the World. Small post 8vo, cloth extra, with Illustrations, 7s. 6d.

Andersen (Hans Christian). Fairy Tales. With Illustrations in Colours by E. V. B. Royal 4to, cloth, 1£ 5s.

Andrews (Dr.) Latin-English Lexicon. 13th edition. Royal 8vo, pp. 1670, cloth extra, price 18s.

Anecdotes of the Queen and Royal Family, collected and edited by J. G. Hodgins, with Illustrations. New edition, revised by J. Timbs. 5s.

Animals Painted by Themselves. Translated from the French of Balzac, Louis Baude, G. Droz, Jules Janin, Georges Sand, E. Lemoine, &c., with upwards of Two Hundred Illustrations from the vignettes of Grandville. [*In the press.*

Assollant (A.) The Fantastic History of the Celebrated Pierrot. Written by the Magician Alcofribas, and translated from the Sogdien by Alfred Assollant, with upwards of One Hundred humorous Illustrations by Yan' Dargent. Square crown 8vo, cloth extra, gilt edges, 7s. 6d.

Backward Glances. Edited by the Author of "Episodes in an Obscure Life." Small post 8vo, cloth extra, 5s.

Bancroft's History of America. Library edition, vols. 1 to 10, 8vo, 6£.

Barrington (Hon. and Rev. L. J.) From Ur to Macpelah; the Story of Abraham. Crown 8vo, cloth, 5s.

THE BAYARD SERIES.

Comprising Pleasure Books of Literature produced in the Choicest Style as Companionable Volumes at Home and Abroad.

"We can hardly imagine better books for boys to read or for men to ponder over."—*Times.*

Price 2s. 6d. each Volume, complete in itself, flexible cloth extra, gilt edges.

The Story of the Chevalier Bayard. By M. D. Berville.

De Joinville's St. Louis, King of France.

The Essays of Abraham Cowley, including all his Prose Works.

Abdallah; or, The Four-leaved Shamrock. By Edouard Laboullaye.

Table-Talk and Opinions of Napoleon Buonaparte.

Vathek: An Oriental Romance. By W. Beckford.

The King and the Commons: a Selection of Cavalier and Puritan Song. Edited by Prof. Morley.

Words of Wellington: Maxims and Opinions of the Great Duke.

Bayard Series (*continued*) :—

Hazlitt's Round Table. With Biographical Introduction.

The Religio Medici, Hydriotaphia, and the Letter to a Friend. By Sir THOMAS BROWNE, Knt.

Ballad Poetry of the Affections. By ROBERT BUCHANAN.

Coleridge's Christabel, &c. Preface by A. C. SWINBURNE.

Lord Chesterfield's Letters, Sentences and Maxims. With Introduction by the Editor, and Essay on Chesterfield by M. De Ste.-Beuve, of the French Academy.

Essays in Mosaic. By THOS. BALLANTYNE.

My Uncle Toby. Edited by P. FITZGERALD.

Reflections; or, Moral Sentences and Maxims of the Duke de la Rochefoucauld.

*Socrates, Memoirs for English Readers from Xeno*phon's Memorabilia. By EDW. LEVIEN.

Prince Albert's Golden Precepts.

Rasselas, Prince of Abyssinia. By DR. JOHNSON.

Beauty and the Beast. An Old Tale retold, with Pictures. By E. V. B. Demy 4to, cloth extra, novel binding. 10 Illustrations in Colours (in same style as those in the First Edition of "Story without an End"). 12s. 6d.

Bees and Beekeeping. By the Times' Beemaster. Illustrated. Crown 8vo. New Edition with additions, 2s. 6d.

Beumer's German Copybooks. In six gradations at 4d. each.

*Bickersteth (Rev. E. H., M.A.) The Reef, and other Para*bles. One Volume square 8vo, with numerous very beautiful Engravings, 7s. 6d.

———— *The Master's Home-Call; or, Brief Memorials* of Alice Frances Bickersteth. 19th Thousand. 32mo, cloth gilt, 1s.
 "They recall in a touching manner a character of which the religious beauty and warmth and grace almost too tender to be definite."—*The Guardian.*

———— *The Shadow of the Rock.* A Selection of Religious Poetry. 6th Thousand. 18mo, cloth extra, 2s. 6d.

———— *The Clergyman in his Home.* Small post 8vo, 1s.

———— *The Shadowed Home and the Light Beyond.* By the Rev. E. H. BICKERSTETH. Third Edition. Crown 8vo, cloth extra, 5s.

Bida. The Authorized Version of the Four Gospels. With the whole of the magnificent Etchings on Steel, after the drawings by M. Bida. The Gospels of St. Matthew, St. John, and St. Mark, appropriately bound in cloth extra, price 3l. 3s. each, are ready. (St. Luke in preparation.)
 "Bida's Illustrations of the Gospels of St. Matthew and St. John have already received here and elsewhere a full recognition of their great merits. To these is now added the Gospel of St. Mark, which is in every respect a fitting pendant to its predecessors. By next season we are promised the complete series."—*Times.*

Bidwell (C. T.) The Balearic Isles. Illustrations and Map, 10s. 6d.

———— *The Cost of Living Abroad.* Crown 8vo, cloth, 6s.

Black (Wm.) Three Feathers. Small post 8vo, cloth extra, 6s. Sixth Edition.

———— *Lady Silverdale's Sweetheart, and other Stories.* 1 vol., crown 8vo, 10s. 6d.

———— *Kilmeny: a Novel.* Small post 8vo, cloth, 6s.

———— *In Silk Attire.* 3rd Edition, small post 8vo, 6s.

———— *A Daughter of Heth.* 13th and Cheaper Edition, crown 8vo, cloth extra, 6s. With Frontispiece by F. Walker, A.R.A.

Blackburn (H.) Art in the Mountains: the Story of the Passion Play, with upwards of 50 Illustrations. 8vo, 12s.

———— *Artists and Arabs.* With Illustrations, 8vo, 7s. 6d.

———— *Harz Mountains: a Tour in the Toy Country.* With numerous Illustrations, 12s.

———— *Normandy Picturesque.* Illustrations, 8vo, 16s.

———— *Travelling in Spain.* Illustrations, 8vo, 16s.

———— *Travelling in Spain.* Cheap Edition, 12mo, 2s. 6d.

———— *The Pyrenees.* Summer Life at French Watering-Places. 100 Illustrations by GUSTAVE DORÉ. Royal 8vo, 18s.

Blackmore (R. D.) Lorna Doone. New Edition. Cr. 8vo, 6s.
"The reader at times holds his breath, so graphically yet so simply does John Ridd tell his tale."—*Saturday Review.*

———— *Alice Lorraine.* 1 vol., 8vo., 6s. Sixth Edition.

———— *Clara Vaughan.* Revised Edition, 6s.

———— *Cradock Nowell.* New Edition, 6s.

———— *Cripps, the Carrier.* Crown 8vo, cloth extra, 6s.

———— *Georgics of Virgil.* Small 4to, 4s. 6d.

Blackwell (E.) Laws of Life. New Edition. Fcp., 3s. 6d.

Blandy (S.) The Little King. 64 Illustrations. Imperial 16mo, cloth extra, gilt edges, 7s. 6d.

Bombaugh (C. C.) Gleanings for the Curious from the Harvest Fields of Literature. 8vo, cloth, 12s.

Book of Common Prayer with the Hymnal Companion. 32mo, cloth, 9d. And in various bindings.

Bosanquet (Rev. C.) Blossoms from the King's Garden. By the Vicar of Christ Church, Folkestone.

Bowker (G.) St. Mark's Gospel. With Explanatory Notes. For the Use of Schools and Colleges. By GEORGE BOWKER. Fcap., cloth.

Bradford (Wm.) The Arctic Regions. Illustrated with Photographs, taken on an Art Expedition to Greenland. With Descriptive Narrative by the Artist. In 1 vol., royal broadside, 25 inches by 20, beautifully bound in morocco extra, price Twenty-Five Guineas.

Brett (E.) Notes on Yachts. Fcap., 6s.

Bristed (C. A.) Five Years in an English University. Fourth Edition, Revised and Amended by the Author. Post 8vo, 10s. 6d.

Broke (Admiral Sir B. V. P., Bt., K.C.B.) Biography. 1l.

Bryant (W. C., assisted by S. H. Gay.) A Popular History of the United States. 4 vols., profusely illustrated with numerous Engravings on Steel and Wood. Super-royal 8vo, cloth extra, gilt top. Vol. I. ready, 42s.

Burritt (E.) Ten Minutes' Talk on all sorts of Topics. With Autobiography of the Author. Small post 8vo, cloth extra, 6s.

Burton (Captain R. F.) Two Trips to Gorilla Land and the Cataracts of the Congo. By Captain R. F. BURTON. 2 vols., demy 8vo, with numerous Illustrations and Map. Cloth extra, 28s.

Butler (W. F.) The Great Lone Land; an Account of the Red River Expedition, 1869-1870, and Subsequent Travels and Adventures in the Manitoba Country. With Illustrations and Map. Fifth and Cheaper Edition. Crown 8vo, cloth extra, 7s. 6d.

——— *The Wild North Land:* the Story of a Winter Journey with Dogs across Northern North America. Demy 8vo, cloth, with numerous Woodcuts and a Map. Fourth Edition, 18s. Crown 8vo, 7s. 6d.

——— *Akim-foo: The History of a Failure.* Demy 8vo, cloth, 16s. Second Edition. Also a Third and Cheaper Edition, 7s. 6d.

Cadogan (Lady A.) Illustrated Games of Patience. By the Lady ADELAIDE CADOGAN. 24 Diagrams in Colours, with Descriptive Text. Foolscap 4to, cloth extra, gilt edges, 12s. 6d. Third Edition.

Cahun (Leon). See Adventures of Captain Mago.

Case of Mr. Lucraft, and other Stories. By the Authors of "Ready-Money Mortiboy." 2 vols., crown, 21s.

Changed Cross (The), and other Religious Poems. 2s. 6d.

Child's Play, with 16 coloured drawings by E. V. B. 7s. 6d.

Chiushingura; or, The Loyal League. A Literary Curiosity. A Japanese Romance. Translated by FREDERICK V. DICKINS. With 30 Full-page Illustrations, Drawn and Engraved by Japanese Artists, and Printed by Japanese Printers. One vol., oblong 8vo, Japanese binding, over 200 pages, price 16s.

Choice Editions of Choice Books. 2s. 6d. each. Illustrated by C. W. COPE, R.A., T. CRESWICK, R.A., F. DUNCAN, BIRKET FOSTER, J. C. HORSLEY, A.R.A., G. HICKS, R. REDGRAVE, R.A., C. STONEHOUSE, F. TAYLER, G. THOMAS, H. J. TOWNSHEND, E. H. WEHNERT, HARRISON WEIR, &c.

Bloomfield's Farmer's Boy.
Campbell's Pleasures of Hope.
Coleridge's Ancient Mariner.
Goldsmith's Deserted Village.
Goldsmith's Vicar of Wakefield.
Gray's Elegy in a Churchyard.
Keat's Eve of St. Agnes.
Milton's L'Allegro.
Poetry of Nature. Harrison Weir.
Rogers' (Samuel) Pleasures of Memory.
Shakespeare's Songs and Sonnets.
Tennyson's May Queen.
Elizabethan Poets.
Wordsworth's Pastoral Poems.

Classified Educational Catalogue of Works, A, published
in Great Britain. Demy 8vo, cloth extra, second edition, greatly revised, 5s.

Cook (Dutton) A Book of the Play. Two vols., crown 8vo, 21s.

Craik (Mrs.) The Adventures of a Brownie. By the Author of "John Halifax, Gentleman." With Illustrations, cloth extra, gilt edges, 5s.

Cumming (Miss C. F. G.) From the Hebrides to the Himalayas; Eighteen Months' Wanderings in Western Isles and Eastern Highlands. By Miss CONSTANCE F. GORDON CUMMING, with very numerous Woodcut Illustrations, from the Author's own Drawings. 2 vols., medium 8vo, cloth extra, 42s.

Cummins (Maria S.) Haunted Hearts (Low's Copyright Series). 16mo, boards, 1s. 6d.; cloth, 2s.

Dana (R. H.) Two Years before the Mast and Twenty-four Years After. Copyright Edition, with Notes and Revisions. 12mo, 6s.

——— *(Jas. D.) Corals and Coral Islands.* Numerous Illustrations, Charts, &c. Crown 8vo, cloth extra, 8s. 6d.

Daughter (A) of Heth. By WM. BLACK. Crown 8vo, 6s.

Davies (Wm.) The Pilgrimage of the Tiber, from its Mouth to its Source. 8vo, with many Illustrations and Map, cloth extra, 18s.

Davies (Wm.) A Fine Old English Gentleman, Exemplified in the Life and Character of Lord Collingwood; a Biographical Study. By WILLIAM DAVIES. 1 vol., cloth extra, crown 8vo, cloth extra, 6s.

Doré's Spain. See Spain.

Dougall (J. D.) Shooting; its Appliances, Practice, and Purpose. *See* Shooting.

English Catalogue of Books (The), published during 1863 to 1871 inclusive, comprising also the Important American Publications.
This Volume, occupying over 450 pages, shows the Titles of 32,000 New Books and New Editions issued during Nine Years, with the Size, Price, and Publisher's Name, the Lists of Learned Societies, Printing Clubs, and other Literary Associations, and the Books issued by them; as also the Publishers' Series and Collections—altogether forming an indispensable adjunct to the Bookseller's Establishment, as well as to every Learned and Literary Club and Association. 30s. half-bound.
*** The previous Volume, 1835 to 1862, of which a very few remain on sale, price 2l. 5s.; as also the Index Volume, 1837 to 1857, price 1l. 6s.

——— *Supplements,* 1863, 1864, 1865, 3s. 6d. each; 1866, 1867, to 1875, 5s. each.

——— *Writers, Essays on. See* Gentle Life Series.

——— *Matrons and their Profession.* By M. L. F., Writer of "My Life, and what shall I do with it." Crown 8vo, cloth, 7s. 6d.

——— *Painters of the Georgian Era.* Hogarth to Turner. Biographical Notices. Illustrated with 48 permanent Photographs, after the most celebrated Works. Demy 4to, cloth extra, 18s.

Erckmann-Chatrian. Forest House and Catherine's Lovers. Crown 8vo, 3s. 6d.

———— *The Brothers Rantzau:* A Story of the Vosges. 2 vols., crown 8vo, cloth, 21s. 1 vol., profusely Illustrated, cloth extra, 5s.

Evans (C.) Over the Hills and Far Away. By C. Evans, Author of "A Strange Friendship." Crown 8vo, cloth extra, 10s. 6d.

———— *A Strange Friendship.* Crown 8vo, cloth, 5s.

E. V. B.'s Beauty and the Beast. See Beauty and the Beast.

Faith Gartney's Girlhood. By the Author of "The Gayworthys." Fcap., with Coloured Frontispiece, 3s. 6d.

Few (A) Hints on Proving Wills. Cloth, 1s.

Fields (J. T.) Yesterdays with Authors. Cr. 8vo, 10s. 6d.

Flammarion (C.) The Atmosphere. Translated from the French of Camille Flammarion. Edited by James Glaisher, F.R.S. With 10 Chromo-Lithographs and 81 Woodcuts. Royal 8vo, cloth extra, bevelled boards, 30s.

Fogg's (W. P.) Arabistan: or, the Land of "The Arabian Nights." Being Travels through Egypt, Arabia, and Persia to Bagdad. By W. P. Fogg, M.A. Demy 8vo, with numerous Illustrations, cloth extra, 14s.

Fool of the Family, and other Tales. By John Dangerfield. 2 vols., crown 8vo, 21s.

Forbes (J. G.) Africa: Geographical Explorations and Christian Enterprise, from the Earliest Times to the Present. By J. Gruar Forbes. Crown 8vo, cloth extra, 7s. 6d.

Forrest (John). Explorations in Australia; being Mr. John Forrest's Personal Accounts of his Journeys. 1 vol., demy 8vo, cloth, with several Illustrations and 3 Maps, 16s.

Forrest (R. W.) Gleanings from the Pastures of Tekoa. By Robert William Forrest, M.A., Vicar of St. Jude's, South Kensington. Small post 8vo, 260 pp., cloth extra, 6s.

Franc (Maude Jeane). Emily's Choice. An Australian Tale. 1 vol., small post 8vo. With a Frontispiece by G. F. Angas, 5s.

———— *Hall's Vineyard.* Small post 8vo, cloth, 4s.

———— *John's Wife.* A Story of Life in South Australia. Small post 8vo, cloth extra, 4s.

———— *Marian; or, the Light of Some One's Home.* Fcp. 3rd Edition, with Frontispiece, 5s.

———— *Silken Cords and Iron Fetters,* 4s.

Franc (Maude Jeane). Vermont Vale. Small post 8vo, 5s.

—— *Minnie's Mission.* Small post 8vo, 4s.

Friswell (Laura) The Gingerbread Maiden; and other Stories. With Illustrations. Square cloth, 3s. 6d.

Garvagh (Lord). The Pilgrim of Scandinavia. By LORD GARVAGH, B.A. 8vo, cloth extra, with Illustrations, 10s. 6d.

Gentle Life (Queen Edition). 2 vols. in 1. 8vo, 10s. 6d.

THE GENTLE LIFE SERIES.

Printed in Elzevir, on Toned Paper, handsomely bound, forming suitable Volumes for Presents. Price 6s. each; or in calf extra, 10s. 6d.

The Gentle Life. Essays in aid of the Formation of Character of Gentlemen and Gentlewomen. Tenth Edition.
"Deserves to be printed in letters of gold, and circulated in every house."—*Chambers' Journal.*

About in the World. Essays by the Author of "The Gentle Life." Fifth Edition.
"It is not easy to open it at any page without finding some handy idea."—*Morning Post.*

Like unto Christ. A New Translation of the "De Imitatione Christi" usually ascribed to Thomas à Kempis. With a Vignette from an Original Drawing by Sir Thomas Lawrence. Second Edition.
"Could not be presented in a more exquisite form, for a more sightly volume was never seen."—*Illustrated London News.*

Familiar Words. An Index Verborum, or Quotation Handbook. Affording an immediate Reference to Phrases and Sentences that have become embedded in the English language. Second and enlarged Edition.
"The most extensive dictionary of quotation we have met with."—*Notes and Queries.*

Essays by Montaigne. Edited, Compared, and Annotated by the Author of "The Gentle Life." With Vignette Portrait. Second Edition.
"We should be glad if any words of ours could help to bespeak a large circulation for this handsome attractive book."—*Illustrated Times.*

The Countess of Pembroke's Arcadia. Written by Sir PHILIP SIDNEY. Edited, with Notes, by the Author of "The Gentle Life." Dedicated, by Permission, to the Earl of Derby. 7s. 6d.
"All the best things in the Arcadia are retained intact in Mr. Friswell's edition."—*Examiner.*

The Gentle Life. Second Series. Seventh Edition.
"There is not a single thought in the volume that does not contribute in some measure to the formation of a true gentleman."—*Daily News.*

Varia : Readings from Rare Books. Reprinted, by permission, from the *Saturday Review, Spectator,* &c.
"The books discussed in this volume are no less valuable than they are rare, and the compiler is entitled to the gratitude of the public."—*Observer.*

The Silent Hour: Essays, Original and Selected. By the Author of " The Gentle Life." Third Edition.
" All who possess ' The Gentle Life ' should own this volume."—*Standard.*

Essays on English Writers, for the Self-improvement of Students in English Literature.
" To all (both men and women) who have neglected to read and study their native literature we would certainly suggest the volume before us as a fitting introduction."—*Examiner.*

Other People's Windows. By J. HAIN FRISWELL. Second Edition.
" The chapters are so lively in themselves, so mingled up with shrewd views of human nature, so full of illustrative anecdotes, that the reader cannot fail to be amused."—*Morning Post.*

A Man's Thoughts. By J. HAIN FRISWELL.

Half-Length Portraits. Short Studies of Notable Persons. By GIBSON CRAIG. Small post 8vo, cloth extra, 6s.

Getting On in the World; or, Hints on Success in Life. By WILLIAM MATHEWS, LL.D. Small post 8vo, cloth boards, 2s. 6d.; superior binding, 3s. 6d.

Gouffé. The Royal Cookery Book. By JULES GOUFFÉ. Translated and adapted for English use by ALPHONSE GOUFFÉ, Head Pastrycook to Her Majesty the Queen. Illustrated with large plates, printed in colours. 161 Woodcuts. 8vo, cloth extra, gilt edges, 2l. 2s.
—————— Domestic Edition, half-bound, 10s. 6d.
" By far the ablest and most complete work on cookery that has ever been submitted to the gastronomical world."—*Pall Mall Gazette.*

—————— *The Book of Preserves; or, Recipes for Preparing* and Preserving Meat, Fish salt and smoked, Terrines, Gelatines, Vegetables, Fruits, Confitures, Syrups, Liqueurs de Famille, Petits Fours, Bonbons, &c., &c. 1 vol., royal 8vo, containing upwards of 500 Receipts and 34 Illustrations, 10s. 6d.

—————— *Royal Book of Pastry and Confectionery.* By JULES GOUFFÉ, Chef-de-Cuisine of the Paris Jockey Club. Royal 8vo, Illustrated with 10 Chromo-lithographs and 137 Woodcuts, from Drawings from Nature by E. MONJAT. Cloth extra, gilt edges, 35s.

Gouraud (Mdlle.) Four Gold Pieces. Numerous Illustrations, small post 8vo, cloth, 2s. 6d. See also Rose Library.

Gower (Lord Ronald). Handbook to the Art Galleries, Public and Private, of Belgium and Holland. 18mo, cloth, 5s.

—————— *The Castle Howard Portraits.* 2 vols. Folio, cloth extra, 6l. 6s.

Greek Testament. See Novum Testamentum.

Green (H. W.) Walter Lee; a Story of Marlborough College. 2 vols., crown 8vo, 21s.

Guillemin (A.) The World of Comets. Translated and Edited by JAMES GLAISHER, F.R.S. Numerous Coloured and other Illustrations. Super-royal 8vo, cloth extra.

Guizot's History of France. Translated by ROBERT BLACK. Royal 8vo. Numerous Illustrations. In 5 volumes, cloth extra, each 24s.

A 3

Guizot's History of England. In 3 volumes of about 500 pp. each, containing 60 to 70 full-page and other Illustrations, cloth extra gilt, 24s. each. [*In the press.*]

Guyon (Mdme.) Life. By UPHAM. Crown 8vo, 6s.

——— *A Short Method of Prayer and Spiritual Torrents.* Translated from the French of Mdme DE LA MOTHE GUYON. 12mo, cloth extra, 2s.

Guyot (A.) Physical Geography. By ARNOLD GUYOT, Author of "Earth and Man." In 1 volume, large 4to, 128 pp., numerous coloured Diagrams, Maps, and Woodcuts, price 10s. 6d., strong boards.

Hacklander (F. W.) Bombardier H. and Corporal Dose; or, Military Life in Prussia. Translated from the German. Crown 8vo, cloth 5s.

Hale (E. E.) In His Name. A Story of the Dark Ages. Small post 8vo, cloth, 3s. 6d.

Hall (S. P.) Sketches from an Artist's Portfolio. See Sketches.

——— *Tour of the Prince of Wales.* See RUSSELL.

Hall (W. W.) How to Live Long; or, 1408 Health Maxims, Physical, Mental, and Moral. By W. W. HALL, A.M., M.D. Small post 8vo, cloth, 2s. Second Edition.

Hans Brinker; or, the Silver Skates. An entirely New Edition, with 59 Woodcuts. Square crown 8vo, cloth extra, 7s. 6d.

Hazard (S.) Santo Domingo, Past and Present; with a Glance at Hayti. With upwards of 150 beautiful Woodcuts and Maps, chiefly from Designs and Sketches by the Author. Demy 8vo, cloth extra, 18s.

——— *Cuba with Pen and Pencil.* Over 300 Fine Woodcut Engravings. New Edition, 8vo, cloth extra, 15s.

Hazlitt (W.) The Round Table. (Bayard Series.) 2s. 6d.

Heber's (Bishop) Illustrated Edition of Hymns. With upwards of 100 Designs engraved in the first style of Art. Small 4to, 7s. 6d.

Heginbotham (Henry). Stockport: Ancient and Modern. In Five Parts, containing 120 pages, and many full-page Illustrations. 10s. 6d. each.

Henderson (A.) Latin Proverbs and Quotations. With Translations and Parallel Passages, and a copious English Index. By ALFRED HENDERSON. Fcap. 4to, 530 pp., 10s. 6d.

Hitherto. By the Author of "The Gayworthys." New Edition, cloth extra, 3s. 6d. Also in Low's American Series, double vol., 2s. 6d.

Hofmann (Carl). A Practical Treatise on the Manufac- ture of Paper in all its Branches. Illustrated by 110 Wood Engravings, and Five large Folding Plates. In 1 vol., 4to, cloth, about 400 pp., 3l. 13s. 6d.

Holland (Dr.) Kathrina and Titcomb's Letters. See Rose Library. Boards, 1s.

——— *Mistress of the Manse,* 2s. 6d. See also Rose Library.

Holmes (Oliver W.) The Guardian Angel. See Rose
Library.
────── *Songs in Many Keys.* Post 8vo, 7s. 6d.
────── *Mechanism in Thought and Morals.* 12mo, 1s. 6d.
Horace (Works of). Translated literally into English
Prose. By C. Smart, A.M. New Edition, 18mo, cloth, 2s.
Horsley (C. E.) A Text-Book of Harmony. For Schools
and Students. Small post 8vo, cloth.
Hugo (Victor). "Ninety-Three." Illustrated, crown 8vo, 6s.
────── *Toilers of the Sea.* Crown 8vo, 6s.; fancy boards.
2s.; cloth, 2s. 6d.; Illustrated Edition, 10s. 6d.
Hunt (Leigh) and S. A. Lee. Elegant Sonnets, with Essay
on Sonneteers. 2 vols., 8vo, 18s.
────── *Day by the Fire.* Fcap., 6s. 6d.
Hutchinson (Thos.) Summer Rambles in Brittany.
Illustrated, cloth extra, 10s. 6d.
Hymnal Companion to Book of Common Prayer. Edited
by the Rev. E. H. Bickersteth, Vicar of Christ Church, Hampstead.

The following is a List of the Editions :— s. d.
No. 1. A Small-type Edition, medium 32mo, cloth limp 0 6
No. 1. B   ditto   roan limp, red edges 1 0
No. 1. C   ditto   morocco limp, gilt edges . . . 2 0
No. 2. Second-size type, super-royal 32mo, cloth limp 1 0
No. 2. A   ditto   roan limp, red edges 2 0
No. 2. B   ditto   morocco limp, gilt edges . . . 3 0
No. 3. Large-type Edition, crown 8vo, cloth, red edges . . . 2 6
No 3. A   ditto   roan limp, red edges 3 6
No. 3. B   ditto   morocco limp, gilt edges . . . 5 6
No. 4. Large-type Edition, crown 8vo, with Introduction and
    Notes, cloth, red edges. 3 6
No. 4. A   ditto   roan limp, red edges 4 6
No. 4. B   ditto   morocco, gilt edges 6 6
No. 5. Crown 8vo, with accompanying Tunes to every Hymn,
    New Edition 3 0
No. 5. A   ditto   with Chants 4 0
No. 5. B The Chants separately 1 6
No. 5. C Large Edition. Tunes and Chants 7 6
No. 6. Penny Edition.
    Fcap. 4to. Organists' Edition. Cloth, 7s. 6d.

The Church Mission Hymn Book. 120 Hymns for Special
Missions and Schoolroom Services. Price 8s. 4d. per 100, or 1½d. each.
*** *Clergymen introducing the Hymnal are allowed Special Terms.*
An 8 pp. prospectus sent post free on application.
☞ The Book of Common Prayer, bound with the Hymnal Companion. 32mo,
cloth, 9d. And in various superior bindings.
The Hymnal Companion is also sold, strongly bound
with a Sunday School Liturgy, in two sizes, price 4d. and 8d.
Illustrations of China and its People. By J. Thomson,
F.R.G.S. Being Photographs from the Author's Negatives, printed in permanent
Pigments by the Autotype Process, and Notes from Personal Observation. 4 vols.,
imperial 4to, each 3l. 3s.

Jacquemart (J.) History of the Ceramic Art. Descriptive and-Analytical Study of the Potteries of all Times and of all Nations. By ALBERT JACQUEMART. 200 Woodcuts by H. Catenacci and J. Jacquemart. 12 Steel-plate Engravings, and 1000 Marks and Monograms. Translated by Mrs. BURY PALLISER. In 1 vol., super-royal 8vo, of about 700 pp., cloth extra, gilt edges, 42s.

Kennan (G.) Tent Life in Siberia. Third Edition, 6s.

Kennedy (Capt. W. R.) Sporting Adventures in the Pacific. With Illustrations, demy 8vo, 18s.

Kerkadec (Vicomtesse de). Madeleine. 2 vols., cr. 8vo, 21s.

King (Clarence). Mountaineering in the Sierra Nevada. Crown 8vo. Third and Cheaper Edition, cloth extra, 6s.

Kingston (W. H. G.) Snow-Shoes and Canoes; or, the Early Days of a Fur-Hunter in the Hudson's Bay Territory. With numerous Illustrations. Imperial 16mo, cloth gilt, 7s. 6d.

Koldewey (Capt.) The Second North German Polar Expedition in the Years 1869-70, of the Ships "Germania" and "Hansa," under Command of Captain Koldewey. Edited by H. W. BATES, Esq. Numerous Woodcuts, Maps, and Chromo-lithographs. Royal 8vo, cloth extra, 1l. 15s.

Lang (Dr. J. D.) An Historical and Statistical Account of New South Wales, from the Founding of the Colony in 1788 to the present day. By JOHN DUNMORE LANG, D.D., Senior Minister of the Scotch Church, Sydney. Fourth Edition. In 2 vols., crown 8vo, cloth extra, 1l. 1s.

Leared (A.) Morocco and the Moors. Being an Account of Travels, with a general Description of the Country and its People. By ARTHUR LEARED, M.D. With Illustrations, 8vo, cloth extra, 18s.

Leavitt (Professor J. M.) New World Tragedies.

Le Duc (Viollet Le). How to build a House. Numerous Illustrations, Plans, &c. Medium 8vo, cloth, gilt edges, 12s.

—— *Annals of a Fortress.* Numerous Illustrations and Diagrams. Demy 8vo, cloth extra, 15s.

—— *The Habitations of Man in all Ages.* 103 Illustrations. Translated by B. BUCKNALL, Architect. 8vo, cloth extra, 16s.

—— *Lectures on Architecture.* Translated by B. BUCKNALL, Architect. In 2 vols., royal 8vo, 3l. 3s.

—— *On Restoration.* With a Notice of his Works in connexion with the Historical Monuments of France, by CHARLES WETHERED. Crown 8vo, with a Portrait on Steel of Viollet le Duc, cloth extra, 2s. 6d.

Lessing's Laocoon: an Essay upon the Limits of Painting and Poetry, with Remarks illustrative of various Points in the History of Ancient Art. By GOTTHOLD E. LESSING. A New Translation. Crown 8vo, cloth extra, 5s.

Lindsay (W. S.) History of Merchant Shipping and Ancient Commerce. Over 150 Illustrations, Maps, and Charts. In 4 vols., demy 8vo, cloth extra. Vols. 1 and 2, 21s. each ; vols. 3 and 4, 24s. each ; 4 vols., 4l. 10s. "Another standard work."—*The Times.*

Little Preacher. 32mo, 1s.

Locker (A.) The Village Surgeon. A Fragment of Autobiography. Crown 8vo, cloth, New Edition, 3s. 6d.

Long (Col. C. Chaillé). Central Africa.—Naked Truths of Naked People: an Account of Expeditions to Lake Victoria Nyanza and the Mabraka Niam-Niam, West of the White Nile. Demy 8vo, numerous Illustrations, 18s.

Low's German Series—
1. THE ILLUSTRATED GERMAN PRIMER. Being the easiest Introduction to the Study of German for all Beginners. 1s.
2. THE CHILDREN'S OWN GERMAN BOOK. A Selection of Amusing and Instructive Stories in Prose. Edited by Dr. A. L. MEISSNER, Professor of Modern Languages in the Queen's University in Ireland. Small post 8vo, cloth, 1s. 6d.
3. THE FIRST GERMAN READER, for Children from Ten to Fourteen. Edited by Dr. A. L. MEISSNER. Small post 8vo, cloth, 1s. 6d.
4. THE SECOND GERMAN READER. Edited by Dr. A. L. MEISSNER. Small post 8vo, cloth, 1s. 6d. (*In preparation.*)

Buchheim's *Deutsche Prosa*. Two volumes, sold separately:—
5. SCHILLER'S PROSA. Containing Selections from the Prose Works of Schiller, with Notes for English Students. By Dr. BUCHHEIM, Professor of the German Language and Literature, King's College, London. Small post 8vo, 2s. 6d. [*Ready.*
6. GOETHE'S PROSA. Selections from the Prose Works of Goethe, with Notes for English Students. By Dr. BUCHHEIM. Small post 8vo. [*In preparation.*

Low's Half-Crown Series, choicely bound, cloth, gilt edges, small post 8vo. :—
1. SEA-GULL ROCK. By JULES SANDEAU. Numerous Illustrations.
2. THE HOUSE ON WHEELS. By Madame STOLZ. Many Illustrations.
3. THE MISTRESS OF THE MANSE. By Dr. HOLLAND.
4. UNDINE, AND THE TWO CAPTAINS. By FOUQUÉ. Illustrations.
5. DRAXY MILLER'S DOWRY AND THE ELDER'S WIFE.
6. THE FOUR GOLD PIECES. By Mdme GOURAUD. Several Illustrations.
7. PICCIOLA; OR, THE PRISON FLOWER. By X. B. SAINTINE. Numerous Illustrations.
8. ROBERT'S HOLIDAYS. Profusely Illustrated.
9. THE TWO CHILDREN OF ST. DOMINGO. Profusely Illustrated.
10. THE PEARL OF ORR'S ISLAND.
11. THE MINISTER'S WOOING.
12. AUNT JO'S SCRAP BAG.

Low's Copyright and Cheap Editions of American Authors, comprising Popular Works, reprinted by arrangement with their Authors:—
1. HAUNTED HEARTS. By the Author of "The Lamplighter." 1s. 6d.
2. THE GUARDIAN ANGEL. By "The Autocrat of the Breakfast Table." 1s. 6d.
3. THE MINISTER'S WOOING. By the Author of "Uncle Tom's Cabin." 1s. 6d.
4. VIEWS AFOOT. By BAYARD TAYLOR. 1s. 6d.
5. KATHRINA, HER LIFE AND MINE. By J. G. HOLLAND. 1s. 6d.
6. HANS BRINKER; OR, LIFE IN HOLLAND. By Mrs. DODGE. 1s. 6d.
7. MEN, WOMEN, AND GHOSTS. By Miss PHELPS. 1s. 6d.
8. SOCIETY AND SOLITUDE. By RALPH WALDO EMERSON. 1s. 6d.
9. HEDGED IN. By ELIZABETH PHELPS. 1s. 6d.
11. FAITH GARTNEY. 1s. 6d.
12. STOWE'S OLD TOWN FOLKS. 2s. 6d.; cloth, 3s.
13. LOWELL'S STUDY WINDOWS. 1s. 6d.
14. MY SUMMER IN A GARDEN. By CHARLES DUDLEY WARNER. 1s. 6d.
15. PINK AND WHITE TYRANNY. By Mrs. STOWE. 1s. 6d.
16. WE GIRLS. By Mrs. WHITNEY. 1s. 6d.
17. OTHER GIRLS. By Mrs. WHITNEY. 2s.
20. BACK-LOG STUDIES. By CHARLES DUDLEY WARNER, Author of "My Summer in a Garden." 1s. 6d.
22. HITHERTO. By Mrs. T. D. WHITNEY. Double Volume, 2s. 6d., fancy flexible boards.
23. FARM BALLADS. By WILL CARLETON. 1s.

Low's Standard Library of Travel and Adventure.
Crown 8vo, bound uniformly in cloth extra :—

1. THE GREAT LONE LAND. By W. F. BUTLER. With Illustrations and Map. Fifth Edition, 7s. 6d.
2. THE WILD NORTH LAND: The Story of a Winter Journey with Dogs across Northern North America. By W. F. BUTLER. With numerous Woodcuts and a Map. Fifth Edition, 7s. 6d.
3. HOW I FOUND LIVINGSTONE. By H. M. STANLEY. Introductory Chapter on the Death of Livingstone, with a brief Memoir. 7s. 6d.
4. THE THRESHOLD OF THE UNKNOWN REGION. By C. R. MARKHAM. With Maps and Illustrations. Fourth Edition, with Additional Chapters, 10s. 6d.
5. A WHALING CRUISE TO BAFFIN'S BAY AND THE GULF OF Boothia. By A. H. MARKHAM. New Edition. Two Maps and several Illustrations, 7s. 6d.
6. CAMPAIGNING ON THE OXUS. By J. A. MACGAHAN. Fourth Edition, 7s. 6d.
7. AKIM-FOO: The History of a Failure. By Major W. F. BUTLER. New Edition, 7s. 6d.

Low's Standard Novels. Crown 8vo, 6s. each, cloth extra :—

THREE FEATHERS. By WILLIAM BLACK.
A DAUGHTER OF HETH. Thirteenth Edition. By W. BLACK. With Frontispiece by F. Walker, A.R.A.
KILMENY. A Novel. By W. BLACK.
IN SILK ATTIRE. By W. BLACK.
ALICE LORRAINE. By R. D. BLACKMORE.
LORNA DOONE. By R. D. BLACKMORE. Eighth Edition.
CRADOCK NOWELL. By R. D. BLACKMORE.
CRIPPS, THE CARRIER. By R. D. BLACKMORE.   [*In the Press.*
CLARA VAUGHAN. By R. D. BLACKMORE.
INNOCENT. By Mrs. OLIPHANT. Eight Illustrations.
WORK: A Story of Experience. By LOUISA M. ALCOTT. Illustrations.
MISTRESS JUDITH: A Cambridgeshire Story. By C. C. FRASER-TYTLER.
NINETY-THREE. By VICTOR HUGO. Numerous Illustrations.
NEVER AGAIN. By Dr. MAYO.
MY WIFE AND I; or, Harry Henderson's History. By H. BEECHER STOWE.
WE AND OUR NEIGHBOURS. By H. BEECHER STOWE.
OLD TOWN TALK. By H. BEECHER STOWE.

Low's Handbook to the Charities of London for 1876.
Edited and Revised to August, 1876, by CHARLES MACKESON, F.S.S., Editor of "A Guide to the Churches of London and its Suburbs," &c. Price 1s.

MacGahan (J. A.) Campaigning on the Oxus and the Fall of Khiva. With Map and numerous Illustrations. Fourth Edition, small post 8vo, cloth extra, 7s. 6d. *See also* Low's Library of Travel and Adventure.

——— **Under the Northern Lights;** or, The Cruise of the "Pandora" to Peel's Straits in Search of Sir John Franklin's Papers. With Illustrations by Mr. DE WYLDE, who accompanied the Expedition. Demy 8vo, cloth extra, 18s.

Macgregor (John). "Rob Roy" on the Baltic. Third Edition, small post 8vo, 2s. 6d.

——— **A Thousand Miles in the "Rob Roy" Canoe.** Eleventh Edition, small post 8vo, 2s. 6d.

——— **Description of the "Rob Roy" Canoe,** with Plans, &c. 1s.

Macgregor (John). The Voyage Alone in the Yawl "Rob Roy." Second Edition, small post 8vo, 5s.

Major (R. H.) The Discoveries of Prince Henry the
Navigator, and their Results. With several Illustrations. Demy 8vo, cloth extra.

Markham (A. H.) The Cruise of the "Rosario." By
A. H. MARKHAM, Commander, R.N. 8vo, cloth, with Map and Illustrations, 16s.

—— *A Whaling Cruise to Baffin's Bay and the Gulf*
of Boothia. With an Account of the Rescue of the Survivors of the Crew of the "Polaris." Third Edition, crown 8vo, 2 Maps and Illustrations, cloth, 7s. 6d.

Markham (C. R.) The Threshold of the Unknown Region.
Crown 8vo, with 4 Maps. Fourth Edition. With additional Chapters, giving the History of our Present Expedition as far as known, and an Account of the Cruise of the "Pandora." Cloth extra, 10s. 6d.

Marsh (G. P.) Origin and History of the English Language. 8vo, 16s.

—— *The Earth, as Modified by Human Action, being*
a New Edition of "Man and Nature." Royal 8vo, cloth, 18s.

—— *Lectures on the English Language.* 8vo, 15s.

Maury (Commander). Physical Geography of the Sea and
its Meteorology. Being a Reconstruction and Enlargement of his former Work, with illustrative Charts and Diagrams. New Edition, crown 8vo, 6s.

Men of Mark; a Gallery of Contemporary Portraits
(taken from Life) of the most Eminent Men of the Day. Printed in Permanent Photography. With brief Biographical Notices. Published Monthly, price 1s. 6d. Vol. I., 4to., cloth extra, gilt edges, 25s.

Mercy Philbrick's Choice. Crown 8vo, 10s. 6d.

Michell (N.) The Heart's Great Rulers, a Poem, and
Wanderings from the Rhine to the South Sea Islands. Fcap. 8vo, 3s. 6d.

Milton's Complete Poetical Works; with Concordance
by W. D. CLEVELAND. New Edition, 8vo, 12s.; morocco, 1l. 1s.

Mistress Judith. A Cambridgeshire Story. By C. C.
FRASER-TYTLER, Author of "Jasmine Leigh." Small post 8vo, cloth extra, 6s.

Mohr (E.) To the Victoria Falls of the Zambesi. By
EDWARD MOHR. Translated by N. D'ANVERS. Numerous Illustrations, four Chromo-lithographs and a Map. 1 vol., demy 8vo, cloth extra, 24s.

Moody (Emma). Echoes of the Heart. A Collection of
upwards of 200 Sacred Poems. 16mo, cloth, gilt edges, price 3s. 6d.

Narrative of Edward Crewe, The. Personal Adventures
and Experiences in New Zealand. Small post 8vo, cloth extra, 5s.

Never Again: a Novel. By Dr. MAYO, Author of
"Kaloolah." New Edition, small post 8vo, 6s., fancy boards, 2s.

New Testament. The Authorized English Version;
with the various readings from the most celebrated Manuscripts, including the Sinaitic, the Vatican, and the Alexandrian MSS., in English. With Notes by the Editor, Dr. TISCHENDORF. Revised and corrected, Tauchnitz's Edition. Cloth flexible, gilt edges, 2s. 6d.; cheaper style, 2s.; or sewed, 1s. 6d.

Noel (Hon. Roden). Livingstone in Africa; a Poem. By
the Hon. RODEN NOEL. Post 8vo, limp cloth extra, 2s. 6d.

Nordhoff (C.) California: for Health, Pleasure, and
Residents. A Book for Travellers and Settlers. Numerous Illustrations. 8vo, 12s. 6d.

—— *Northern California, Oregon, and the Sandwich*
Islands. Square 8vo, cloth extra, price 12s. 6d.

Nothing to Wear, and Two Millions. By WILLIAM ALLEN BUTLER. 1s.

Novum Testamentum Græce. Edidit OSCAR DE GEB-HARDT. 18mo, cloth, 3s. 6d.

Oliphant (Mrs.) Innocent. A Tale of Modern Life. By Mrs. OLIPHANT, Author of "The Chronicles of Carlingford," &c., &c. With Eight full-page Illustrations. Small post 8vo, cloth extra, 6s.

Our Little Ones in Heaven. Edited by Rev. H. ROBBINS. Fcap. cloth extra, New Edition, with Illustrations, price 5s.

Painting. A Brief History of the Painters of all Schools. By LOUIS VIARDOT and other writers. Illustrated with 90 full-page and other Engravings. Super-royal 8vo (440 pp.), cloth extra, 25s.

Palliser (Mrs.) A History of Lace, from the Earliest Period. A New and Revised Edition, with additional Cuts and Text, with upwards of 100 Illustrations and Coloured Designs. 1 vol., 8vo, 1l. 1s., Third Edition.

"One of the most readable books of the season; permanently valuable, always interesting, often amusing, and not inferior in all the essentials of a gift book."—*Times.*

—— *Historic Devices, Badges, and War Cries.* 8vo, 1l. 1s.

—— *The China Collector's Pocket Companion.* With upwards of 1000 Illustrations of Marks and Monograms. Second Edition, with Additions. Small post 8vo, limp cloth, 5s.

Paris (Comte de). History of the Civil War in America. By the COMTE DE PARIS. Translated, with the approval of the Author, by LOUIS F. TASISTRO. Edited by HENRY COPPÉE, LL.D. Volume I. (embracing, without abridgment, the First Two Volumes of the French Edition). With Maps faithfully engraved from the Originals, and Printed in Three Colours. 8vo, cloth, 18s.

Phelps (Miss). Gates Ajar. 32mo, 6d.

—— *Men, Women, and Ghosts.* 12mo, sewed, 1s. 6d.; cloth, 2s.

—— *Hedged In.* 12mo, sewed, 1s. 6d.; cloth, 2s.

—— *Silent Partner.* 5s.

—— *Trotty's Wedding Tour.* Small post, 8vo, 3s. 6d.

—— *What to Wear.* Foolscap 8vo, fancy boards, 1s.

Phillips (L.) Dictionary of Biographical Reference. 8vo, 1l. 11s. 6d.

Phipson (Dr. T. L.) Familiar Letters on some Mysteries of Nature and Discoveries in Science. Crown 8vo, cloth extra, 7s. 6d.

Pike (N.) Sub-Tropical Rambles in the Land of the Aphanapteryx. In 1 vol., demy 8vo, 18s. Profusely Illustrated from the Author's own Sketches, also with Maps and valuable Meteorological Charts.

Plutarch's Lives. An entirely New and Library Edition.
Edited by A. H. CLOUGH, Esq. 5 vols., 8vo, 2*l*. 10*s*. ; half morocco, top gilt, 3*l*.

—— *Morals.* Uniform with Clough's Edition of
"Lives of Plutarch." Edited by Professor GOODWIN. 5 vols., 8vo, 3*l*. 3*s*.

Poe (E. A.), The Works of. 4 vols., 2*l*.· 2*s*.

Poems of the Inner Life. A New Edition, Revised, with
many additional Poems, inserted by permission of the Authors. Small post 8vo, 5*s*.

Polar Expedition. *See* Koldewey and Markham.

Portraits of Celebrated Women. By C. A. STE.-BEUVE.
12mo, 6*s*. 6*d*.

Purdy (William). The City Life, its Trade and Finance.
Crown 8vo, cloth extra, 7*s*. 6*d*.

Preces Veterum. Collegit et edidit Joannes F. France.
Crown 8vo, cloth, red edges, 5*s*.

Prejevalsky (N. M.) Travels in Mongolia. By N. M.
PREJEVALSKY, Lieut.-Colonel, Russian Staff. Translated by E. DELMAR MORGAN, F.R.G.S., and Annotated by Colonel YULE, C.B. 2 vols., demy 8vo, cloth extra, with numerous Illustrations and Maps, 42*s*.

Price (Sir Rose, Bt.) The Two Americas. Demy 8vo,
with Illustrations. [*In the press.*

Queen (The) of the Colonies ; or, Queensland as I saw it.
Second Edition, crown 8vo, 6*s*.

Rasselas, Prince of Abyssinia. By Dr. JOHNSON. With
Introduction by the Rev. WILLIAM WEST, Vicar of Nairn. (Bayard Series.) 2*s*. 6*d*.

Read (S.) Leaves from a Sketch Book: Pencillings of
Travel at Home and Abroad By SAMUEL READ. Royal 4to, containing about 130 Engravings on Wood, cloth extra. 25*s*.

Retzsch (M.) Outlines to Burger's Ballads. Etchings by
MORITZ RETZSCH. With Text, Explanations, and Notes. Designs. Oblong 4to, cloth extra. 10*s*. 6*d*.

—— *Outlines to Goethe's Faust.* 26 Etchings. Oblong
4to, 10*s*. 6*d*.

—— *Outlines to Schiller's " Fight with the Dragon,"*
and " Fridolin." 26 Etchings. Oblong 4to, cloth extra, 10*s*. 6*d*.

—— *Outlines to Schiller's " Lay of the Bell."* 42 Etch-
ings. With Lord Lytton's Translation. New Edition. Oblong 4to, cloth extra, 10*s*. 6*d*.

Reynard the Fox. The Prose Translation by the late
THOMAS ROSCOE. With about 100 exquisite Illustrations on Wood, after designs by A. J. ELWES. Imperial 16mo, cloth extra, 7*s*. 6*d*.

Richardson (A. S.) Stories from Old English Poetry.
Small post 8vo, cloth, 5*s*.

Rivington (F.) Life of St. Paul. With Map. 5*s*.

Rochefoucauld's Reflections. (Bayard Series.) 2s. 6d.

Rogers (S.) Pleasures of Memory. See "Choice Editions of Choice Books." 2s. 6d.

Rohlfs (Dr. G.) Adventures in Morocco and Journeys through the Oases of Draa and Tafilet. By Dr. GERHARD ROHLFS. Translated from the German. With an Introduction by WINWOOD READE. Demy 8vo, 12s.

Rose Library (The). Popular Literature of all Countries. 1s. each volume. Many of the books are Illustrated. The following volumes are now ready:—

1. SEA-GULL ROCK. By JULES SANDEAU. Illustrated. 1s.
2. LITTLE WOMEN. By LOUISA M. ALCOTT. 1s.
3. LITTLE WOMEN WEDDED. (Forming a Sequel to "Little Women.") 1s.
4. THE HOUSE ON WHEELS. By MADAME DE STOLZ. Illustrated. 1s.
5. LITTLE MEN. By LOUISA M. ALCOTT. Double Vol.), 2s.
6. THE OLD-FASHIONED GIRL. By LOUISA M. ALCOTT. (Double Vol.), 2s.
7. THE MISTRESS OF THE MANSE. By J. G. HOLLAND. 1s.
8. TIMOTHY TITCOMB'S LETTERS TO YOUNG PEOPLE, SINGLE AND MARRIED. 1s.
9. UNDINE, AND THE TWO CAPTAINS. By Baron DE LA MOTTE FOUQUE. A new Translation by F. E. BUNNETT. Illustrated. 1s.
10. DRAXY MILLER'S DOWRY AND THE ELDER'S WIFE. By SAXE HOLM. 1s.
11. THE FOUR GOLD PIECES. By Madame GOURAUD. Numerous Illustrations. 1s.
12. WORK: A Story of Experience. First Portion. By LOUISA M. ALCOTT. 1s.
13. BEGINNING AGAIN: being a Continuation of "Work." By LOUISA M. ALCOTT. 1s.
14. PICCIOLA: or, The Prison Flower. By X. B. SAINTINE. Numerous graphic Illustrations. 1s.
15. ROBERT'S HOLIDAYS. Illustrated. 1s.
16. THE TWO CHILDREN OF ST. DOMINGO. Numerous Illustrations. 1s.
17. AUNT JO'S SCRAP BAG. 1s.
18. STOWE (Mrs. H. B.) THE PEARL OF ORR'S ISLAND. 1s.
19. ——— THE MINISTER'S WOOING. 1s.
20. ——— BETTY'S BRIGHT IDEA. 1s.
21. ——— THE GHOST IN THE MILL. 1s.
22. ——— CAPTAIN KIDD'S MONEY. 1s.
23. ——— WE AND OUR NEIGHBOURS. (Double Vol.), 2s.
24. ——— MY WIFE AND I. (Double Vol.) 2s.
25. HANS BRINKER; or, The Silver Skates. 1s.
26. LOWELL'S MY STUDY WINDOW. 1s.
27. HOLMES (O. W.) THE GUARDIAN ANGEL.
28. WARNER (C. D.) MY SUMMER IN A GARDEN.

The Volumes in this Series are also published in a more expensive form on fine toned paper, cloth extra, gilt edges, at 2s. 6d. or 3s. 6d. each, according to size, &c. *See* Low's Half-Crown Series.

Russell (W. H.), LL.D. The Tour of the Prince of Wales in India. Illustrated entirely by SYDNEY P. HALL, Esq., M.A. Super royal 8vo, cloth extra, gilt, 2l. 2s.

Ruth and Gabriel. A Novel. By LAURENCE CHENY.
"The reader's interest is sustained from the first page to the last."—*Scotsman.*

Sanitary Drainage of Houses and Towns. By GEORGE E. WARING, Jun. One vol., crown 8vo, cloth extra, 10s. 6d.

Sauer (E.) Handbook of European Commerce. What to buy and Where to buy it, &c. By GEORGE SAUER, for many years Correspondent of the *New York Herald.* Crown 8vo, cloth, 5s.

Schiller's Lay of the Bell. Translated by Lord Lytton.
With 42 Illustrations after Retsch. Oblong 4to, 10s. 6d.

Schuyler (E.) Turkistan. See Turkistan.

Schweinfurth (Dr. G.) The Heart of Africa; or, Three Years' Travels and Adventures in the Unexplored Regions of the Centre of Africa. By Dr. GEORG SCHWEINFURTH. Translated by ELLEN E. FREWER. 2 vols., 8vo, upwards of 500 pages each, with 130 Woodcuts from Drawings made by the Author, and 2 Maps, 42s. Second Edition.

―――― *Artes Africanæ.* Illustrations and Descriptions of Productions of the Natural Arts of Central African Tribes. With 26 Lithographic Plates. Imperial 4to, boards, 28s.

Sea-Gull Rock. By JULES SANDEAU, of the French Academy. Translated by ROBERT BLACK, M.A. With Seventy-nine very beautiful Woodcuts. Royal 16mo, cloth extra, gilt edges, 7s. 6d. Cheaper Edition, cloth gilt, 2s. 6d. *See also* Rose Library.

Shakespeare. The Boudoir Shakespeare. Arranged for reading aloud. Part I.—Cymbeline, 1s. Part II.—The Merchant of Venice, 1s.

Shooting: Its Appliances, Practice, and Purpose. By JAMES DALZIEL DOUGALL, F.S.A., F.Z.A., Author of "Scottish Field Sports," &c. Crown 8vo, cloth extra, 10s. 6d.

"The book is admirable in every way . . We wish it every success."—*Globe.*
"A very complete treatise. . . Likely to take high rank as an authority."—*Daily News.*

Sketches from an Artist's Portfolio. By SYDNEY P. HALL. Folio, cloth extra, 3l. 3s. Containing about 60 Facsimiles of the original Sketches by this well-known Artist during his travels in various parts of Europe.
"A portfolio which any one might be glad to call their own."—*Times.*

Sketches of Life and Scenery in Australia. By a Twenty five Years' Resident. 1 vol., demy 8vo, cloth extra, 14s. Crown 8vo, 6s.

Smith (G.) Assyrian Explorations and Discoveries. By GEORGE SMITH (of the British Museum). Illustrated by Photographs and numerous Woodcut Illustrations of his recent Discoveries. Demy 8vo, 18s. Fifth Edition.

―――― *The Chaldean Account of Genesis.* Containing the Description of the Creation, the Fall of Man, the Deluge, the Tower of Babel, the Times of the Patriarchs, and Nimrod; Babylonian Fables, and Legends of the Gods; from the Cuneiform Inscriptions. By GEORGE SMITH, of the Department of Oriental Antiquities, British Museum, Author of "History of Assurbanipal," "Assyrian Discoveries," &c., &c. With many Illustrations. Demy 8vo, cloth extra, 16s. Fourth Edition.

Smith and Hamilton's French Dictionary. 2 vols., cloth, 21s.; half roan, 22s.

Spain. Illustrated by GUSTAVE DORÉ. Text by the Baron CH. D'AVILLIER. Over 240 Wood Engravings, half of them being full-page size. All after Drawings. Imperial 4to, cloth extra, gilt edges, 3l. 3s.

Socrates. (Bayard Series.)

Spooner (Very Rev. E.) St. Oswald's Sunday School. Small post 8vo, cloth, 3s. 6d.

Spry (W. J. J.) The Cruise of H.M.S. "Challenger." 1 Vol., cloth extra, with Map and numerous Illustrations.

Stanley (H. M.) How I Found Livingstone. Crown 8vo, cloth extra, 7s. 6d.

—— *"My Kalulu," Prince, King, and Slave.* A Story from Central Africa. Crown 8vo, about 430 pp., with numerous graphic Illustrations, after original Designs by the Author. Cloth, 7s. 6d.

—— *Coomassie and Magdala.* A Story of Two British Campaigns in Africa. Demy 8vo, with Maps and Illustrations, 16s. Second Edition.

Stolz (Madame). The House on Wheels. Small post 8vo, 2s. 6d. *See also* Rose Library.

Story without an End. From the German of CAROVE, by the late Mrs. SARAH T. AUSTIN. Crown 4to, with 15 exquisite Drawings by E. V. B., printed in Colours in facsimile of the Original Water-Colours, and numerous other Illustrations. New Edition, 7s. 6d.

—— Square 16mo, with Illustrations by HARVEY, 2s. 6d.

Stowe (Mrs. Beecher). Dred. 12mo, in boards, 1s.

—— *Geography,* with 60 Illustrations, cloth, 4s. 6d.

—— *Minister's Wooing.* 5s.; Copyright Series, 1s. 6d.; cloth, 2s.

—— *Old Town Folk.* 6s.; Cheap Edition, 2s. 6d.

—— *Old Town Fireside Stories.* Cloth extra, 3s. 6d.

—— *My Wife and I; or, Harry Henderson's History.* Small post 8vo, cloth extra, 6s.

—— *We and Our Neighbours.* Small post 8vo, 6s.

—— *Pink and White Tyranny.* Small post 8vo, 3s. 6d. Cheap Edition, 1s. 6d. and 2s.

—— *Chimney Corner.* 1s.; cloth, 1s. 6d.

—— *The Pearl of Orr's Island.* Crown 8vo, 5s.

—— *Women in Sacred History.* Illustrated with 15 Chromo-lithographs and 200 pages of Letterpress. 4to, cloth extra, gilt edges, 1l. 5s.

Studies from Nature. Twenty-four Plates, with Descriptive Letterpress. By STEPHEN THOMPSON. Imperial 4to, 35s.

Sullivan (G. C.) Dhow Chasing in Zanzibar Waters and on the Eastern Coast of Africa; a Narrative of Five Years' Experiences in the Suppression of the Slave Trade. With Illustrations. Demy 8vo, cloth extra, 16s.

Tauchnitz's English Editions of German Authors. Each Volume, cloth flexible, 2s.; or sewed, 1s. 6d. The following are now ready:—
ON THE HEIGHTS. By B. AUERBACH. 3 vols.
IN THE YEAR '13. By FRITZ REUTER. 1 vol.
FAUST. By GOETHE. 1 vol.
L'ARRABIATA. By PAUL HEYSE. 1 vol.
THE PRINCESS, AND OTHER TALES. By HEINRICH ZSCHOKKE. 1 vol.
LESSING'S NATHAN THE WISE, AND EMILIA GALLOTTI.
HACKLANDER'S BEHIND THE COUNTER. Translated by MARY HOWITT. 2 vols.
THREE TALES. By W. HAUFF.
JOACHIM v. KAMMERN: Diary of a Poor Young Lady. By M. NATHUSIUS.
POEMS BY FERDINAND FREILIGRATH. Edited by his Daughter.
GABRIEL. From the German. By ARTHUR MILMAN.
THE DEAD LAKE, AND OTHER TALES. By P. HEYSE.
THROUGH NIGHT TO LIGHT. By GUTZKOW.
FLOWER, FRUIT, AND THORN PIECES. By JEAN PAUL RICHTER. 2 vols.
THE PRINCESS OF THE MOOR. By Miss MARLITT. 2 vols.
AN EGYPTIAN PRINCESS. By G. EBERS. 2 vols.
EKKEHARD. By J. V. SCHEFFEL. 2 vols.
BARBAROSSA, AND OTHER TALES. By PAUL HEYSE. From the German. By L. C. S.
WILHELM MEISTER'S APPRENTICESHIP. By GOETHE. 2 vols.
PRINCE BISMARCK. A Biographical Sketch by WILHELM GORLACH. 1 vol.
DOUBTFUL PLAYS OF SHAKESPEARE.

Tauchnitz (B.) German and English Dictionary. Paper, 1s.; cloth, 1s. 6d.; roan, 2s.

―― *French and English.* Paper, 1s. 6d.; cloth, 2s.; roan, 2s. 6d.

―― *Italian and English.* Paper, 1s. 6d.; cloth, 2s.; roan, 2s. 6d.

―― *Spanish and English.* Paper, 1s. 6d.; cloth, 2s.; roan, 2s. 6d.

―― *New Testament.* Cloth, 2s.; gilt, 2s. 6d.

Tennyson's May Queen. See Choice Series, 2s. 6d.

Theophilus and Others. By the Author of "Hans Brinker and the Silver Skates." Crown 8vo, cloth extra, 10s. 6d.

Thomson (J.) The Straits of Malacca, Indo-China, and China; or, Ten Years' Travels, Adventures, and Residence Abroad. By J. THOMSON, F.R.G.S. Upwards of 60 Woodcuts, from the Author's own Photographs and Sketches. Demy 8vo, cloth extra, 21s.

Thompson (Stephen). Old English Homes. A Summer's Sketch-Book. By STEPHEN THOMPSON, Author of "Swiss Scenery," &c. 25 very fine Permanent Photographs by the Author. Demy 4to, cloth extra, gilt edges, 2l. 2s.

Thornwell Abbas. By GRANT LLOYD. 2 vols., Crown 8vo. 21s.

Ticknor (George), Life, Letters, and Journals. 2 vols., crown 8vo, cloth extra, 21s.
"No matter what your peculiar taste in this style of composition, no matter what your range of acquirement, rest assured that you will rise from the careful perusal of his journals and correspondence with a lively sense of self-satisfaction, amused, instructed, and (we will venture to add) improved."—*Quarterly Review.*

Timothy Titcomb's Letters to Young People, Single and Married. Cloth, 2s. (See also Rose Library.)

Tinné (J. E.) The Wonderland of the Antipodes: Sketches of Travel in the North Island of New Zealand. Illustrated with numerous Photographs. Demy 8vo, cloth extra, 16s.

Tischendorf (Dr.) See New Testament.

*Tissandier (Gaston). A History and Handbook of Photo-*graphy. Translated from the French of GASTON TISSANDIER; edited by J. THOMSON, F.R.G.S. Imperial 16mo, 75 Wood Engravings and a Frontispiece, cloth extra, 6s.

Tolhausen (A.) The Technological Dictionary in the French, English, and German Languages. Containing the Technical Terms used in the Arts, Manufactures, and Industrial Affairs generally. Revised and Augmented by M. LOUIS TOLHAUSEN, French Consul at Leipzig. The First Part, containing French German-English, crown 8vo, 2 vols., sewed, 8s.; 1 vol., half roan, 9s. The Second Part, containing English-German-French, crown 8vo, 2 vols., sewed, 8s.; 1 vol., bound, 9s. The Third Part, containing German-English-French, crown 8vo, 2 vols., sewed 8s.; 1 vol., bound, 9s.

Trégane (Louis.) See Adventures in New Guinea, 6s.

Trollope (A.) Harry Heathcote of Gangoil. A Story of Bush Life in Australia. Illustrations. Small post, cloth extra, 5s.

Trowbridge (A. C.) The Young Surveyor. 1 vol., small post 8vo, cloth extra, with numerous Illustrations, 5s.

Turkistan. Notes of a Journey in the Russian Provinces of Central Asia and the Khanates of Bokhara and Kokand. By EUGENE SCHUYLER, Secretary to the American Legation, St. Petersburg. Numerous Illustrations. 2 vols., demy 8vo, cloth extra, 2l. 2s.

Turner (Rev. F. S.) British Opium Policy. 8vo, cloth, 6s.

Vincent (F.) The Land of the White Elephant: Sights and Scenes in South-Eastern Asia. With Maps and Illustrations. 8vo, cloth extra, 18s.

Waller (Rev. C. H.) The Names on the Gates of Pearl. Being those of the twelve Tribes of Israel, and other Studies. By the Rev. C. H. WALLER, M.A. Crown 8vo, cloth extra, 6s.

—— *Adoption and the Covenant.* Some Thoughts on Confirmation. Super-royal 16mo, cloth limp, 2s. 6d.

Warburton (Col. Egerton). Journey across Australia. An Account of the Exploring Expedition sent out by Messrs. Elder and Hughes, under the Command of Colonel WARBURTON. With Illustrations and Map. Edited, with an Introductory Chapter, by H. W. BATES, Esq., F.R.G.S. 8vo, cloth, 16s.

Waring (George E., Jun.) See Sanitary Drainage.

JULES VERNE'S WORKS.

SPECIAL NOTICE.—Messrs. SAMPSON LOW & Co. beg to inform the public, in reply to many inquiries with reference to an announcement of Cheap Editions of JULES VERNE'S WORKS by other houses, that they are the sole Proprietors of the Copyright in all the Translations of the Works by this Author published by themselves, as testified by the following : —

To ENGLISH READERS OF THE WORKS OF M. JULES VERNE.

" *The undersigned, exclusive Proprietors and Publishers of the Works of* M. JULES VERNE, *hereby certify that* Messrs. SAMPSON LOW & CO. *are alone authorized to translate into English the following Works of this Author:—*

MICHAEL STROGOFF. 10s. 6d.
THE MYSTERIOUS ISLAND, in 3 vols. 22s. 6d.
THE SURVIVORS OF THE CHANCELLOR. 7s. 6d.
DR. OX'S EXPERIMENT.* 7s. 6d.
      A WINTER AMID THE ICE, &c.*
AROUND THE WORLD IN EIGHTY DAYS.* 7s. 6d.
THE FUR COUNTRY. 10s. 6d.
MERIDIANA: OR, THE ADVENTURES OF THREE RUSSIANS AND THREE ENGLISHMEN IN SOUTH AFRICA.* 7s. 6d.
FIVE WEEKS IN A BALLOON.* 7s. 6d.
A FLOATING CITY.* 7s. 6d.
THE BLOCKADE RUNNERS.* 1s. only.
FROM THE EARTH TO THE MOON.* } 10s. 6d.
AROUND THE MOON.*
TWENTY THOUSAND LEAGUES UNDER THE SEA.* 10s. 6d.
MARTIN PAZ, THE INDIAN PATRIOT. 1s.

and that all other Copies of these Works are unauthorized and counterfeit reprints. (Signed)   "J. HETZEL & CO."

" *Je soussigné certifie que* M. HETZEL, *mon éditeur, a seul droit d'autoriser ou de refuser la reproduction de mes livres.*" (Signed)   "JULES VERNE."

** Besides the more expensive Editions, Messrs. Low have issued handsome Shilling Illustrated Editions of each of the Books marked with an asterisk, thus (*). Complete Lists of all the Editions and full particulars may be had on applying to the English publishers.

Warner (C. D.) My Summer in a Garden. 1s., cloth, 2s.

—— *Back-log Studies.* 1s. 6d.; cloth, 2s.

—— *Mummies and Moslems.* Demy 8vo, cloth, 12s.

Westropp (H. M.) A Manual of Precious Stones and Antique Gems. By H. M. WESTROPP, Author of "The Travellers' Art Companion," "Pre-Historic Phases," &c. Numerous Illustrations. Small post 8vo, cloth extra, 6s.

Wheaton (Henry). Elements of International Law. New Edition. [*In the press.*

Whitall (Alice B.) On the Rock. A Memoir of Alice B. WHITALL, by Mrs. PEARSALL SMITH. Small post, cloth, 2s.

Whitney (Mrs. A. D. T.) The Gayworths. Small post 8vo, 3s. 6d.

—— *Faith Gartney.* Small post 8vo, 3s. 6d.; paper, 1s.

—— *Real Folks.* Small post 8vo, 3s. 6d.

—— *Hitherto.* Small post 8vo, 3s. 6d. and 2s. 6d.

—— *Sights and Insights.* 3 vols., crown 8vo, 31s. 6d.

—— *Summer in Leslie Goldthwaite's Life.* Small post 8vo, 3s. 6d.

—— *The Other Girls.* Small post 8vo, 3s. 6d.

—— *We Girls.* Small post 8vo, 3s. 6d. Cheap Edition, 1s. 6d. and 2s.

Wilkes (George). Shakespeare from an American Point of View. Demy 8vo, cloth extra.

Wills, A Few Hints on Proving, without Professional Assistance. By a PROBATE COURT OFFICIAL. Fourth Edition, revised and enlarged, with Forms of Wills, Residuary Accounts, &c. Fcap. 8vo, cloth limp, 1s.

Woolsey (C. D., LL.D.) Introduction to the Study of International Law; designed as an Aid in Teaching and Historical Studies. Crown 8vo, cloth extra, 8s. 6d.

Worcester (Dr.) New and Greatly Enlarged Dictionary of the English Language. Adapted for Library or College Reference, comprising 40,000 Words more than Johnson's Dictionary. 4to, cloth, 1834 pp., price 31s. 6d., well bound; ditto, half morocco, 2l. 2s.

"The volumes before us show a vast amount of diligence; but with Webster it is diligence in combination with fancifulness.—with Worcester in combination with good sense and judgment. Worcester's is the soberer and safer book, and may be pronounced the best existing English Lexicon."—*Athenæum.*

Words of Wellington, Maxims and Opinions, Sentences and Reflections of the Great Duke, gathered from his Despatches, Letters, and Speeches (Bayard Series), 2s. 6d.

Wrinkles and Recipes: a Collection of Practical Suggestions, Processes, and Directions for the Mechanic, the Engineer, the Farmer, and the Housekeeper. Edited by PARK BENJAMIN. Illustrated, 12mo, roan, 8s.

Xenophon's Anabasis; or, Expedition of Cyrus. A Literal Translation, chiefly from the Text of DINDORF, by GEORGE B. WHEELER. Books I. to III. Crown 8vo, boards, 2s.

—— Books I. to VII. Boards, 3s. 6d.

Young (L.) Acts of Gallantry. Giving a detail of every Act for which the Silver Medal of the Royal Humane Society has been granted during the last Forty-one Years. Crown 8vo, cloth, 7s. 6d.

Young (J. F.) Five Weeks in Greece. Crown 8vo, 10s. 6d.

London:
SAMPSON LOW, MARSTON, SEARLE, & RIVINGTON,
CROWN BUILDINGS, 188, FLEET STREET.

www.ingramcontent.com/pod-product-compliance
Lightning Source LLC
Chambersburg PA
CBHW030602300426
44111CB00009B/1079